Familienunternehmen und KMU

Edited by
A. Hack, Berne
A. Calabrò, Witten/Herdecke
H. Frank, Vienna
F. W. Kellermanns, Tennessee
T. Zellweger, St. Gallen

Both Family Firms and Small and Medium Sized Enterprises (SME) feature a number of distinct behaviors and characteristics which could provide them with a competitive advantage in the market but could also lead to certain risks. The scientific series at hand presents research which provides an empirical and theoretical contribution to the investigation on these specific characteristics and their impact on business practice. The overall aim of this series is to advance the development of theory in the areas of family firm and SME management.

Oliver Ahlers

Family Firms and Private Equity

A Collection of Essays on Value Creation, Negotiation, and Soft Factors

Foreword by Prof. Dr. Andreas Hack

Springer Gabler

Oliver Ahlers
Vallendar, Germany

Dissertation WHU – Otto Beisheim School of Management, Vallendar, 2013

ISBN 978-3-658-04093-2 ISBN 978-3-658-04094-9 (eBook)
DOI 10.1007/978-3-658-04094-9

The Deutsche Nationalbibliothek lists this publication in the Deutsche Nationalbibliografie; detailed bibliographic data are available in the Internet at http://dnb.d-nb.de.

Library of Congress Control Number: 2014945239

Springer Gabler

Printed on acid-free paper

Springer Gabler is a brand of Springer DE.
Springer DE is part of Springer Science+Business Media.
www.springer-gabler.de

Foreword

"Family companies are living experiments in holding on and letting go. The good ones know how to do both well." (John A. Davis)

Ensuring succession is a key challenge for all family businesses. However, passing the baton to the next family generation and keeping the business sound in the long run is tremendously difficult. It is a well known fact that many family businesses do not survive beyond the first or second generation.

Researchers on family businesses have not been inactive on the issue of family business succession. An impressive stock of knowledge has been generated on how the succession of the family business could work well. Surprisingly, previous research strongly focused on internal family solutions to succession. Indeed, research so far has often disregarded succession paths involving situations in which the family would "let go" of the business and transfer ownership and management to "outsiders".

This is the point of departure for the thesis at hand. In his work, Oliver Ahlers investigates the external succession route for family firms and in particular management buyouts that involve private equity (PE) firms who assume ownership and/or take over the management of the former family business. In particular, Mr. Ahlers investigates different facets of the buyout deal such as the valuation of the family business, negotiations between family and non-family sellers, and how soft factors such as trust and commitment play a role in deal-making.

Oliver Ahlers uses different theories and methodological approaches to shed light on buyout deals. He is among the first to apply real options theory to family business research and to develop a conceptual valuation model. Mr. Ahlers' valuation model is specific to family firms and puts the family at the center of business valuation whose role can be value-enhancing or value-decreasing. But Mr. Ahlers does not limit his work to conceptual thoughts. He collected a unique and singular empirical sample which comprises responses from high-profile PE managers who realized buyout deals across Europe. Getting data on buyouts is highly difficult due to the confidentiality that accompanies buyouts. This makes his extensive statistical analysis extremely valuable.

The empirical sample was used to investigate negotiations and soft factors affecting buyouts. His empirical results indicate that bidder competition, expertise, and seller's time pressure do have effects on the acquiring PE firm's bargaining power. Additionally, PE firm's specialization on the size of buyout deals and certain structures of family firms are found to have moderating effects on the PE firm's bargaining power. Furthermore, Mr. Ahlers points out that affective commitment, a key determinant of strong relationships, plays a role in buyouts and that goal congruence and trust are its antecedents. He also shows that family sellers show higher affective commitment and moderate the role of trust – indicating a higher need for positive relationships and trust.

Mr. Ahlers` thesis makes a truly valuable research contribution. It deals with a topic in family business research that certainly deserves more attention and coverage. Not only is it based on convincing and diverse theoretical reasoning, but also on an in depth review of the literature and a strong empirical analysis. In fact, this thesis goes beyond that which is generally expected of a doctoral dissertation.

I do believe that Mr. Ahlers thesis deserves high attention among researchers and management practitioners alike. It is especially recommended for private equity managers, family business CEOs and managers or shareholders, advisors to family businesses, and ultimately all those with an interest in family firms and private equity.

Prof. Dr. Andreas Hack

Preface

When I entered university to study business administration, I was surprised to find special courses on family businesses available in the university's course calendar. Until then, I did not consciously perceive that there was a difference between family and non-family businesses. I thought at the time "It was certainly nothing that deserved special lectures and seminars". Growing up in a family business myself, it naturally appeared to me as the most common form of business organization. Since being a little boy, it was clear that the production halls of our family business could be used as a giant playground for my friends and I. Listening to my parents talking about successful sales pitches, non-paying clients, sick employees, or new tax regulations over dinner was nothing special. Working in the business was a regular duty to earn a little pocket money.

Nevertheless, I was curious and decided to enroll for the aforementioned family business course to find out more about it. I did not really expect much but then it turned out that it was all there! It was fascinating to reflect and to understand what this type of business is all about. I could easily connect theory and practice and began to make sense of what I had already experienced for quite some time. In fact, I understood that I was the researcher and the object of study at the same time. This was the beginning of my scientific interest in family businesses. Now, more than 10 years later, this book is my doctoral thesis, and still, there is this fascination and interest that inspired me to start the doctoral journey.

I submitted my doctoral thesis at the WHU- Otto Beisheim School of Management. It was chaired by Professor Dr. Andreas Hack & Professor Franz W. Kellermanns, Ph.D. whom I would both sincerely like to thank for supervising my thesis. I highly appreciate their guidance, support, and advice over the course of my dissertation project and I always loved to discuss my thoughts and ideas with them. There was no idea or thought that Andreas was not able to challenge to take it to the next level and no statistical problem Franz could not give advice on. Contrary to commonly held beliefs that professors do not invest time in their students, Andreas and Franz were always approachable and available. It was hard to meet their standards, but rewarding when this was achieved. Without their deep commitment and professional expertise, this doctoral thesis would not have been possible.

Furthermore, I express my deep gratitude to my parents, Anke and Fritz. They never pushed me, but gave me the freedom and support to follow my own path. They are my role models, both as parents as well as entrepreneurs. I also thank my grandmother Gerda whose discipline and optimism has always been a source of inspiration and my brother Michael whom I can always count on.

Next, I appreciate the support of my colleagues and fellow doctoral students at the WHU. In particular, I appreciate the company of Stephan Wessel with whom I shared many doctoral seminars and countless phone calls that helped both of us to improve not only our doctoral thesis, but also to develop a close friendship. I would also like to thank David Gorecki, Cristian A. Herrera Riquelme, and Tommaso Rooms for an unforgettable time at the London School of Economics and Political Science and a friendship that connects the four of us despite significant geographical distance.

Finally, I cannot thank my wife Berith enough. Whenever I felt down, Berith was there to cheer me up. Whenever I tended to descend into the world of research, Berith pulled me back to reality. Whenever I lost faith, Berith brought it back - always with a smile. I cannot think of more fortunate circumstances than her sitting at the desk just opposite mine during the time of my thesis. I just had to look up from my papers and there it was: her beautiful smile that made my world look brighter. To her I dedicate this thesis.

Oliver Ahlers

Contents

Figures[1]

[1] Figure coding example: Figure 3–11 implies the figure is in chapter three and it is the 11th figure of the thesis

Tables[2]

[2] Table coding example: Table 4–5 implies the table is in chapter four and it is the 5th table of the thesis

Abbreviations

BATNA	Best Alternative to a Negotiated Agreement
bn	billion
CEO	Chief Executive Officer
CFA	Confirmatory Factor Analysis
CFI	Comparative Fit Index
DCF	Discounted Cash Flow
Dr.	Doctor
DV	Dependent Variable
Ed./Eds.	Editor/-s
e.g.	exempli gratia (for example)
e-mail	electronic mail
EU	European Union
EFA	Exploratory Factor Analysis
FF	Family Firm
FFAV	Family Firm Acquisition Value
FOaR	Family Options at Risk
F-PEC	Family power (P), experience (E), and culture (C)
FUM	Funds Under Management
GP	General Partners
i.e.	id est (that is)
IFI	Incremental Index of Fit
IPO	Initial Public Offering
IV	Independent Variable
LBO	Leveraged Buy-out
LP	Limited Partners
m	million(s)
M	Moderator
MBO	Management Buy-Out
MBI	Management Buy-In
Mgmt.	Management
MM	Mitigation Measures
n/a	not applicable

NED	Non-Executive Directors
NfO	Non-family Options
NfFV	Non-family Firm Value
NPV	Net Present Value
OLS	Ordinary Least Squares
PDF	Portable Document Format
PE	Private Equity
RBV	Resource-based View of Strategy
ROA	Real Options Analysis
RMSEA	Root Mean Square Error of Approximation
SEW	Socioemotional Wealth
SME	Small and Medium Enterprise
TLI	Tucker-Lewis Index
TMT	Top-Management Team
U.K.	United Kingdom
U.S.	United States
USD	US-Dollar
VC	Venture Capital
VIF	Variance Inflation Factor
vs.	versus
WHU	Wissenschaftliche Hochschule für Unternehmensführung
WTA	Willingness To Accept

1 Introduction

1.1 Relevance and background

Family firms are of particular significance for the global economy (IFERA, 2003; Anderson & Reeb, 2003; Morck & Yeung, 2003; Astrachan & Shanker, 2003; Klein, 2000). Prior research acknowledges that family firms are considerably different from non-family firms and the source of distinction clearly is the "family" (Sharma, 2004). Although family firms are a heterogeneous group with varying degrees of family influence, differences in size, industry and geography (Chua, Chrisman, Steier et al., 2012; Chrisman, Chua, Pearson et al., 2012; Tsang, 2002), they all face the same challenge sooner or later—to ensure succession, and the survival of the firm as a family-owned entity (Cabrera-Suárez, de Saá-Pérez, & García-Almeida, 2001).

Succession is a highly difficult issue for family businesses. When family owners have to secure family succession, it is a decision overshadowed by emotions (Sharma, Chrisman, & Chua, 2003; Miller, Steier, & Le Breton-Miller, 2003). This is unsurprising, as a key driver for many family firms is to secure trans-generational control over the business (Zellweger, Kellermanns, Chrisman et al., 2011). Emotional attachment is what most family entrepreneurs feel when it comes to the question of how their "lifetime achievement" will continue once they leave the business (Zellweger & Astrachan, 2008). There are a number of reasons why family succession might fail. Most importantly, the incumbent family CEO is unwilling to let go or there simply is no willing and/or qualified family successor available (Kets de Vries, 1993; Sharma, Chrisman, Pablo et al., 2001; Sharma & Irving, 2005).

The risks of family succession have significant macroeconomic implications. In Germany it was estimated that ~100,000 family firms have to secure succession between 2010 and 2014 and of these firms a majority will be unable to find a successor within the boundaries of the family (Hauser, Kay, & Boerger, 2010). The increasing difficulty to secure succession of the family business is not only present in Germany, but a pressing global issue (PWC, 2012). For example, the EU estimated that the ownership of ~450,000 SMEs (a majority of them are family firms)[3] is being transferred each year in Europe and among them ~150,000 firms with ~600,000 employees are at risk because ownership transfer is conducted "inefficiently" (Calogirou, Houdard-Duval, & Perrin-Boulonne, 2010). What opportunities do family firms have to ensure succession if no family successor is available?

It is possible to take a succession route outside of the family. "External" family succession is when a non-family member takes over a business. Prior family business research has been primarily concerned with how to secure intra-family succession and neglected the external succession route (Howorth, Westhead, & Wright, 2004; Niedermeyer, Jaskiewicz, & Klein, 2010). There are multiple options to ensure ownership transition in the external succession route, such as trade sale, IPO and management buyouts (Scholes, Westhead, & Burrows, 2008; Goossens, Manigart, & Meuleman, 2008). Trade sale involves the sale to another company, which might even be a competitor (Scholes, Wright, Westhead et al., 2007). However, in a trade sale the identity and culture of the former family firm can be put at risk (Scholes et al., 2007). An initial public offering (IPO), the start of public quotation, is a complex and costly process, and thus, only an option for large family firms (Scholes et al., 2008). Management buyouts which usually involve private equity (PE) firms are another option. In general, a buyout is when PE firms together with the incumbent and/or external management take over the business (Meuleman, Amess, Wright et al., 2009).

Buyouts can have some advantages over IPO and trade sale. Firstly, in a buyout the former family business could ensure independent ownership and maintain (at least part of) the family culture, as PE firms usually treat their portfolio firms on a standalone basis, i.e. they remain independently run companies (Jensen, 1989; Scholes et al., 2007). Secondly, members

[3] The EU study specifically refers to SMEs—which is not fully congruent with the term "family firm". However, it is estimated that the majority of SMEs are family firms (IFB, 2011).

of the family could stay associated with the business if they prefer to do so (Scholes et al., 2008; Niedermeyer et al., 2010). Thirdly, the majority of the management team could remain in place if the management buyout is structured accordingly (Scholes et al., 2007).

There is certainly potential for conflict between PE investors and family firms. Family firms constitute an important deal source for PE firms (Scholes, Wright, Westhead et al., 2009). However, according to existing research, there is considerable potential for conflict because family firms and PE firms may follow very different business "philosophies" (Dawson, 2011; Poech, Achleitner, & Burger-Calderon, 2005). Family firms are known to have a long-term perspective on the business and often pursue non-financial goals (Berrone, Cruz, & Gómez-Mejía, 2012) whereas PE firms buy businesses in order to resell them with a profit (Braun, Zacharias, & Latham, 2011; Tappeiner, Howorth, Achleitner et al., 2012). Furthermore, PE firms have been widely criticized for unsustainable performance effects in portfolio firms (Wright, Amess, Weir et al., 2009).

PE firms increasingly face competition from peers and have to specify their value proposition as well as build up capabilities to succeed in a difficult market environment (Wilson, Wright, Siegel et al., 2012; Cressy, Munari, & Malipiero, 2007). Specifically, PE firms need to source deals and have to successfully increase the economic value of their portfolio companies (Kaplan & Strömberg, 2009). However, PE firms are not always able to successfully create value in former family firms (Wulf, Stubner, Gietl et al., 2010) and the general perception PE firms have of family firms tends to be negative (Granata, 2010; Dawson, 2011). In order for PE firms to successfully buy a family business, they may need to build up their knowledge on how to target and deal with family firms over the lifecycle of a management buyout (Tappeiner et al. 2012; Burkhardt, 2008).

Prior research has largely neglected the subject of family firms and PE. The status quo of research on family firms and PE has been described as being still in an early stage of development (Tappeiner et al., 2012). This is surprising for a number of reasons. Firstly, buyouts of non-family businesses are very complex and adding the familial dimension only adds to this complexity. Secondly, ownership transition of family firms is of tremendous economic importance because of the prevalence of family firms in the global economy (Calogirou et al., 2010; Hauser et al., 2010). Thirdly, management buyouts as means for transfer of ownership in family firms are often related to the main strategic challenge of family firms, i.e., succession (Cabrera-Suárez et al., 2001). Therefore all means available for accomplishing transfer of ownership should be thoroughly investigated (Howorth et al., 2004; Niedermeyer et al., 2010). Lastly, it is particularly interesting how different business philosophies (i.e. family firms and PE) interact and how they could create mutually beneficial outcomes (Poech et al., 2005; Dawson, 2011).

The main objectives of this Ph.D. thesis are as follows. Firstly, this thesis intends to investigate the neglected topic of buyouts in family firms involving PE. The focus is on topics that have been previously regarded as either "puzzling", such as the valuation of family firms in buyouts, or "pressing", because such issues have been particularly neglected by previous researchers, including issues surrounding the negotiation stage.[4] Furthermore, some previous research findings lack sound quantitative empirical evidence, such as "relationship factors" in buyout deals.[5] This thesis relies largely on quantitative empirical research in order to verify and validate previous research. Secondly, this thesis hopes to inform practitioners of both buyers (PE firms) and sellers (family firm owners) in buyouts. Although the essays that make up this thesis usually employ the perspective of the buyer, they certainly also imply important insights of great relevance for the seller. The findings of this thesis may help to facilitate management buyouts in family firms and make them more successful by creating win-win situations for buyers and sellers alike.

[4] See the literature review of this thesis (chapter 1.3)
[5] See the literature review of this thesis (chapter 1.3)

1.2 Basic terms

In the following descriptions the basic terms of this research project will be explained and defined. The basic terms are "family firms", "private equity", "buyouts", and the "stylized investment process".

1.2.1 Family firms

The task of defining the term "family firm"[6] is challenging for researchers. Although family firm researchers have acknowledged the importance of an accurate and consistent definition of the family firm, still no widely accepted definition prevails (Handler, 1994; Litz, 1995; Hack, 2009; Sharma, 2004). For example, one paper identified 44 different definitions of family firms over a period of ten years (Habbershon, Williams, & Daniel, 1998). Another recent work has reviewed a total of 28 definitions (Miller, Le Breton-Miller, Lester et al., 2007). Early research on family firms already encountered a "paradox" when family firms have to be defined (Lansberg, 1988). Landsberg (1988) argues people usually have an intuitive understanding of family firms, but struggle with giving precise and consistent definitions. Having no consistent definition of family firms is problematic for all research efforts because such a definition is needed to differentiate family from non-family firms, to ensure reliability of research efforts, and to make research studies comparable (Smyrnios, Tanewski, & Romano, 1998; Habbershon & Williams, 1999; Klein, 2000). Although some progress has been made in this debate, considerable differences remain (Astrachan, Klein, & Smyrnios, 2002; Chrisman, Chua, & Sharma, 2005). The key works and insights on how to define family firms are discussed below. This section concludes with a definition on how the term "family firm" is used in this thesis.

Initial attempts to describe and to distinguish family firms have been made by conceiving family firms as a collection of systems or institutions. Early conceptions of family

[6] The terms "family business" or "family-owned business" are understood to be synonymous.

firms illustrate them as two overlapping circles—that of the family and that of business (Landsberg, 1983). Later on, a third circle was introduced by Taguiri & Davis (1983, reprinted 1996) adding to those of family and business with one representing the ownership system. The key lesson from these models is that different "circles" create divergent role requirements, perceptions, needs, objectives, pressures, and conflicts for the family (Landsberg, 1983; Tagiuri & Davis, 1996). The overlaps of circles can also represent the strategic challenges for the family business, such as how to ensure succession (Hoy & Verser, 1994). The circle models can assist in understanding how family firms differ and highlight important parameters of family firm configurations, such as ownership, management, and the family (Gersick, 1997). However, it remains challenging to derive a clear definition of family firms from the circle models because one can think of multiple possible combinations of circles and associated characteristics. Much of the recent research on family firms has addressed this issue and two main approaches to define family firms have evolved—"components-of-involvement" and "essence" approaches (Chrisman et al., 2005).

"Components-of-involvement" and "essence" approaches define family firms from two different perspectives. Approaches in the "components-of-involvement" category consider family firms as observable configurations of family involvement in businesses which could be in management, ownership, or governance roles and often conceptually built upon the three-circle model (Chrisman et al., 2005). Definitions in the "components-of-involvement" category vary in terms of specific boundaries, such as minimum share of ownership or participation in management roles by family members used to distinguish family firms from non-family firms. For example, the minimum share of ownership used by researchers to classify a firm as a family firm differs widely—ranging from 100% to 5% (Chua, Chrisman, & Sharma, 1999; Villalonga & Amit, 2006). The "components-of-involvement" approach has been criticized due to a lack of theoretical reasoning on how certain levels of family influence translate into distinct family firm behavior (Chua et al., 1999; Hack, 2009). This criticism has led to more theory-driven definitions that put the "essence" or outcome of family involvement at the center of family firm definitions (Chrisman et al., 2005). Outcomes of family behavior can become apparent in multiple dimensions such as in the firms' strategies influenced by the family (Ward, 1988; Sharma, Chrisman, & Chua, 1997), the firms' resources and capabilities (Habbershon, Williams, & MacMillan, 2003; Habbershon & Williams, 1999; Sirmon & Hitt, 2003; Eddleston, Kellermanns, & Sarathy, 2008), and the need for forms of family control over the business (Litz, 1995; Sharma, 2004; Zellweger et al., 2011). Thus, family involvement as such is a necessary, but insufficient alone as a condition for defining the family firm, i.e. capturing its essence (Chrisman et al., 2012; Chrisman et al., 2005). However, Hack (2009) argues the main theoretical difficulties known from the "components-of-involvement" approach also apply to the "essence" approaches because it is still questionable whether specific levels allow for a distinction between family and non-family firms.

"Components-of-involvement" and "essence" approaches to define family firms are converging somewhat in the "F-PEC scale". Astrachan, Klein & Smyrinos (2002) proposed to capture the varying degree of family influence with the F-PEC scale of family influence which is comprised of the three subscales of power (P), experience (E), and culture (C). In the logic of the F-PEC, the subscales are consolidated as one metric variable (Klein, Astrachan, & Smyrnios, 2005). Of key importance is the power scale that comprises the sub-dimensions of family influence through ownership, management, and/or governance (Klein et al., 2005). The experience scale covers the quantitative and generational involvement of family members in the business (Astrachan et al., 2002). The culture scale examines how family values are reflected in the business (Klein et al., 2005). The main contribution of F-PEC to the debate on family firm definitions is the variety of family influence dimensions it covers and the conception of family influence as being interchangeable, leading to a "continuum" of family firms (Sharma, 2004). However, the interchangeability of the F-PEC components may simultaneously be the greatest weakness of this approach, as very different family configurations can yield the same level on the F-PEC scale (Hack, 2009). By simplifying different dimensions of family influence into one variable, one could neglect the importance of each individual dimension. Further, the F-PEC has been criticized for significant data requirements which are needed for its calculation and also because measurement of several variables is not possible on the basis of cross-sectional data (Zellweger, 2006).

Raising awareness of the heterogeneity of family firms has still not triggered a universal definition. Current research debates acknowledge that family firms display a considerable degree of heterogeneity, rather than being a homogenous group (Tsang, 2002; Chua et al., 2012; Melin & Nordqvist, 2007). While some typologies of family firms have emphasized their heterogeneity instead of dichotomous treatments (Sharma, 2004; Westhead & Howorth, 2007), these approaches often suffer from a certain degree of simplification (Hack, 2009). Presently, the composition of objectives in family firms, governance structure, resources and capabilities, as well as the industry (environment), are seen as key sources for heterogeneity of family firms (Chua et al., 2012). Statistical techniques of mediation and moderation analysis have triggered more differentiated results often combining elements from the "involvement" and "essence" definitions. For example, Chrisman et al. (2012) identified factors of "family essence" to mediate the relationship between family involvement ("components of involvement") and adoption of non-financial objectives. Other researchers have emphasized that the composition of family firms' objectives can be shaped by considerations of different dimensions of SEW[7]. For example, some family firms could accept higher risks to ensure family control while others would be willing to pollute less to create a

[7] SEW is a key theory used in family firm research and will be explained in chapter 2.

positive company image (Gómez-Mejía, Haynes, Nuñez-Nickel et al., 2007; Gómez-Mejía, Makri, & Larraza-Kintana, 2010; Berrone, Cruz, Gómez-Mejìa et al., 2010). The importance of non-financial goals that contribute to the affective endowment of the family is ultimately what distinguishes a family firm from a non-family firm—"its essence" (Berrone et al., 2010). The recent emphasis on heterogeneity of family firms makes it even more difficult to agree on a consistent definition of family firms. However, research approaches that capture various aspects of family firms' distinctiveness might be required and justified given the diversity of family firms.

If one accepts the diversity of family firms, every research consequently has to justify and explicitly give a definition of family firms. In empirical studies of family firms, quantifiable operationalizations are usually based on structural criteria such as ownership, which can serve as proxies for more sophisticated measurement (Astrachan et al., 2002; Engelskirchen, 2007). For example, high correlations between power and culture subscales are found for the F-PEC (Klein et al., 2005). For this thesis, family firms are defined as those firms with at least 50% of ownership concentrated among family owners, and which have member(s) of the family active in the business, whether it be in management or governance roles. This definition is consistent with those of leading researchers in the field (Eddleston & Kellermanns, 2007; Eddleston, Kellermanns, & Zellweger, 2012; Eddleston et al., 2008). When there is no comparison of family with non-family firms as in chapter 5, various factors of family influence such as "generational ownership dispersion" and "family members in the business" are used to account for and investigate the variations among the sample of family firms (Ling & Kellermanns, 2010).

1.2.2 Private equity firms

In this section, the nature of private equity (PE) firms is explained, including how such firms invest and how they are different from "traditional" companies. Furthermore, it describes how PE firms try to increase the value of their portfolio companies.

PE firms are investment companies focused on the acquisition of established companies. In general, PE "*(...) provides capital to invest in unquoted companies including public companies that are de-listed as part of the transaction. These investments may take the form of a purchase of shares from an existing shareholder (a buy-out if control is acquired) or an investment in new shares providing fresh capital to the investee company (development capital).*" (Gilligan & Wright, 2008, p. 10).[8] In the early 1980s, the first PE firms appeared in the U.S. and became prominent by realizing a rising number of acquisitions often involving large amounts of debt to finance transactions (Jensen, 1989). Since then, PE firms have spread globally and received considerable media attention and criticism (Wright et al., 2009). PE firms usually acquire the majority stakes in corporations and focus their investments on established companies which are usually characterized by stable cash flow streams. Investment in more developed companies ("later stage") rather than investments in companies that are just emerging or newly found ("early stage") is what distinguishes PE from VC as an investment class (Cumming & Johan, 2009). Businesses which are acquired by PE firms are usually referred to as "portfolio firms" or "PE-backed firms" or "investee company".

PE firms differ from "traditional" companies. PE firms are active investors, i.e. actively monitor, advise, and support the companies they are invested in and intend to re-sell or IPO the business to realize financial gains (Bottazzi, Da Rin, & Hellmann, 2008; Kaplan & Strömberg, 2009). Put differently, PE firms "buy to sell" (Barber & Goold, 2007, p. 54). PE firms show different characteristics related to size and composition of respective investment

[8] A broader definition of the term private equity would include funding for early stage (venture capital) investments (Klöckner, 2009).

portfolios as well as their investment strategy (Gupta & Sapienza, 1992; Amram & Kulatilaka, 1999; Cressy et al., 2007). Interaction with portfolio firms is the responsibility of PE firms' investment managers, who regularly meet management teams of portfolio firms and who are represented on governance boards (Klöckner, 2009). Some researchers consider the way PE firms do business as being superior and already predicted the "eclipse of the public corporation" due to its widespread inefficiencies in the use of free cash flow which is suppressed by PE firms (Jensen, 1989). Essentially, PE firms exist as intermediaries who raise certain funds which in turn are invested in acquisition targets, i.e. portfolio firms (Axelson, Strömberg, & Weisbach, 2009).[9] PE funds are comprised of capital provided by various investors over many years (e.g. pension funds) (Wright et al., 2009). Technically, PE funds are structured as limited partnerships where investors act as limited partners (LPs) and PE firms take over the role of general partners (GPs) (Axelson et al., 2009). Portfolio firms remain legally independent and PE firms are able to gain profits if the value of portfolio firms at the time of exit exceeds the acquisition price.

A key issue of PE firm research is how PE firms perform. It has been shown in prior research that PE-backed buyouts often lead to superior performance of portfolio firms (Boucly, Sraer, & Thesmar, 2011; Brown, Fee, & Thomas, 2009; Cumming, Siegel, & Wright, 2007; Amess, 2002; Amess, 2003; Gottschalg & Wright, 2008; Cressy et al., 2007; Wilson et al., 2012), and PE firms can provide their own investors with significant returns, although with some variance (Nikoskelainen & Wright, 2007; Cumming et al., 2007; Kaplan & Schoar, 2005). PE firms can use multiple instruments to achieve profitable performance. Dimensions of value creation in portfolio firms can be divided into financial, governance, and operational "engineering" (Kaplan & Strömberg, 2009). In particular, managers are motivated by incentives such as provision of substantial equity stakes (Kaplan, 1989; Heel & Kehoe,

9 In this Ph.D. thesis the term "PE firm" and "buyout fund" are used synonymously unless a distinction is required.

2005; Jensen, 1989) and disciplined in their use of free cash flows due to regular repayment of debt, typically put on the balance sheet of the buyout target (Wright et al., 2009; Jensen, 1986). Additionally, PE firms continuously monitor the performance of their portfolio companies, participate in smaller governance boards, frequently meet management teams, and do not hesitate to lay-off underperforming management teams (governance engineering) (Heel & Kehoe, 2005; Acharya, Kehoe, & Reyner, 2009). Operational engineering consists of all measures designed to improve operational performance (Kaplan, 1989; Smith, 1990), but which also add value to their portfolio firms via strategic advice often focused on growth initiatives (Nikoskelainen & Wright, 2007; Wilson et al., 2012). Thus, PE firms are able to complement existing resources and capabilities of management teams (de Clercq & Dimov, 2008; Meuleman et al., 2009). To do so, PE firms increasingly develop industry specializations (Cressy et al., 2007), which is recognized as the main factor in the success of PE firms' future ability to create value in buyout firms, marginalizing the role of financial engineering, governance engineering, and multiple arbitrage (Kaplan & Schoar, 2005; Kaplan, 2007; Heel & Kehoe, 2005).

1.2.3 Buyouts

PE firms typically achieve investments through buyout deals. The acquisition of portfolio firms is realized through buyouts in which PE firms and the (incumbent) management combine financing with equity and debt to acquire the majority of shares from the current owner and set up a new corporate entity (Meuleman et al., 2009). Buyouts are usually financed with a considerable amount of debt, up to 90% of the purchase price, which is why transactions are often referred to as leveraged buyouts (LBO) (Demiroglu & James, 2010). However, buyout deals are not necessarily the same and different forms can be distinguished (Wright et al., 2009). Most prominent buyout classifications differentiate buyouts by "type of acquirer" or the vendor's main intention for the sale (Jakoby, 2000; Klöckner, 2009). Other authors have grouped buyout deals by "mindset" and distinguish, for example, between "efficiency" or "revitalization" buyouts (Wright, Hoskisson, & Busenitz, 2001).

Buyout deals can be distinguished by type of acquirer involved in addition to PE firms. In a "Management Buy-In' (MBI), management external to the buyout target participates in the acquisition, i.e. is introduced as a new management team, usually with ownership shares (Gilligan & Wright, 2008; Cumming et al., 2007). In a "Management Buyout" (MBO), the incumbent management team (insiders) participates in the acquisition of the buyout target with significant shares (Gilligan & Wright, 2008; Cumming et al., 2007). A "Buy-In Management Buyout" (BIMBO) refers to the combination of both MBO and MBI (Meuleman et al., 2009).

Buyout deals can also be distinguished by reasons for the sale of the business. The vendor can have different reasons for selling the business in a buyout, including securing succession, turnaround, privatization, and spin-off (Klöckner, 2009; Jacoby, 2010). For example, "succession buyouts" are used to ensure succession of the family business (Scholes et al., 2008). "Turnaround buyouts" refers to buyouts involving companies in a crisis which need a restructuring process (Klöckner, 2009). "Privatization buyouts" (public-to-private) involve public companies transferring to private ownership (Gilligan & Wright, 2008). "Spin-off buyouts" refer to transactions in which certain divisions of larger corporate entities are carved out and are transferred to private ownership (Klöckner, 2009).

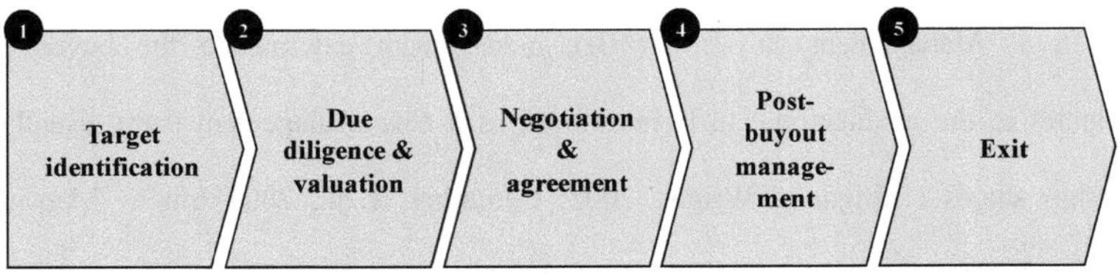

Figure 1-1: Buyout investment process
Source: Modified, based on Klöckner (2009)

1.2.4 Investment process

We can structure a stylized PE firm buyout investment into a process which consists of five steps as illustrated in ***Figure 1*** (Shepherd, Zacharakis, & Baron, 2003; Klöckner, 2009; Achleitner & Fingerle, 2003).

In step one, PE firms screen the market for attractive investment opportunities. Multiple sources can be used in this step such as personal networks of investment managers or advisors, announced auctions, and other available market information (Batjargal & Liu, 2004; de Clercq & Dimov, 2008; Klöckner, 2009). Certain attractive investment targets are selected by PE firms for further consideration and are contacted accordingly. The deal can also be initiated by the selling side, i.e. where potential sellers contact PE firms (Klöckner, 2009).

In step two, PE firms thoroughly analyze the investment target—a process called "due diligence". The primary goal of due diligence is to gather and interpret information about the investment target which allows the PE firm to determine its value and whether a deal would be promising (Crilly, 1998; Puranam, Powell, & Singh, 2006). Analysis in the due diligence step can be related to financial, legal, managerial, and strategic aspects of the business among others (Harvey & Lusch, 1995). Due diligence is essentially about "detecting signals" related to risks and opportunities associated with the buyout target (Puranam et al., 2006). Information generated from due diligence is ultimately translated into PE valuation models. Firm valuation is essential for expressing the economic value of a firm in monetary terms and thus establishing a basis for price negotiations (Damodaran, 2002; Granata & Chirico, 2010). Determining an appropriate value of the family firm is important before the PE buyer makes a bid or the vendor agrees to sell. According to financial theory, perceptions of firm value have to be supported by expected cash flows likely to be generated from the firm's assets (Damodaran, 2002).

In step three, negotiations take place between buying and selling side in order to achieve a transaction agreement. Buyout transactions are complex and include a number of financial, tax, and legal issues that need to be resolved between the negotiating parties (Reed, Lajoux, & Nesvold, 2007; Cumming & Johan, 2009). Often PE firms try to minimize risks with specific contractual terms that are negotiated with the seller (e.g. earn out).

In step four, PE firms act as active investors and together with the existing or new management try to increase the economic value of the portfolio firm (Barber & Goold, 2007; Kaplan & Strömberg, 2009).

In step five, the PE firm exits after a certain holding period (typically 3-7 years) (Wright et al., 2009). The exit can take several forms, such as trade sale, IPO or secondary buyout (Achleitner & Fingerle, 2003; Scholes et al., 2007).

1.3 Literature review

Every research project requires a point of departure from which it develops a distinct research contribution. A scientific point of departure is established if one comprehensively reviews previous literature in a particular field to evaluate the current stock of knowledge (Reuber, 2010). By doing so, it becomes obvious what prior research has contributed to date, its shortcomings and research gaps, and where future research can make valuable contributions (Reuber, 2010; Tranfield, Denyer, & Smart, 2003). The literature review process of this Ph.D. thesis has been structured as follows: Firstly, a clear methodology of review is developed, i.e. the principles by which the literature review is conducted. Secondly, the literature is analyzed following the previously developed methodology. By doing so, key characteristics and key aspects of existing literature are identified and summarized. Thirdly, research gaps which might require future consideration are highlighted. Lastly, the review is concluded by underlining key insights with relevance for the further course of this thesis.

1.3.1 Methodology

A clear methodology is required to conduct a literature review. The "systematic" literature review procedure (Tranfield et al., 2003) was structured into five steps which are *(1) identification of search terms*, *(2) selection criteria*, *(3) selection of databases*, *(4) literature identification*, and *(5) analysis strategy*—illustrated in ***Figure 2***. In the following, each step is briefly explained to maximize transparency, objectivity, replicability, and reliability of the literature review (Tranfield et al., 2003).

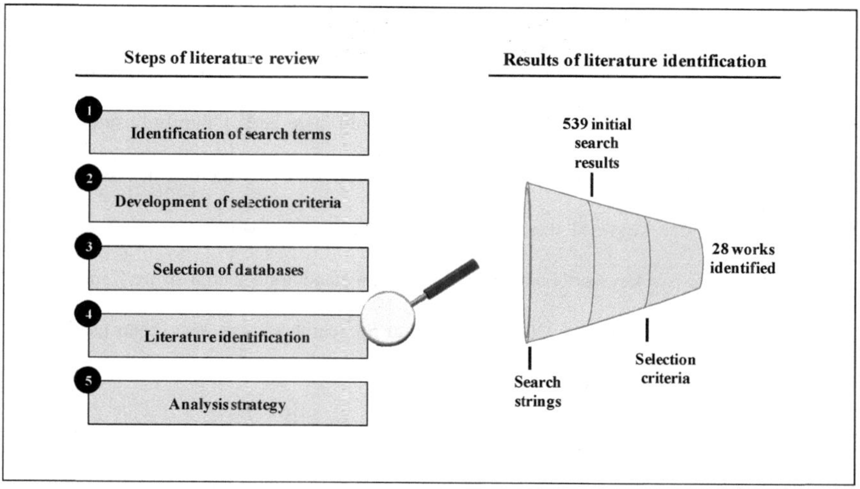

Figure 1-2: Literature review procedure
Source: Author

(1) Identification of search terms. This literature review deals with the research interface of (a) PE and (b) family firms. Comprehensive literature reviews for each singular research topic and multiple sub-issues are already available for family firms (Handler, 1994; Sharma et al., 1997; Casillas & Acedo, 2007; Debicki, Matherne III, Kellermanns et al., 2009) and PE (Wright Robbie, 1998; Cumming et al., 2007; Wood & Wright, 2009). Thus, this review is specifically focused on the interface of PE and family firms which usually takes place when PE firms invest in family firm buyout targets. Research which goes beyond or has no particular implications for the research interface is of minor interest for this review. Accordingly, the identification of search terms began with keywords related to each side of the interface—(a) PE and (b) family firms. The initial list of keywords resort to the author's prior experience and is complemented by three interviews conducted with two experienced academics in the field of family business research and one practitioner from the PE industry.

For part (a) PE, 13 keywords were identified.[10] For part (b) family firm, four keywords were identified.[11] Part (a) and part (b) keywords were combined and resulted in the creation of 52 search strings (13*4). For example, search strings could have been ["family business" AND "LBO"] or ["family firm" AND "private equity"]. Additionally, it seemed necessary to add three keywords—one keyword was used on a standalone basis which was "entrepreneurial exit" and the other two keywords were used to create a standalone search string ["succession" AND "private equity"]. In total, 20 keywords and 53 search strings have been used as the basis for the literature review.

(2) Selection criteria. Selection criteria were used to specify the scope of the literature review, i.e. to make it manageable. Firstly, the review only included peer-reviewed journals, peer-reviewed conference contributions, and Ph.D. theses to ensure academic quality of reviewed works. Working papers were only added if they seemed to provide the very latest research insights. Secondly, only research published after 1995 was utilized in order for the research to be current. Thirdly, all industries and all countries in which research was undertaken relating to this subject was considered. Fourth, research on PE minority investments (i.e. deals involving no majority control of PE firms) was included. Inclusion of PE minority investments research was needed because it could reveal insights about the relationship between family firms and PE and because minority investments can trigger buyouts later on (Tappeiner et al., 2012). Fifth, only academic work was considered, be it conceptual or empirical, and hence, work dedicated primarily to practitioners was excluded. Sixth, works focusing on technical specifics of deal-making only relevant for specialists such as legal, tax or accounting issues were not included. Seventh, academic work focused on early stage investments (i.e. venture capital) was excluded. However, since the use of the terms "venture capital" and "private equity" is sometimes confusingly similar, papers dealing with

[10] The keywords are: acquisition, business transfer, business exit, buyout, divestment, divestiture, emotional value, financial investor, LBO, MBI, MBO, private equity, and takeover

[11] The keywords are: family business, family firm, family ownership, privately-owned business

venture capital when the definition was apparently referring to private equity were also included. Eighth, academic work which did not devote a significant proportion of its content to the interface of PE and family firms or did not have significant implications was eliminated. For example, some papers on entrepreneurial exit that did not focus particularly on family firms or on the PE/buyout route were removed (DeTienne, 2010; DeTienne & Cardon, 2012). However, papers on "emotional value" were included because they could have significant implications for valuation in buyout deals, a key part of deal-making (Granata & Chirico, 2010). It is acknowledged that some form of academic "judgment" is needed for this criterion. Ninth, only papers written in either English or German were considered for the review.

(3) Selection of databases. For the literature search, two prominent databases for management research were used which are "EBSCO host" (Business Source Premier) and "ScienceDirect". Coverage of research outlets within the aforementioned databases is subject to change and was complemented by "manual search" for which "Google Scholar" was employed. The search strings generated in step (1) were used in the respective databases. Furthermore, search in the databases was narrowed to include only the title, abstract and author-provided keywords to make the number of search results manageable.

(4) Literature identification. For the database "EBSCO host", a total of 380 unique search results were identified, i.e. duplicative results due to similar search strings were eliminated. "ScienceDirect" yielded 159 unique search results. The 539 papers were reviewed and used to refine the selection criteria described in step (2). Using the selection criteria, 14 papers were selected from "EBSCO host", along with four papers from "ScienceDirect" (after removing duplicates with "EBSCO host"), and ten were selected from "manual search". Thus, a total of 28 papers were identified and selected for the literature review.

(5) Reviewing strategy. To review all 28 papers in a consistent and systematic manner, each work was summarized and classified in terms of (a) "specific research topic", (b) "research question", (c) "research perspective", (d) "theories applied", (e) "characteristics of the sample", (f) "geographic scope", and (g) "key findings". All work was further grouped into five (largely) distinct content categories. The categories are "market", "information asymmetry", "PE firms' perception and decision-making", "family firms' perception and decision-making", and "strategic change".

"Market" refers to works which assess the distinctiveness of the market for family firm buyouts, i.e. what quantitative characteristics (e.g. deal size, number of deals) apply to family firm buyouts compared to non-family buyouts. "Information asymmetry" refers to all works which investigate the distribution of information between the deal parties, its antecedents and consequences. "PE firms' perception and decision-making" refers to works dealing with the PE firms' perception of the target family firm and how investment decisions for family firm (buyouts) are made. "Family firms' perception and decision-making" includes works related to the family firm's general perception of PE firms, particularly about the buyout route and the specific needs as well as selection criteria used to select among different PE firms. "Strategic change" refers to forms of strategic change such as growth, efficiency, or governance settings triggered by changing ownership from family to PE ownership following a buyout. The summary of each work and composition of each category is given in ***Table 1***. Findings of the literature review are discussed in the next section.

Authors / Year of publication	Topics	Research question	Perspective	Type of research	Theory	Sample	Country / region	Key message
(A) Market								
Scholes, Wright, Westhead, Bruining, Kloeckner (2009)	Market overview Strategic changes	What is the market size for FF buyouts in Europe? How do former FFs change strategically in the post-buyout period?	Neutral; management for 2nd research question	Empirical	N/a	Database with ~30 tsd buyout deals; sample with 104 managers in FFs which underwent a buyout	Europe	• ~29% of all buyouts in Europe between 1998 and 2007 are classified as FF buyouts; in 2007 this corresponds to 559 family deals and an average deal size of ~€45 m • Strategic changes related to efficiency improvements and company growth are higher when a founder leads the family business pre-buyout and the TMT is run and controlled by family members
(B) Information asymmetry								
Howorth, Westhead, Wright (2004)	Level of information asymmetries Inhibitors of information asymmetries Deal satisfaction	How do information asymmetries impact the buyout process when FFs are concerned?	Buyer/ vendor	Empirical	Agency, trust, negotiation	8 case studies	UK	• Buyouts comprise a high degree of information asymmetries between vendor and buyer especially in MBI deals • Information asymmetries are lower if the buyout is part of the FFs' long-term plan, mutual involvement of vendor/seller sides, and positive relationships (trust, friendship, understanding) • Deal satisfaction is higher with low information asymmetries, positive relationships, trust, mutual involvement and co-operative negotiation behavior • Continuous involvement post-buyout of the former family owner mitigates information asymmetries

Authors / Year of publication	Topics	Research question	Perspective	Type of research	Theory	Sample	Country / region	Key message
Scholes, Wright, Westhead, Burrows, Bruining (2007)	Information sharing Price agreement	How are FFs' ownership and governance structures associated with balanced information sharing and a mutually agreed sale price?	Buyer	Empirical	Agency, game theory	114 respondents each representing a buyout	Europe	• Information-sharing: founder-run FFs and those with a priority for financial objectives are associated with equal information sharing; explanation: founders prefer to stay involved post-buyout and financial objectives suggest a de-prioritization of family goals • Mutually agreed price: FFs without a family successor, a priority for financial goals, and early involvement of investors more likely report a mutually agreed sale price
Scholes, Westhead, Burrows (2008)	Information sharing Price agreement	How are FFs' ownership and governance structures associated with balanced information sharing and a mutually agreed sale price?	Buyer	Empirical	Agency	114 respondents each representing a buyout	Europe	• Information-sharing: mutual involvement of FF owners and management in succession planning leads to lower information asymmetries • Agreed price: mutually involvement in succession planning and information-sharing increases the probability for a mutually agreed sale price • PE firm involvement negatively affects a mutually agreed sale price because it could more effectively challenge the vendor
Dehlen, Zellweger, Kammerlander, Halter (2012)	Succession paths	How do information asymmetries on potential external successors affect the probability for internal (family) succession vs. external succession via buyout?	Successors	Empirical	Information asymmetry theory, SEW	613 respondents	Germany, Switzerland	• Information asymmetries between owners and potential external entrants as successors lead to a higher likelihood for intra-family succession • External succession through MBI/MBO can become more likely if owners increase screening efforts (inverted U-shape relationship) and potential external successors signal suitability (e.g. experience, education) • Above mentioned relationships are weakened with increasing firm age as a driver of emotional attachment

Authors / Year of publication	Topics	Research question	Perspective	Type of research	Theory	Sample	Country / region	Key message
(C) PE perceptions and decision-making								
Upton, Petty (2000)	Investment criteria	What perceptions and criteria of investors regarding FFs are important for succession financing?	Buyer/ vendor	Empirical	N/a	53 PE investors, 85 family owners	U.S.	• Financing of family succession is of high relevance for FFs, but owners prefer to use family capital, the firm's cash flow, or bank loans • PE firms are willing to participate in succession financing and are compensated for by debt, shares, and warrants or conversion rights • PE firms' evaluation of transition investments considers successor qualification, future business strategy, and family harmony
Silva (2005)	Perceptions Investment criteria	Is investing in FFs any different for PE managers?	Buyer	Empirical	N/a	7 interviews	Finland	• FFs are considered an important source of deal flow but in comparison to non-FFs, they are more complex and riskier • The same investment criteria are used for family- and non-FFs, but deal structuring could differ because PE firms recognize families' need for control
Granata (2010)	Perceptions	How do PE managers perceive FFs?	Buyer	Empirical	N/a	154 respondents	Western Europe	• Differences between family and non-FFs are recognized, but do not necessarily trigger different evaluations • PE managers that perceive FFs differently associate higher investment risks and less professional mgmt. structures with FFs
Granata, Chirico (2010)	Evaluation	How do buyers value the family business?	Buyer	Empirical	RBV, stewardship	73 matched pairs of family and non-FFs	Western Europe	• FFs are acquired at a discount of ~16% • Investors do not recognize FFs' true value because FFs are perceived as rather unprofessional and inefficient

Authors / Year of publication	Topics	Research question	Perspective	Type of research	Theory	Sample	Country / region	Key message
Dawson (2011)	Investment criteria	Which investment criteria are used by PE managers for FF targets?	Buyer	Empirical	Agency, RBV	41 respondents, 1312 observations in conjoint analysis	Italy	• Aspects specific to FF are used to make investment decisions • Professionalized FFs (with family members who posess outside work experience and nonfamily managers) and future reduction of family involvement after deal closure are considered positive by PE managers
(D) Family perceptions and decision-making								
Poutziouris (2001)[12]	Capital preferences Family concerns	Do family and non-FFs have different rationales and perceptions for dealing with PE investors?	Buyer	Empirical	Pecking order theory	240 companies, 150 non-family and 90 FFs	UK	• FFs prefer to rely on internal capital to ensure growth and survival • Families' greatest concern is to share control and displacement of family managers
Poech, Achleitner, Burger-Calderon (2005)	Psychological barriers Intermediaries	What psychological barriers inhibit deal closure?	Buyer	Empirical	Sender-receiver model	21 interviews	Germany	• Different mindsets, stereotypes, and selective information processing between family owners and PE firms inhibits collaboration • Intermediaries are suggested as mitigating relationship difficulties
Astrachan, Jaskiewicz, (2008)	Valuation	How do family sellers value their business?	Buyer	Conceptual	Utility theory	-	U.S.	• Sellers value their business based on emotional returns and costs • Depending on whether emotional returns or costs weigh more, the family business is perceived as worth more or less compared to non-family firms

[12] Poutziouris subsumes under venture capital what is usually referred to as PE/buyout investments

Authors / Year of publication	Topics	Research question	Perspective	Type of research	Theory	Sample	Country / region	Key message
Zelleweger, Astrachan, (2008)	Evaluation	How do family sellers value their business?	Buyer	Conceptual	Endowment, possession attachment	-	Europe/ U.S.	• "Emotional value" is the residual between the financial value of the firm and the sellers' WTA driven by emotional returns and costs • Emotional value unrelated to the financial value of the firm inhibits transfer of ownership • Multiple factors such as the owner's demographics or marketability of the firm influence effects of emotional costs and returns on WTA
Burkhardt, (2008) [Dissertation]	Selection criteria	What drives success of FF buyout transaction?	Buyer/ vendor	Empirical	-	6 case studies	Switzer-land	• For family or entrepreneurial sellers, the buyout sale is often the "last option" • Family sellers emphasize trust and "serious interest" as key decision criteria for selecting PE investors
Niedermeyer, Jaskiewicz, Klein (2010)	Drivers of deal satisfaction	What drives family sellers' satisfaction when selling the family business?	Vendor	Conceptual (Empirical)	Utility theory	one exemplary case study	Germany	• Family sellers' initial sale satisfaction is affected by the level of perceived fairness during interactions, the level of control, flexibility to select buyers, goal alignment, and realization of adequate sale price • Family sellers' retrospective satisfaction is affected by ongoing association with the business, information exchange with new owners, and the pursuit of new entrepreneurial activities
Graebner, Eisenhardt (2010)	Selection criteria	What is important for owners in privately owned businesses when selling the business?	Vendor	Empirical	N/A	12 cases; 80 interviews	U.S.	• Entrepreneurial sellers adopt an active and influential role in the sale process which centers around a long-term and sustainable perspective for the business • Sellers' decision-making is comprised of multiple factors which go beyond price maximization and self-interest • Sellers feel more inclined to sell the business to investors who offer potential for business synergies

Authors / Year of publication	Topics	Research question	Perspective	Type of research	Theory	Sample	Country / region	Key message
								and to whom they feel connected (organizational rapport)
Salvato, Chiricio, Sharma (2010)	Role of family heritage	What psychologically affects family sellers when selling the business?	Vendor	Empirical	Strategic change, commitment	one case study	Italy	• Selling the business or parts of it can be a source of strategic renewal for the FF • Family has to identify a suitable pathway that ensures preservation of institutional identity and anchoring in the founders' heritage when selling parts of the business
Zellweger, Kellermanns, Chrisman, Chua (2011)	Evaluation	How do family sellers value their business?	Vendor	Empirical	SEW, Prospect theory	83 respondents in Swiss sample and 148 in German sample	Germany, Switzer-land	• Family sellers require SEW which increases with the need for transgenerational control • Due to SEW, family sellers would sell the business for a lower price to family members
Tappeiner, Howorth, Achleitner, Schraml (2012)	Selection criteria for minority financing	What shapes FFs' demand for PE minority investments?	Buyer / vendor/ management	Empirical	Agency	21 case studies	Germany	• FFs' demand and likelihood for PE investment is driven by three factors: (1) financing need, (2) PE firms' non-financial resource contribution, (3) costs for ceding control rights • Incompleteness of pecking-order hypothesis for FFs because factors of family influence are ignored • PE firms are granted increased control rights if family conflicts are solved, PE firm's neutrality is assumed, and relational trust exists
(E) Strategic change								
Goossens, Manigart, Meuleman (2008)	Growth and efficiency	How does the new ownership post-buyout influences growth and efficiency of the	N/A	Empirical	Agency	167 buyouts, 43 FFs	Belgium	• Family- and non-FF buyouts with and without PE involvement are compared • If strategic change is measured as "growth" in total assets, sales, and employees—no significant differences occur between family and non-family

Authors / Year of publication	Topics	Research question	Perspective	Type of research	Theory	Sample	Country / region	Key message
		former FF?						buyouts; PE involvement is associated only with employee growth • If strategic change is measured as "efficiency" improvements, neither previous family ownership nor involvement of PE have an significant differentiating effect
Klöckner, (2009)	Value creation	What are the changes associated with FF buyouts for corporate governance, managerial control instruments and finance?	Buyer/ vendor	Empirical	Agency, Sewardship	32 case studies	Germany	• Buyouts create value in FFs through "professionalization" and "economization" while potentially creating higher agency costs when FFs change from stewardship to agency governance • "Professionalization" refers to enhancement of corporate governance and organizational processes—PE firms enable strategies of internationalization and M&A, hire more professional managers, increase monetary incentives, introduce ambitious targets, establish supervisory boards to tighten control, and improve planning, accounting, and performance management practices • "Economization" refers to new corporate goals that prioritize financial over non-financial goals
Scholes, Wright, Westhead, Bruining, (2010)	Growth and efficiency Effects of family configurations	How do family characteristics pre-buyout effect growth and efficiency changes post-buyout?	Management	Empirical	Agency, Stewardship	104 buyouts	Europe	• Univariate analysis: strategic change measured as efficiency gains and strategic growth are higher in PE-backed buyouts if the founder was present, no NED and no non-family management existed before deal closure; involvement of PE firms or internal management pre-buyout also triggered these changes • Multivariate analysis: only non-family management without equity shares pre-buyout is confirmed to

Authors / Year of publication	Topics	Research question	Perspective	Type of research	Theory	Sample	Country / region	Key message
								induce strategic change (efficiency, growth) post-buyout
Achleitner, Herman, Lerner, Lutz (2010)	Governance/ value creation	Do FFs offer potential for value creation based on governance engineering?	Buyer / vendor/ management	Empirical	Agency	one case study	Germany	• Value creation through governance engineering by PE firms does not originate in ownership concentration, but changes in strategy, operations, and incentives through PE firms' board representation • Buyouts can be a force to reinforce family entrepreneurship
Wulf, Stubner, Gietl, Landau (2010)	Performance enhancing activities of PE	What is the effect of PE firms' involvement on former FFs?	Company	Empirical	RBV	118	Europe	• Many support activities (e.g. financial mgmt, operational, strategic) of PE firms do not add performance to the former family business except if PE fosters cooperation and networking with other portfolio firms • For a sub-group of under-performing FFs pre-buyout, PE firms support activities related to professionalization of organizational structures and systems is positively related to performance—the impact can be negative if PE firms get involved in operational activities
Braun, Zacharias, Latham (2011)	Differences in governance structures	How do governance structures between FFs and LBOs differ and what are its performance implications?	Company	Conceptual	Agency, stewardship	-	U.S.	• FFs' governance structures are characterized by long-term business orientation and both financial and non-financial objectives • LBOs' governance structures reflect short-termism and shareholder value maximization • FFs' governance structures have performance advantages during times of economic stagnation whereas LBO structures outperform in economic growth cycles

Authors / Year of publication	Topics	Research question	Perspective	Type of research	Theory	Sample	Country / region	Key message
Grundström, Öberg, Rönnbäck (2012)	Innovation Succession paths	How is innovative behavior affected when comparing internal (family) succession to external succession (e.g. buyouts)?	Buyer/ vendor	Empirical		5 internal succession cases, 5 external succession cases (mainly buyouts)	Sweden	• New owners in external succession exhibit higher orientation towards innovating behavior • Family successors tend to focus on incremental innovation and diversify businesses so that resource shedding can be avoided • Intermediating factors such as customer involvement or acquirers' motives need to be considered
Chrisman, Chua, Steier, Wright, McKee (2012)	Governance/ value creation	How do agency costs develop post-buyout?	Company	Conceptual	Agency	-	U.S./ Europe	• Value creation in MBOs is conceived as a reduction in agency costs • Agency cost reduction is dependent on pre-buyout agency costs associated with different family configurations (e.g. solely owned vs. dispersed ownership), minimization of agency costs between upper and lower level management, and balancing the relationship of agency control costs and residual losses

Table 1-1: Literature review: overview of selected works

Source: Author

1.3.2 Key findings

The key findings of the literature review will be presented as follows. Firstly, the sample of selected studies is described in terms of publication date, research approach, key research journals, and theories applied. Secondly, the literature is reviewed based on five content categories into which the selected works have been grouped. Lastly, the key overall findings of each content category are summarized and evaluated.

1.3.2.1 Description of selected studies

The majority of selected studies (~79%) were published in the last 5 years, i.e. between 2007 and 2012, which indicates a rising interest and relevance of the research subject. The research is predominantly empirical (~82%) and a lower proportion is conceptual (~18%). Empirical research is almost evenly split between quantitative studies (~52%) and qualitative studies (~48%)—the latter almost exclusively based on case study research. When research on PE firms and family firms is quantitative, many of the studies are characterized by small sample sizes, which might be due to difficulties in gathering and accessing appropriate data. The number of buyout deals is limited and most deals occur under agreements of confidentiality. Additionally, key informants participating in these deals are distinguished TMT members and highly qualified PE investment managers with limited free time at their disposal (Fenn, Liang, & Prowse, 1997).

Many of the selected studies were published in family-firm-specific or PE-specific journals such as "Family Business Research" (four studies), "Journal of Family Business Strategy" (three studies), and "Journal of Private Equity" (three studies), but also within leading management journals such as "Journal of Business Venturing" (three studies). The overall number of publications, although the number is rising, indicates that research on the specific topic of family firms and PE is still in an early stage of development (Tappeiner et al., 2012).

The large majority of the studies use agency theory (~39%), followed by stewardship theory (~14%), and RBV (~11%). The dominance of the aforementioned theories is not surprising in this research context. Agency theory assumes that individuals will follow self-interest and will be incentivized by financial objectives (Ross, 1973; Jensen & Meckling, 1976; Fama, 1980; Fama & Jensen, 1983). Additionally, agency theory focuses on situations of information asymmetry, with conflicting goals between a "principal" and an "agent" (Akerlof, 1970; Eisenhardt, 1989). Essentially, the principals need to protect themselves against the agents' potentially opportunistic behavior by utilizing control mechanisms and appropriate incentives to align potentially conflicting interests (Eisenhardt, 1989; Jensen & Meckling, 1976). As PE-backed buyouts usually take place in markets less transparent for corporate control (Capron & Shen, 2007) and PE firms' primary goal is reckoned to be the maximization of shareholder value (Wright et al., 2009), the relationship between PE firms and portfolio firms can be conceived as a "principal-agent" setting (Sahlman, 1990). Thus, the application of the agency theory appears warranted in this research context.

"Stewardship theory" differs to agency theory and has been frequently applied to family firms. Stewardship theory has been used to distinguish between family firms and non-family firms (Davis, Allen, & Hayes, 2010; Eddleston et al., 2012). According to this theory, individuals may naturally act as stewards of the firm, i.e. act in the interest of the principal, the organization, and/or the firms' stakeholders (Davis, Schoorman, & Donaldson, 1997). Formal control mechanisms of agency theory are replaced by relationship elements of trust, common values, culture, and reciprocity which could mitigate the risk of exploitation by the principals (Mayer, Davis, & Schoorman, 1995; Davis et al., 1997). The RBV, similarly to stewardship theory, has been applied frequently to family firms because special resource bundles are considered as an explanation for family firms' competitive advantage (Sirmon & Hitt, 2003). In general, RBV explains that family firms hold a sustainable competitive advantage against other firms because of the unique character of resources they possess

(Penrose, 1959; Wernerfelt, 1984; Barney, 1991; Peteraf, 1993). According to Barney, these resources can be defined as *"...all assets, capabilities, organizational processes, firm attributes, information, knowledge, etc., controlled by the firm that enable the firm to conceive of and implement strategies that improve its efficiency and effectiveness"* (Barney, 1991, p. 101). Resources provide a sustainable competitive advantage if they are "valuable", "scarce", "inimitable", and "non-substituable" (Barney, 1991).

1.3.2.2 Identified research categories

Five (largely) distinct categories can be distilled from the findings of this prior research. The categories are (A) "market", (B) "information asymmetry", (C) "PE firms' perception and decision-making", (D) "family firms' perception and decision-making", and (E) "strategic change". The categories are illustrated in ***Figure 3***.

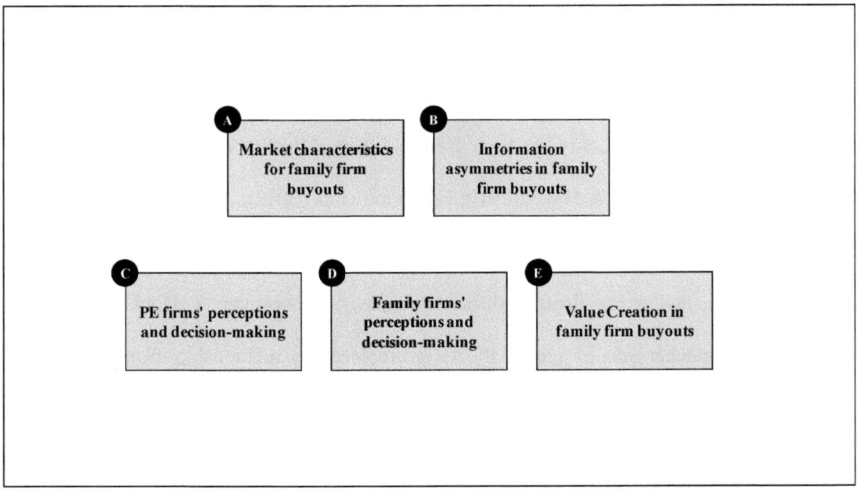

Figure 1-3: Identified categories of literature review
Source: Author

(A) Market. There is very limited information available on the market size and quantitative characteristics of family firm buyouts. Only one of the studies comprises a detailed review of market information on family firm buyouts (Scholes et al., 2009). Unfortunately, information is only given until 2007 and no follow-up studies are available. Although buyout markets have been undergone changes since 2007, including contraction during the financial market crises (Wilson et al., 2012), the information available sheds some light on specific characteristics of family firm buyouts. Market information from European countries from 1998 until 2007 reveals that family buyout deals are generally smaller in size, i.e. the average deal size over the past 10 years is largely constant at ~ €26 m whereas non-family firm deal size is steadily increasing, reaching its climax in 2007 at ~ €120 m. If PE firms are involved in family buyouts, the transaction size is considerably higher at ~ €41 m whereas it is only ~ €7 m when PE firms are not involved. The total number of family buyout transactions represents on average ~29% of all buyout transactions between 1998 and 2007 (total number of buyouts in 2007 ~1,930 deals), but only accounts for a value share of ~11% of the total buyout market (total value of buyouts in 2007 ~ €16.6 bn). Additionally, there is considerable difference in size of family firms involved in buyouts across European countries. In Germany, for example, the 10-year average for the number of employees per deal is 794 whereas it is only 339 in Italy and 224 in the UK.

Three aspects can be concluded from the market-related research study. Firstly, family buyouts are usually smaller in size. It is important to recognize the size of family buyout deals because smaller firms (SMEs) might have distinct characteristics in deal-making due to size and not due to family influence. Thus, one needs to be cautious when attributing phenomena to family influence when it could occur because of the firm size. For example, smaller firms might face expertise disadvantages when dealing with PE firms because they possess insufficient resources and capabilities (Barney, 1986; Barney, 1991; Peteraf, 1993). Secondly, family firms constitute a key source of deals for PE firms and thus represent a large share of the buyout market. Thirdly, one needs to be cautious when interpreting the information on family buyout markets. It has already been acknowledged that definitions of family firms differ and the reviewed work only employs one of many definitions (Astrachan et al., 2002; Klein, 2000; Klein et al., 2005; Chua et al., 2012). Thus, other definitions of family firms might yield considerably different results.[13] ***Figure 4*** displays all data from 1998 until 2007.

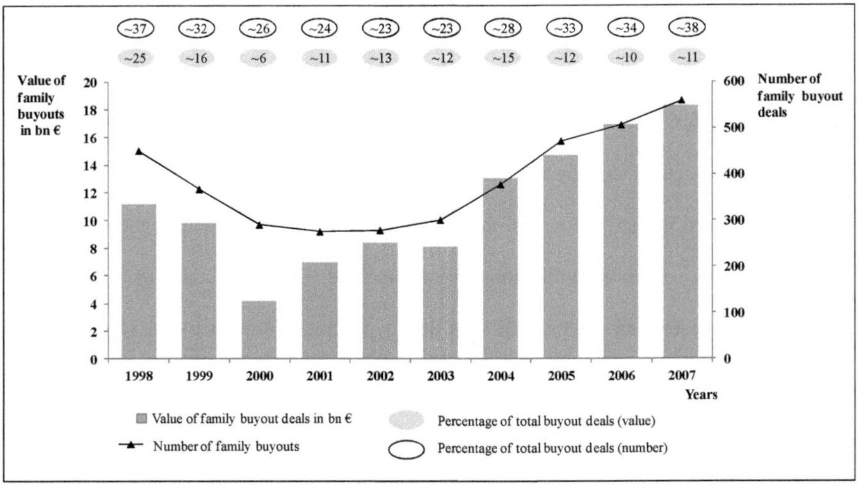

Figure 1-4: Buyout market for family firms
Source: Modified, based on Scholes et al. (2009)

(B) Information asymmetries and decision-making. Four studies dealing with aspects of information asymmetry could be identified. In particular, one study highlights the role of information asymmetries in selecting a succession route (Dehlen, Zellweger, Kammerlander et al., 2012) and three studies deal with information asymmetries in buyouts (Howorth et al., 2004; Scholes et al., 2007; Scholes et al., 2008). Howorth, Westhead, & Wright (2004) emphasize the role of positive relationships and relational factors such as trust and mutual involvement between the deal parties when planning for the buyout which facilitates the flow

[13] Scholes et al. (2009) have defined family firms as where a single family group has >50% ownership of a firm.

of information. The work of Scholes et al. (2007) illustrates how family firm characteristics such as the involvement of the founder and professionalized management structures can contribute to improved information-sharing. Scholes et al. (2008) show that mutual involvement of the management team and the selling family firm owner when planning the succession is beneficial, in that it limits information asymmetries and helps address conflicts of interest in family firm buyouts.

A mutually agreed sale price is more likely to result when no family successor was available or financial objectives are of the family firms' priority (Scholes et al., 2007). However, the role of PE firms for a mutually agreed sale price remains unclear—Scholes et al. (2007) show that a mutually agreed sale price is more likely when the PE firms are involved in buyout planning whereas in the subsequent study of Scholes et al. (2008) PE firms' involvement leads to a mutually agreed sale price being less likely.

The study of Dehlen et al. (2012) underlines the role of information asymmetries one step earlier, i.e. when the decision for a succession path is made by (family) owners. It illustrates that family firms are generally biased towards intra-family succession paths (Dehlen et al., 2012). However, if family owners undertake efforts to reduce information asymmetries, such as screening, the external succession through a buyout can become more likely (Dehlen et al., 2012). Socioemotional wealth (SEW)[14], measured by age of firm can limit screening activities and the authors conclude that emotional attachment makes family succession more likely and leads to increased difficulties for family departure from business activities (Dehlen et al., 2012).

The prominent role of information asymmetries is unsurprising given adjacent literature. Most family firms are often privately held (Klein, 2000; Wang, 2006). The quality and quantity of information available about private firms is usually lower compared to information about public firms (Capron & Shen, 2007). Limited information availability on

[14] See chapter 2.1.1

privately held companies is due to a weaker market for corporate control (analysts, investment banks etc.) and less stringent regulations on information disclosure (Shen & Reuer, 2005; Ragozzino & Reuer, 2010). The market for corporate control has an important function in providing information and supporting asset evaluation (Capron & Shen, 2007). In addition, information availability could be further constrained by family firms' high degree of tacitness and a lower willingness to share information with those outside the family (Cabrera-Suárez et al., 2001; Lee, Lim, & Lim, 2003; Nonaka & Takeuchi, 1995). In particular, MBI deals might suffer from information asymmetries because the existing management is not part of the buying coalition (Howorth et al., 2004).

A few preliminary conclusions can be drawn from the selected literature on information asymmetries. Firstly, family firm owners and the incumbent management team potentially face conflicts of interest, especially in MBI deals, in which case the buying and selling side should be wary (Howorth et al., 2004). Secondly, the high complexity of a buyout route requires long-term planning in order to prepare and to achieve a sound information basis for successful deal-making. The collaboration of management and family owners appears to be beneficial in this process (Scholes et al., 2008). Families' needs for SEW potentially lead to a "biased" or "postponed" succession process (Dehlen et al., 2012). Thirdly, the actual relationship between buyer and seller in buyouts deals can play a key role in facilitating information flows and cooperative bargaining solutions (Howorth et al., 2004). Lastly, advisors might play a valuable role to facilitate the buyout process and to brokerage deals (Scholes et al., 2009).

(C) PE firms' perceptions and decision-making. Another category of studies examines if and how family firms are perceived by PE investors, compared to non-family firms. There are five identifiable papers in this category (Upton & Petty, 2000; Silva, 2006; Granata & Chirico, 2010; Granata, 2010; Dawson, 2011). Family firms are often perceived differently by potential acquirers, compared to non-family buyout targets—which is highlighted in several studies (Silva, 2006; Granata, 2010; Dawson, 2011). In particular, family firms are considered riskier investment targets because of the higher complexity resulting from the intertwinement of family and business systems (Silva, 2006; Granata, 2010). Additionally, family firms are associated with less professional management that could favor particular family interests and by doing so emphasize non-financial goals over financial ones (Granata, 2010), leading to lower company valuations (Granata & Chirico, 2010). Dawson (2011) argues that family firm investment targets could be perceived more positively by PE investors if selling owners exit the business soon after the buyout and if management structures are already professionalized. If PE investors participate in succession financing (usually minority investments), the qualifications of the successor, the business strategy, and the degree of harmony in family relationships are considered by PE firms (Upton & Petty, 2000).

Two main findings can be concluded from this review category. Firstly, family firms are indeed perceived by PE investors as being different from non-family firm targets. Secondly, the difference in perception is rather negative, i.e. PE investors emphasize the negative side of family influence and in particular the additional risks associated with family firm investments (e.g. owner-centricity). However, these findings contrast with research on family firms highlighting performance advantages of family firms (Anderson & Reeb, 2003; Villalonga & Amit, 2006) and prior research that argues family firms can be both a source of performance advantage, but also disadvantage (Sirmon & Hitt, 2003; Miller & Le Breton-Miller, 2006).

(D) Family firms' perceptions and decision-making. The perception of PE firms represents only one perspective on the relationship between family firms and private equity firms. It is not surprising that another strand of studies examine the family or vendors' perspective. A total of ten works fall into this category (Poutziouris, 2001; Poech et al., 2005; Astrachan & Jaskiewicz, 2008; Zellweger & Astrachan, 2008; Burkhardt, 2008; Niedermeyer et al., 2010; Graebner & Eisenhardt, 2004; Salvato, Chirico, & Sharma, 2010; Zellweger et al., 2011; Tappeiner et al., 2012). Poutziouris (2001) shows how family firms are hesitant to use external sources of financing and in particular sources that would require them to give up ownership control, which applies to PE financing—indicating that the pecking-order hypothesis could apply to family firms. The pecking-order hypothesis proposes preference of internal funds over debt, and, once debt capacities are maximized, external equity is used (Myers, 1984). However, Tappeiner et al. (2012) argue the pecking-order hypothesis needs modification and refinement for family firms. In particular, the authors illustrate that family firms' demand and the likelihood for utilizing PE (minority) investment is driven not only by financing needs, but also by how well PE firms are equipped to provide non-financial resources, the costs associated with ceding control rights, and how relational factors play out (Tappeiner et al., 2012). Furthermore, it is important to consider family influence such as the need for SEW to understand financing decisions of family firms (Tappeiner et al., 2012). For example, family owners would be willing to cede control rights if family conflicts can be resolved due to PE firm involvement, the PE firm is able to provide complementary expertise, and if the PE firm is regarded as trustworthy (Tappeiner et al., 2012).

SEW seems to play a bigger role when families exit the business. Family firm owners struggle to sell their business and have difficulties letting go of the business due to emotional attachment which is driven by the emotional costs and benefits that occurred over time (Astrachan & Jaskiewicz, 2008; Zellweger & Astrachan, 2008). In particular, it can be a feeling of responsibility to carry on the family's heritage that makes it difficult to make decisions as to how to shed resources (Salvato et al., 2010). Zellweger & Astrachan (2008) emphasize how family business owners' emotional attachment is a key dimension of SEW that can develop over time and may distort family business owners' value perception, i.e. family sellers attach a higher value to the firm that cannot be explained by the financial value of business performance but rather by "emotions". This might make it difficult to transfer the business to a PE firm in a buyout, as "emotions" cannot help justify to the market what might be an acceptable price for the family firm (Zellweger & Astrachan, 2008). However, emotional value can also lower the market price when family CEOs sell to family members—as shown by Zellweger and colleagues (2011). Moreover, it is not only the type of buyer but also the quality of the buyer-seller relationship (with factors such as organizational rapport, relational trust, cultural fit and a long-term interest shown by the buyer in the prosperity of the business) that plays an important role (Burkhardt, 2008; Graebner & Eisenhardt, 2004). Unsurprisingly, Niedermeyer et al. (2011) hypothesize how families' deal satisfaction can be driven not just by an adequate sales price, but also by factors of procedural fairness, goal alignment, opportunities to select among different buyers, and an ongoing post-sale connection with the former family business (Niedermeyer et al., 2010).

Psychological "barriers" might exist when family firms are dealing with PE firms. The study of Poech, Achleitner & Burger-Calderon (2005) illuminates how family sellers often feel confronted with a different "mindset" which does not match family firm philosophy when dealing with PE firms (Poech et al., 2005). Family perceptions, however, might be biased according to stereotypes and a lack of prior experience/knowledge when dealing with PE, and accentuated by selective information processing (Poech et al., 2005).

From the literature on family business sellers' perceptions and decision-making, the following conclusions can be made: Firstly, sellers assume an active role when selling the business. Secondly, family firm sellers might be concerned to whom and how the business is sold while the maximization of the sale price is only one of many sale objectives. Thirdly, reciprocal perceptions of family firms and PE could be a source of conflict and a positive relationship might be critical in relationships between family firms and PE firms.

(E) Value creation. Eight papers can be identified as falling into the "value creation" category (Goossens et al., 2008; Klöckner, 2009; Scholes, Wright, Westhead et al., 2010; Achleitner, Herman, Lerner et al., 2010; Wulf et al., 2010; Braun et al., 2011; Grundström,

Öberg, & Öhrwall Rönnbäck, 2012; Chrisman et al., 2012). Klöckner (2009) subsumes the effects PE buyouts can have on the former family firm broadly under "economization" and "professionalization"—the former referring to all activities, be it strategic (e.g. M&A) or operational (e.g. planning) and the latter comprises a general shift from partially non-financial goals to purely financial ones (Klöckner, 2009). Thus, "economization" and "professionalization" stimulate the creation of economic value in family firm buyouts (Klöckner, 2009). "Professionalization" is also emphasized in the work of Braun, Zacharias, & Latham (2011) who argue that governance structures of family firms and buyout vehicles represent two different "business philosophies". While family firms are generally regarded as having a long-term orientation and show co-existence of financial and non-financial objectives, buyout structures especially in the form of LBOs are reckoned to be characterized by short-termism and purely financial goals (Braun et al., 2011). Furthermore, the authors argue that LBOs are more successful in economic growth cycles, whereas family firms have performance advantages in economic downward cycles (Braun et al., 2011). In another work related to innovative behavior, the case study's evidence suggests that family successors show cautious innovation behavior whereas external succession through buyouts is associated with a higher degree of strong innovation behavior (Grundström et al., 2012).

Achleitner et al. (2010) agree with prior research that changes in corporate governance ("governance engineering") can stimulate value creation in buyouts, but "how" it occurs in family business buyouts is distinctively different from non-family buyouts. While value creation in non-family buyouts, in particular those involving publicly held companies, originates in creating more concentrated ownership structures with lower agency costs (Jensen, 1989)—this line of argument could not be applied to family firm buyouts who most commonly already have concentrated ownership (Achleitner et al., 2010). Thus, according to Achleitner et al. (2010) value creation in family buyouts originates from strategic and operational improvements achieved by the representation of PE managers in supervisory boards as well as higher incentivization of the top management in portfolio firms. Similarly, the work of Chrisman et al. (2012) highlights how different family firm governance configurations (ownership, management) create different levels of agency costs pre-buyout, which leads to greater unpredictability of agency cost reduction in the post-buyout period. This is in line with related literature on family firm governance, which argues that family influence can be both beneficial and detrimental to firm performance—the potential agency cost advantage might be lost due to owner-manager or owner-owner agency problems leading to asymmetric altruism, managerial entrenchment, and hold-up (Schulze, Lubatkin, Dino et al., 2001; Schulze, Lubatkin, & Dino, 2003a, Schulze, Lubatkin, & Dino, 2003b; Villalonga & Amit, 2006). Furthermore, Chrisman et al. (2012) hypothesize agency cost reductions in family firm buyouts could occur on other levels than previously thought, i.e. not between owners and managers, but between upper and lower management. Former asymmetric altruism (e.g. favoring family members) with detrimental effects on agency costs (Schulze et al., 2001) can be reduced in the post-buyout phase. Lastly, it is also emphasized that buyouts in family firms will shift the composition of agency costs from residual losses (due to opportunism) to newly created agency control costs as former family firms rely less on formal control mechanisms (Chrisman et al., 2012).

Empirical studies that use a quantitative approach do not entirely confirm that value creation in family firm buyouts is any different from non-family buyouts. Goosens, Manigart & Meulemann (2008) could not find differences in post-buyout performance where changes in efficiency and company growth are concerned. On the contrary, Scholes et al. (2010) could confirm for family configurations with no "non-family management with equity stakes" (who would have no incentive to perform higher because they have no equity stake) in the former family firm is associated with higher growth and efficiency. Wulf et al. (2010) only found positive effects of PE involvement on performance for formerly under-performing family firms when it comes to professionalization of organizational structures and systems. The impact of PE firms could turn negative if PE firms' involvement becomes operational (cost-saving activities) in nature (Wulf et al., 2010).

Three conclusions can be drawn from the literature on value creation. Firstly, family firms might undergo strategic changes after a buyout. These changes stem from a greater orientation towards financial goals in the post-buyout period. Secondly, strategic changes and financial value creation is not certain and sound empirical evidence remains scarce. Thirdly, different family configurations might need investigating to determine whether und under what circumstances value creation occurs.

1.3.2.3 Literature gaps and future research

After having reviewed the works dealing with the interface of family firms and PE, literature gaps become evident. Literature gaps in this Ph.D. thesis are structured according to (1) opportunities for methodological or theoretical improvement which is needed in future research, (2) research issues within current research categories not yet covered, and (3) new research categories requiring consideration in the future.

(1) Methodology and theory. High-quality research requires both a strong theoretical basis and an appropriate as well as reliable methodology (Bird, Welsch, Astrachan et al., 2002). Concerning the papers in this literature review, the methodologies used offer opportunities for improvement and future research.

Future research might rely more on quantitative empirical research. The majority of reviewed studies are either conceptual or, if empirical, rely heavily on case study evidence.[15] Case study research is especially appropriate in early stages of research development to provide inductively a foundation upon which quantitative research methods can be deductively built (Eisenhardt & Graebner, 2007; Miles & Huberman, 1985). Thus, case study research's key objective is to identify and recognize key elements, structures, and

[15] See *Table 1* in this chapter.

relationships of a "field situation" (Barzelay, 2007; Eisenhardt & Graebner, 2007). Given the comparably low number of publications on family firms and PE, case study research can be considered as being a suitable means to prepare the ground work for further quantitative research. The results of multiple case study research are typically more reliable than those of single case studies (Graebner & Eisenhardt, 2004). However, a total of three works in this literature review rely on single case studies to deduct research insights, which somewhat limits empirical validity (Niedermeyer et al., 2010; Salvato et al., 2010; Achleitner et al., 2010). In general, future research should focus on and complement existing research with quantitative empirical research, so that insights from case study evidence can be statistically verified with larger sample sizes (Debicki et al., 2009).

Existing quantitative empirical research in existing literature would have benefitted from greater methodological rigor, such as the application of more sophisticated statistical techniques, including multiple regression, moderation and mediation analysis, structural equation modeling, and the use of statistical constructs confirmed by factor analysis (Baron & Kenny, 1986; Kline, 2005; Hair, 1987). For example, Scholes et al. (2007) acknowledge that their use of logistic regression analysis for cross-sectional data would benefit from techniques of structural equation modeling to establish causality and interactions between variables. Furthermore, Scholes et al (2007) or Wulf et al. (2010) use singe-item variables which could suffer from measurement error compared to statistical constructs (Scholes et al., 2007). In the work of Scholes et al. (2008), bivariate non-parametric statistical tests (such as Mann-Whitney “U” test, Chi-square test) were used to analyze whether statistically significant differences between respondent groups exist. However, these kind of statistical tests require the complementary use of statistical techniques such as moderation or mediation analysis in multiple regression so that control variables can be included (Hair, 1987). Scholes et al. (2010) use univariate analysis and when testing also multivariate analysis have to relativize their results. There are notable exceptions in this literature review whose authors exhibit great methodological rigor such as the works of Dehlen et al. (2012) and Zellweger et al. (2011). Also, relatively new statistical approaches—such as conjoint analysis in the study of Dawson (2011) who examines tradeoffs in decision-making—can be considered a promising route for future research (Lohrke, Holloway, & Woolley, 2009). Future empirical research might try to validate current research findings by using robust and state-of-the-art statistical techniques.

The treatment of family firms also needs more sophistication in current work on family firms and PE. It was previously mentioned that family firms exhibit great heterogeneity, so simple dichotomous differentiations might be misleading (Tsang, 2002; Hack, 2009; Chua et al., 2012; Chrisman et al., 2012). In the prominent study of Villalonga & Amit (2006), it was shown how a change from defining family based solely on ownership rights leads to different forms of family involvement and thus renders family firm performance from being positive to negative (Hack, 2009). Therefore, it may be necessary to test various forms and configurations of family firms to appropriately differentiate between varying degrees of family influence and its consequences. If family influence is not investigated comprehensively, research might fall victim to unjustified generalizations (Melin & Nordqvist, 2007). Moderation and mediation analysis might be appropriate means to ensure more sophisticated treatment of family firm configurations in statistical analysis, but researchers also need to capture different characteristics of family influence (e.g. ownership, management) in surveys as a precondition. A greater differentiated treatment of family influence might provide further needed evidence on currently contradictory research findings, such as those on value creation in family firm buyouts (Wulf et al., 2010; Scholes et al., 2010; Goossens et al., 2008).

Multiple respondent studies and larger sample sizes could also contribute to higher statistical reliability. Most quantitative empirical studies rely on the key informant approach (Kumar, Stern, & Anderson, 1993) and studies often either take the perspective of the buyer or seller (Dawson, 2011; Niedermeyer et al., 2010). New insights and more representativeness might be achieved if multiple respondents from both the buying and selling side are investigated simultaneously to capture a less biased perspective (Eddleston & Kellermanns, 2007). Additionally, most studies rely on comparably low sample sizes (Dawson, 2011; Granata & Chirico, 2010) compared to other fields of management research. This is likely due to the difficulty to get access to data, given the confidentiality that surrounds buyout deals.

The use of novel theories could inspire new research insights. Established theories such as agency theory, stewardship theory, and the RBV dominate works in this literature review. However, management theory is not limited to the aforementioned theories, but offers a broader spectrum of theories. More diverse theoretical approaches could point out interesting insights. A number of prominent theories such as upper-echelon (Hambrick & Mason, 1984), institutional theory (DiMaggio & Powell, 1983; Meyer & Rowan, 1977), commitment-trust theory (Allen & Meyer, 1990; Meyer & Allen, 1991) or insights from the field of behavioral finance (Thaler, 1993; Ackert & Deaves, 2010) might provide promising paths for future research.

(2) Research gaps within current categories. The literature review followed the different research categories that had been identified. Within the *"Market"* category, there is a need to provide more recent information on the dimension and characteristics of family firm buyouts. Furthermore, it might be necessary to distinguish between different definitions of family firms that could yield different results for the market characteristics of family firm buyouts and PE activity. Additionally, it would be beneficial to have more detailed insights on the contractual terms of family deals vs. non-family deals (e.g. covenants, degree of control) and potential antecedents.

Within the *"Information asymmetries"* category, it would be complementary to existing research if long-term consequences of information asymmetries for buyout deals were investigated, i.e. the consequences for financial success and deal satisfaction of the involved parties. In particular, for the buying side it could be insightful to evaluate whether specific strategies in the due diligence process of PE firms focused on family aspects reduce information asymmetries (Puranam et al., 2006). Furthermore, it might be interesting to identify specific types of information asymmetries and assess how each type could be mitigated.

Research within the category *"PE perceptions and decision-making"* has not yet assessed how perceptions on family firms might lead to cognitive biases in the investment decision-making of PE firms (e.g. overconfidence) (Thaler, 1993; Kahneman, Slovic, & Tversky, 1999; Ackert & Deaves, 2010). For example, PE firms might not recognize company strengths in family firms because family firms are cognitively associated with certain weaknesses. Furthermore, PE managers might refrain from investments in family firms as they try to avoid higher perceived risk due to family involvement or use certain strategies to mitigate risks. For example, PE firms might negotiate specific investment contracts (e.g. earn out) or use certain monitoring arrangements.

Within the category *"Family firm perceptions and decision-making"*, literature gaps become apparent when specific selection criteria of family sellers are concerned. While there is a strong indication that the relationship side matters to family sellers (Poech et al., 2005; Burkhardt, 2008; Graebner & Eisenhardt, 2004; Niedermeyer et al., 2010; Tappeiner et al., 2012), the specific elements of the relationship that matter the most are yet to be fully discovered. Conjoint analysis could be a methodological instrument to investigate decision trade-offs of family owners (Dawson, 2011). Specifically, it needs to be evaluated how financial and non-financial objectives are weighted relative to each other, given that family firms have a preference for non-financial goals (Corbetta & Salvato, 2004; Chrisman, Chua, Kellermanns et al., 2007; Gómez-Mejía et al., 2007). For example, how does a characteristic of the relationship, such as trust, have an effect on sellers' financial objectives during the sale? Additionally, there is a need to understand whether and how negative perceptions of family sellers on PE firms might change once family sellers interact with PE firms (Poech et al., 2005).

The *"Value creation"* literature needs to close the gap on whether value creation strategies for family firms need to be different and how. It is necessary to understand how family influence pre-buyout can trigger effective strategies for value creation post-buyout and what role the departing family plays in this context. In particular, it could be beneficial to identify whether forms of family influence post-buyout are successful given adjacent literature who claims family influence can be both a source of high performance and low performance (Sirmon & Hitt, 2003). Combined influence of former family business owners and PE management could create value, as complementary expertise could be combined to achieve competitive advantage. All these facets need to be investigated over longer time periods to effectively differentiate between short-term and long-term effects.

(3) Future research categories. The reviewed literature does not touch some areas that can have importance in family-firm buyout deals. Firstly, the negotiation phase of deal-making is neglected, yet is considered as highly important in many transactions due to complexity of deals and a lack of market transparency (Reed et al., 2007; Cumming & Johan, 2009; Tyebjee & Bruno, 1984; Birley, 1984). Multiple aspects of negotiations could be important, such as bargaining power or bargaining tactics (Kim, Pinkley, & Fragale, 2005). Secondly, there are literature gaps regarding the role of advisors and intermediaries. For example, we don't know if family sellers employ advisors to support them in deal-making and the selection of PE partners and how family sellers select such advisors. Thirdly, literature gaps exist when it comes to the initiation of buyout deals. It might be particularly interesting to find out how family sellers and PE firms get into contact with each other and how network structures and PE firms' strategies can have an effect on successful deal initiation. Fourth, the whole planning process family firms undergo to prepare a buyout and how this affects the success of the deal could be of great research interest. Fifth, future literature might resolve contradictory issues arising from different research categories—such as the valuation of family targets given findings related to lower valuations in the marketplace (Granata & Chirico, 2010; Granata, 2010), but higher valuations by family sellers (Zellweger et al., 2011; Zellweger & Astrachan, 2008).

1.3.2.4 Conclusion

From this literature review, some key messages from the identified research categories can be distilled. Information asymmetries might be characteristic for buyout deals when family firms and PE firms are involved. It is also evident that two different management philosophies could "clash" when PE firms interact with family firms in buyout deals. Reciprocal perceptions might not be entirely positive and decision-making criteria and deal objectives might place different emphases on financial and non-financial objectives. In addition, family firms and PE firms might possess different capabilities and resources. More research is needed to fill the outlined research gaps within the existing and entirely new categories. Future research might also be concerned with more quantitative empirical research and the methodological rigor needed to address the complexity of buyout deals as well as the breath and diversity among family firms. More diverse theories should be able to stimulate new insights.

1.4 Research questions of this thesis

Not all research gaps can be addressed entirely in this thesis. However, quite a few of them are targeted. Specifically, this dissertation addresses the following research questions:

Question 1: *How can the role of the family be understood for value creation in family firm buyouts?*

Question 2: *What factors generate bargaining power in buyout negotiations?*

Question 3: *What factors give bargaining power in buyout negotiations when different family firm characteristics are concerned?*

Question 4: *What is the role of relationship factors in buyout transactions and how are family firms different from non-family firms?*

Each research question is addressed in a separate essay. The first essay deals with the question of value creation in buyouts and by doing so tries to solve the "valuation puzzle". It combines the aforementioned literature review categories on "value creation" and "perceptions and decision-making" of both PE firms and family firms. The essay conceptually tries to reconcile findings on lower valuations of family firms in the market place (Granata & Chirico, 2010; Granata, 2010), but higher valuations by family sellers (Zellweger et al., 2011; Zellweger & Astrachan, 2008).

The second essay and third essay address the research gap on negotiations in buyouts. In particular, the second essay investigates bargaining power in negotiations. Essay three builds upon the multifaceted definition of family firms (heterogeneity) and how this might affect bargaining power. The fourth essay tries to identify relationship factors in buyout deals—i.e., how family sellers might be different from non-family sellers—emphasized in previous research (Graebner & Eisenhardt, 2004; Burkhardt, 2008; Niedermeyer et al., 2010; Tappeiner et al., 2012). In doing so, further insights are provided on how family sellers select PE firms and how the value of relationship factors is considered in relation to financial factors.

All essays rely on theories not used before in this specific research context. The second, third and fourth essay rely on quantitative empirical research using multiple regression and testing of interaction effects (Baron & Kenny, 1986). By doing so, this thesis hopes to bridge the existing research gap while simultaneously raising new research questions.

1.5 Thesis overview and main contributions

This doctoral thesis is concerned with providing insights on the research questions outlined above and is structured into seven chapters.

Chapter 2 *"Research approach"* illustrates what theories and methodologies are used to address the research questions raised in the previous section. Further information is given on what statistical methods have been used for the quantitative empirical examinations.

In ***chapter 3*** *"Stepping into the buyers' shoes: looking at the value of family firms through the eyes of private equity investors"* research question "1" is addressed. More and more families have to sell their business to external investors because no family successor is available or willing to take over the family firm. Potential buyers are often PE firms who take over the business in a buyout. A key question is what the family firm is worth without the family being part of the business, but with a new owner who has a different perspective on the business independent from family considerations? The essay provides a buyers' perspective on the value of the family business and hopes to continue the discussion on the valuation of and value creation in family firm buyouts. It is argued that the involvement and influence of a family provides the PE buyer with a distinct landscape of real options[16] requiring consideration when valuing a family firm.

In ***chapter 4*** *"Opening the black box: power in buyout negotiations and the moderating role of private equity specialization"* bargaining power in buyout negotiations between PE firms and current owners who sell their business is studied. A hand-collected sample of buyouts is used to identify sources of bargaining power from a buyer/PE perspective. "Competition", "expertise", and "time pressure" are identified as key sources of bargaining power in buyouts. It is also examined whether and how different forms of PE firm specialization such as "industry" and "size" moderate sources of bargaining power in buyout negotiations.

[16] See chapter 2.1.2 for explanation.

Chapter 5 *"Bargaining power in family firm buyouts: does family influence make a difference?"* studies bargaining power in buyout transactions between PE firms and current family firm owners who sell their business. As such, chapter 5 complements chapter 4 on the role of "the family". A sub-sample of family firm buyouts from those used in chapter 4 is studied and resulted in confirmation of bargaining power sources pointed out in chapter 3. Further tests reveal factors of family influence such as "family members in the business" and "generational ownership dispersion" to have moderating effects on sources of bargaining power—in particular on competition and expertise. This is attributed to the moderating effects of different degrees of SEW associated with variations of family influence.

In ***chapter 6*** *"Sellers' affective deal commitment – buyout transactions as courtship"* sellers' affective deal commitment in buyout transactions between PE firms and current owners who sell their business is studied. The chapter emphasizes the sellers' perspective and uses a hand-collected sample from chapter 4 to identify sources of affective deal commitment. Trust, goal congruence, and PE reputation are tested as potential antecedents of deal commitment; and a positive relationship for trust and goal congruence is confirmed. Furthermore, it is examined whether and how different type of sellers, i.e. family and non-family firms, moderate sources of affective deal commitment which is an affirmation of the importance of trust. In summary, evidence is found that non-financial factors play a role in buyout transactions, suggesting that "courtship" might be a suitable term to characterize buyout deals especially where family sellers are concerned.

Chapter *7 "Conclusion"* summarizes chapters 1–6 and the conclusions derived. Additionally, the key theoretical and practical implications of this thesis are outlined and discussed.

Chapters 3, 4, 5 and 6 are each composed as stand-alone essays with the same structure common to management research journals in which publication is intended. Thus, each paper comprises an introduction, theoretical background, hypothesis development, methods and sample characteristics, research results, and discussion sections. Some redundant elements occur across chapters 3–6 and in particular between chapters 4 and 5 which could not be entirely avoided given the cumulative nature of this thesis. ***Figure 5*** visualizes the structure of this thesis.

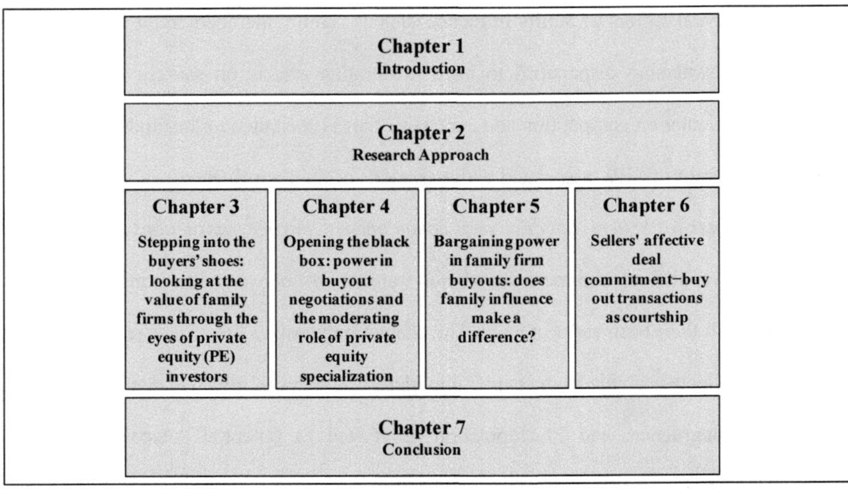

Figure 1-5: Structure of this Ph.D. thesis
Source: Author

2 Research approach

In this chapter, it is explained how the research questions outlined in chapter 1 are addressed theoretically and methodologically in this thesis. Firstly, the theories applied in the subsequent chapters 3–6 are summarized (the theoretical framework). Secondly, the sample used for the quantitative empirical chapters 4, 5, and 6 as well as the data collection process is described. Lastly, statistical techniques to investigate the generated hypotheses are outlined.

2.1 Theoretical framework

The subsequent chapters 3–6 employ different theories. Real option analysis is used in chapter 3, bargaining power theory is used in chapters 4 and 5, and commitment-trust theory is used in chapter 6. These theories are complemented by socioemotional wealth theory (SEW) used in chapters 3, 5 and 6. SEW is a "homegrown" theory of family business researchers (Gómez-Mejía, Cruz, Berrone et al., 2011a) and complements the aforementioned theories to facilitate insights particularly related to family firms. Overall, it can be said that this thesis is theoretically "grounded" in SEW theory. An overview of what theories are used in which chapter is given in ***Figure 6***.

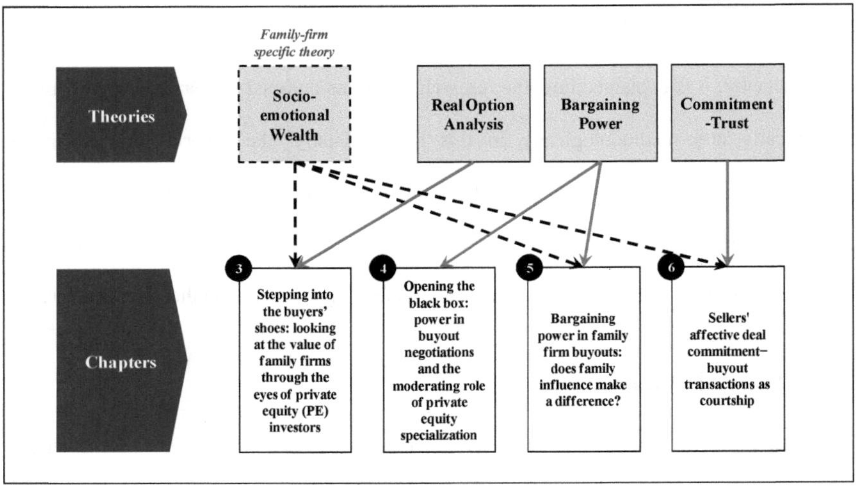

Figure 2-6: Theories and corresponding chapters
Source: Author

2.1.1 Socioemotional wealth

Socioemotional wealth (SEW) theory represents the theoretical reference point for the explanation of family-firm-specific behavior throughout this thesis. SEW theory is essentially about the importance of non-economic goals for family firms (Berrone et al., 2012). According to SEW theory, family firms try to realize high levels of SEW so that SEW becomes a reference point for family firms' decision-making (Berrone et al., 2010; Berrone et al., 2012; Gómez-Mejía et al., 2007; Gómez-Mejía et al., 2010; Zellweger et al., 2011). Consequently, decisions in the family firm are often implicitly judged by their contribution to SEW endowment (Berrone et al., 2012), which is not always in the interest of the firms' stakeholders or does not contribute to the financial performance of the family business (Kellermanns, Eddleston, & Zellweger, 2012; Gómez-Mejía et al., 2007). SEW includes a number of affectively motivated needs such as the need for family affiliation and family harmony, preservation and continuation of family values, family control over the family business and the intention to build a family dynasty, the need for trust and family reputation as well as the preservation of social capital, among others (Gómez-Mejía et al., 2010; Gómez-Mejía et al., 2007; Gómez-Mejía, Nuñez-Nickel, & Gutierrez, 2001; Berrone et al., 2010). The specific importance of SEW for family firms' actions is dependent on forms and the degree of family influence (Berrone et al., 2012). Family influence comprises multiple sources such as ownership, participation in management functions, generations involved in the business, and/or age of the business, among others (Chua et al., 2012; Astrachan et al., 2002, Klein et al., 2005; Ling & Kellermanns, 2010; Dehlen et al., 2012).

SEW can become a dominant motive for family firm sellers in buyouts. In general, family firm ownership is often associated with strong emotional attachment so that the value of the business is, "in the eye of the owner", biased by emotions (Zellweger & Astrachan, 2008; Zellweger et al., 2011; Astrachan & Jaskiewicz, 2008). Through the identification of the family (members) with the business, the family firm becomes a defining component of the family (Zellweger & Astrachan, 2008; Dyer & Whetten, 2006). Moreover, the family firm represents prestige, recognition, and reputation for the family (Chrisman, Chua, & Litz, 2004; Westhead, Cowling, & Howorth, 2001; Berrone et al., 2010), and families will try to secure control over the business (Zellweger et al., 2011). Consequently, the buyout might be accompanied by feelings of regret, as in the sale the family loses control over the business as the generating mechanism of SEW (Shepherd, 2009; Pellegrin, 1999; Niedermeyer et al., 2010).

2.1.2 Real options analysis

Real options analysis (ROA) is concerned with the value of flexibility in investment decision-making. The foundations of ROA were laid by financial options theory (Myers, 1977; Trigeorgis, 1996). The difference between financial and real options is that financial options are created for financial transactions and real options involve "real" assets (Black & Scholes, 1973; Trigeorgis, 1995). In general, ROA is mainly concerned with the value of flexibility in managerial decision-making under conditions characterized by uncertainty (Pindyck, 1988; Dixit & Pindyck, 1994; Trigeorgis, 1995). As such, ROA can be used to evaluate the favourability of investments (Wang & Lim, 2008; Howell, 2001), to support company valuation (Myers, 1977), and to improve strategic decision-making (Bowman & Hurry, 1993; Bowman & Ambrosini, 2007). It is assumed in ROA that investments and/or decisions have follow-up opportunities and outcomes can be estimated with probabilities (Leiblein, 2003).

The functioning of real options is analogous to financial options. A *financial* call option generates ex post returns when the stock price exceeds the predetermined exercise price, and a put option generates returns when the stock price falls below the exercise price (Trigeorgis, 1996; Hull, 2009). A *real* option can be defined as the *"right, but not the obligation, to take an action in the future"* (Amram & Kulatilaka, 1999; p. 5). Consequently, a financial option's stock price turns into the real option's net present value (NPV) of the potential investment; volatility is the risk of future cash flows, and the exercise price is the cost needed for the follow-on investment (Howell, 2001). The underlying asset is the potential investment, and the option holder's right is given by the opportunity to invest (call option) or to divest (put option) (Howell, 2001).

ROA is applied in chapter 3 for the valuation of family firm in buyouts. Options can be viewed as an important part of firms' valuation, complementing the discounted cash flow (DCF) value (static component) with the value derived from future flexibility or real options (dynamic component) (Myers, 1977; Trigeorgis, 1995). In particular, situations of uncertainty and irreversibility are viewed as essential for applying ROA (Adner & Levinthal, 2004; McGrath, Ferrier, & Mendelow, 2004). Family firm buyouts are considered being high-risk transactions affected by information asymmetries and strong investment irreversibility once a firm is acquired. Thus, ROA is highly suited for application in family firm buyouts.

2.1.3 Bargaining power

Negotiations occur all the time, not only in the world of business, and can be defined as *"... the deliberate interaction of two or more complex social units which are attempting to define or redefine the terms of their interdependence"* (Walton & McKersie, 1965, p. 35). "Power" in negotiations is usually referred to as "bargaining power" and is defined as the potential to influence others for obtaining desired outcomes (Kelley & Thibaut, 1978; Bacharach & Lawler, 1981; Dreu & van Kleef, 2004; Kim et al., 2005). Power is subject to individuals' perception, interpretation, assessments, preferences, experiences, values and how available information is processed (Cyert & March, 1963; Bacharach & Lawler, 1976; Leap & Grigsby, 1986; Wolfe & McGinn, 2005; Poppo, Zhou, & Ryu, 2008).

Dependency theories conceive the nature of bargaining power as being related to the dependency of negotiators. The relational aspect of power was emphasized in power-dependence theory, which postulates that A's negotiation power increases when B's dependence on the negotiation relationship grows (Emerson, 1962; Blau, 1964; Wolfe & McGinn, 2005). Thus, a negotiation party provided with a broader set of alternatives can engage in alternatives to the current negotiation relationship and will be less willing to make concessions (Fisher, 1981). Previous research uses the term "context-based bargaining power" to refer to dependency derived from availability of alternatives (Yan & Gray, 2001b). "Resource-based bargaining power" is a derivative of power-dependence theory and assumes that power in relationships originates in the possession of critical resources potentially valuable in the negotiation relationship (Pfeffer & Nowak, 1976; Aldrich, 1977; Pfeffer & Salancik, 1978; Yan & Gray, 2001b).

Power base theories do not directly link to the dependency aspect of the parties involved and rather analyze power from an individual actor's point of view (French & Raven, 1959; Patchen, 1974; Bacharach & Lawler, 1980; Kim et al., 2005). French & Raven (1959) gained prominence with their typology of power bases, such as reward, coercion, expertise, legitimacy and referent power. The overall efficacy of power (sources) largely depends on the individual negotiation situation and hence no universally applicable framework for negotiation power has yet been developed (Astley & Sachdeva, 1984; Leap & Grigsby, 1986). However, both power-dependence theory and power base theory emphasize that power can only be established in a relationship and thus power is viewed as a relational concept (Yan & Gray, 2001b; Dreu & van Kleef, 2004).

2.1.4 Commitment-trust theory

Prior research developed a range of different commitment definitions and established levels at which commitment exists such as between individuals, between individuals and organizations or between organizations (Becker, 1960; Anderson & Weitz, 1992; Beamish & Banks, 1987; Cullen, Johnson, & Sakano, 1995). This thesis follows the definition of Meyer & Herscovitch (2001, p. 301) of commitment as a "*force that binds an individual to a course of action that is of relevance to a particular target*". Commitment is driven by similar values, goals, and attachments that lead to relationship continuation (Mäkelä & Maula, 2006; Beamish, 1984; Mowday, Porter, & Steers, 1982).

Prior research acknowledged the importance of commitment for business relationships (Dwyer, Schurr, & Oh, 1987; Lund, 1985; Scheer & Stern, 1992). Commitment has been associated with—along with other effects—higher tendencies of cooperation and desires of relationship partners to achieve mutual profitability, loyalty, as well as long-term relationship stability (Gundlach, Achrol, & Mentzer, 1995; Anderson & Weitz, 1992; Gounaris, 2005) despite relationship alternatives being available (Anderson & Weitz, 1992; Morgan & Hunt, 1994; Ghemawat, 1991). Thus, if an individual or organization is provided with commitment, it is likely to benefit from that commitment.

Different forms of commitment can be distinguished. Commitment is usually differentiated based on the underlying motivation into an "affective" and a "calculative" form (Becker, 1960; Mowday, Steers, & Porter, 1979; Mathieu & Zajac, 1990). While the former form is reckoned to be emotional, the latter is motivated by economic advantages and rationality (Allen & Meyer, 1990; Bansal, Irving, & Taylor, 2004; Fullerton, 2003). It is important for this thesis to differentiate between affective and calculative commitment so that antecedents can be distinguished effectively (Geyskens, Steenkamp, & Kumar, 1998).

2.2 Data collection and sample description

Data collection focused on the buying side of management buyouts. In order to test the hypotheses in chapters 4, 5, and 6, cross-sectional data was collected using a key informant approach (Kumar et al., 1993). Two main categories of respondents were identified as appropriate sources for the research questions outlined in the previous chapter—the buying and the selling side. For a number of reasons, it was decided to contact only the buying side, i.e. PE firm investment managers. Firstly, it is highly difficult to identify a substantial number of family sellers having been involved in management buyouts due to confidentiality reasons and because family buyouts usually take place in less information-efficient private takeover markets (Capron & Shen, 2007). Secondly, it was relatively easy to identify PE firms and managers because industry associations and company websites disclose much of the needed information (EVCA, 2011). Thirdly, PE investment managers were considered particularly suitable because they regularly engage in buyouts and usually deal with both family and non-family buyout targets. Thus, PE managers are well suited to identify and assess differences between family firm and non-family firm buyouts.

Two steps were taken to generate an appropriate target population of PE firms for sampling. Firstly, PE firms appropriate for serving as potential respondents were identified. In doing so, 856 European PE firms were identified based on membership directories of PE associations and internet search. Elimination of 348 PE firms was necessary, as some PE firms focused on early stage investments, were fund-of-funds[17] PE investors, were mezzanine capital providers[18], had no deal record, or stopped doing business. 508 individual PE firms remained as suitable targets for the survey.

Secondly, individual investment managers for each PE firm were researched and contacted via email. Individual contact details are beneficial for surveys because personalized surveys are usually more successful than anonymous surveys and lead to higher "quality" of responses (Heerwegh, Vanhove, Matthijs et al., 2005). The electronic survey procedure was chosen because it usually outperforms paper-based mailings in terms of costs, response rates, and response speed (Sheehan, 2001). The survey also contained a short introduction and assurance of confidentiality and anonymity. Respondents' answers to the questionnaire were qualified by using three conditions for participation. Firstly, respondents had to relate their answers to a randomly selected buyout in which their PE firm represented the buying coalition. Secondly, respondents had to be actively involved in the negotiation process. Thirdly, the buyout deal had to have occurred during the last three years.

A high response rate was achieved. 188 PE investment professionals from different PE firms filled-in and returned the electronic survey. Thus, the response rate amounts to ~37 %. Most respondents hold positions as partner or managing director (42%), investment director (43%), investment associate (10%); some provided no information on position (5%). The majority of respondents are from Germany (~27%), Italy (~14%), France (~10%), UK (9%), and Spain (~6%) with manufacturing being the dominant industry of buyout deals in the sample. The transaction value shows a mean of ~ € 224 million. The mean of employees

[17] Fund-of-fund PE firms invest in other PE funds usually without investing into portfolio firms directly (Brophy & Guthner, 1988).

[18] Mezzanine capital is a form of financing usually for SMEs. Financially speaking, mezzanine debt is "senior" to the original equity of the firm, but "junior" to bank debt (Bean, 2008).

involved in reported buyout targets is ~1159 and the mean of sales is ~ € 192 million. The average PE firms' fund under management (FUM) is ~ € 3199 million. A more detailed description of the sample is given in ***Figures** 7, 8, 9, and 10.* In ***Figure*** *7* it can be easily observed that variables are skewed which requires consideration and countermeasures in statistical analysis. Also, it is necessary to acknowledge that the sample sizes and characteristics in chapters 4, 5, and 6 could (slightly) deviate because respective outliers were eliminated and a family firm subsample was created accordingly for chapter 5.

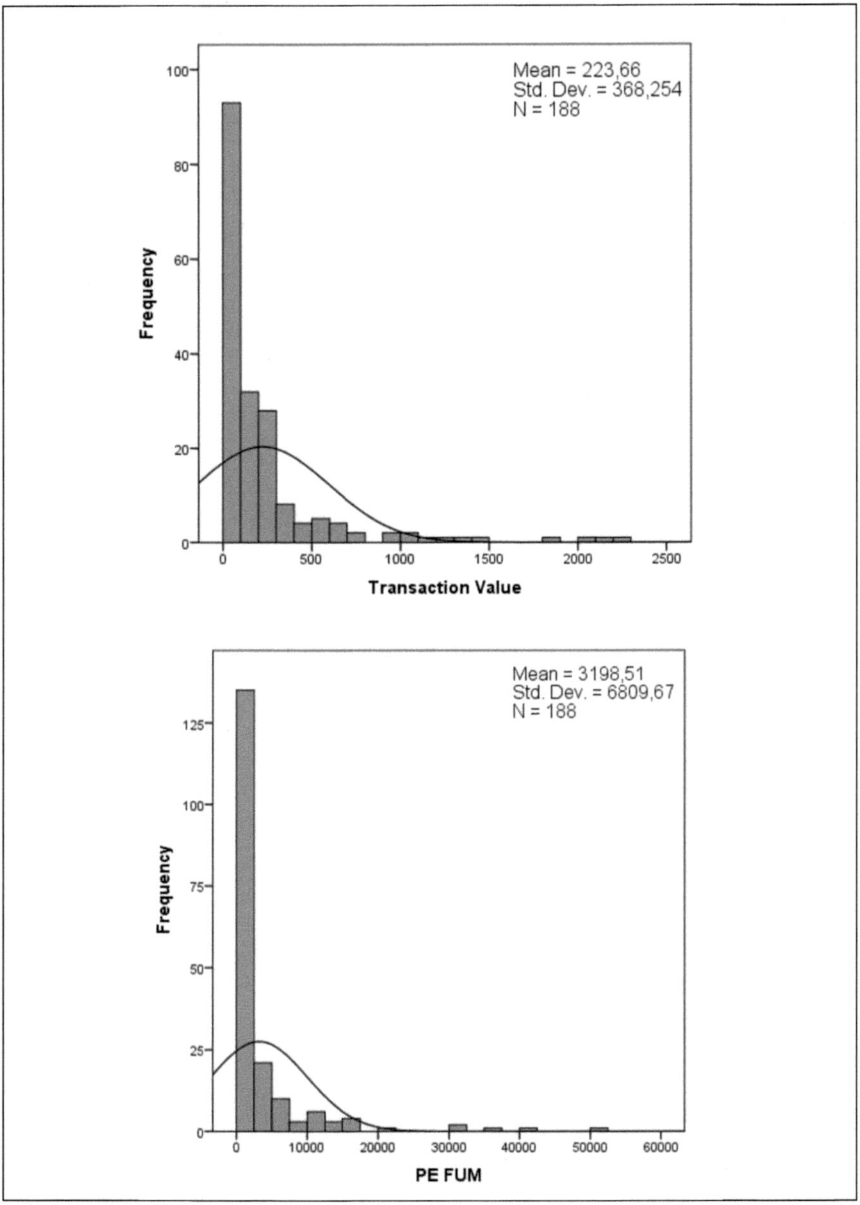
Mean = 223,66
Std. Dev. = 368,254
N = 188
Frequency
100
80
60
40
20
0
0
500
1000
1500
2000
2500
Transaction Value
Mean = 3198,51
Std. Dev. = 6809,67
N = 188
Frequency
125
100
75
50
25
0
0
10000
20000
30000
40000
50000
60000
PE FUM

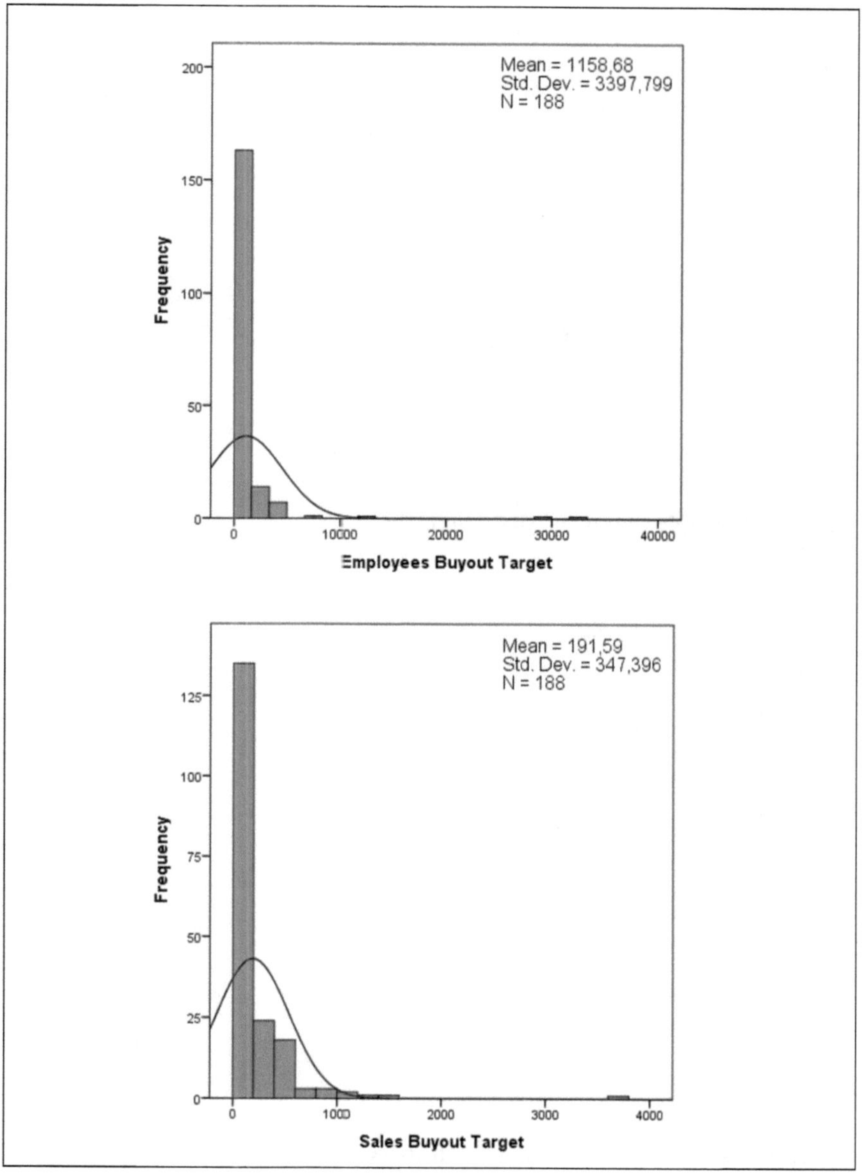

Notes: 1) Numbers might deviate from those shown in chapters due to different sample sizes; 2) Except for employees all numbers given in million €

Figure 2-7: Sample characteristics – key descriptive statistics

Source: Author

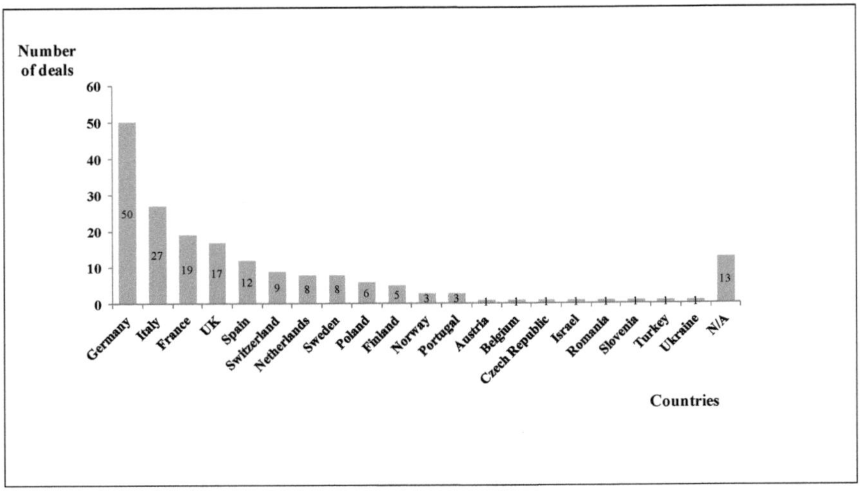

Figure 2-8: Sample characteristics – countries
Source: Author

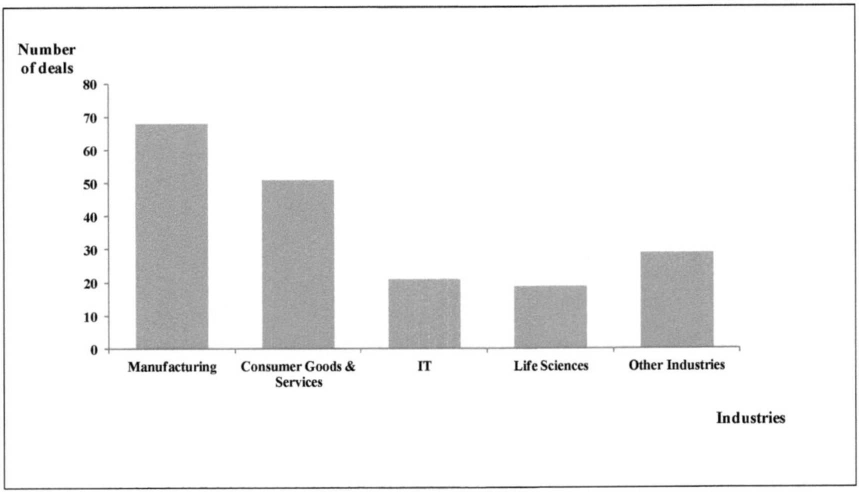

Figure 2-9: Sample characteristics – industries
Source: Author

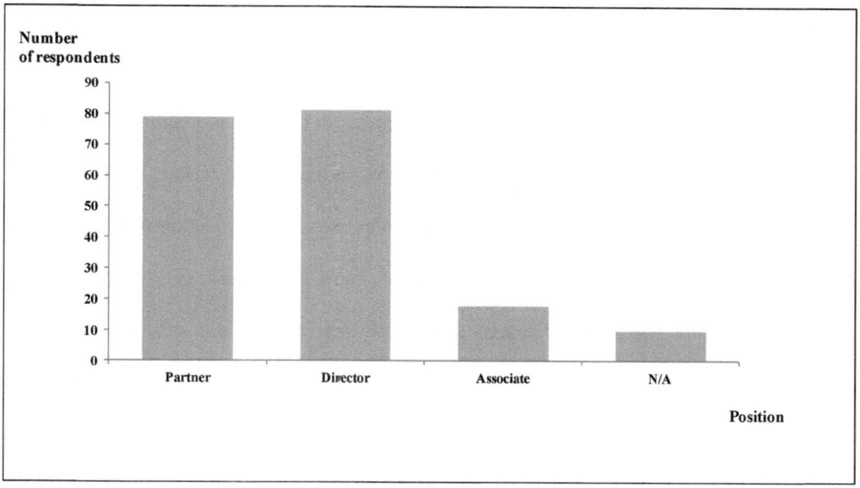

Figure 2-10: Sample characteristics – job title of respondents
Source: Author

2.3 Methodology

Multiple regression analysis was used to test the empirical hypotheses in chapters 4, 5, and 6. Multiple regression analysis is generally used to *"analyze the relationship between a single dependent and several independent variables"* (Hair (1987), p. 19). Most commonly, a regression model is used to predict the dependent variable, almost always based on techniques of Ordinary Least Squares (OLS); regression coefficients are estimated by minimizing the sum of the squared residuals between the values which are observed and those that are expected (Weisberg, 2005). (Linear) multiple regression is based on a number of assumptions such as non-zero variance, quantitative or categorical nature, and normality of variables used in the model[19], as well as normality and homoscedasticity of residuals, independence and linearity of the dependent variable, and the absence of multicollinearity of independent variables (Field, 2009; Hair, 1987). Multicollinearity refers to linearity between two or more variables and can be checked via calculation of variance-inflation-factor (VIF), condition

[19] Field (2009) argues that normality of used variables is not necessarily required.

index and/or analyzing variance proportions related to eigenvalues (Hair, 1987). If normality assumptions are violated, counter measures are indicated such as calculating the logarithm of affected variables (Hair, 1987). Significance of regression coefficients requires using t-tests and outliers (large residual values) require elimination from the sample (Hair, 1987).

Multiple regression analysis was applied in this thesis in conjunction with moderation analysis, which is a means to test for "third factors". Here, a moderator is *"(...) a qualitative (e.g. sex, race, class) or quantitative (e.g. level of reward) variable that affects the direction and/or strength of the relationship between an independent variable or predictor variable and a dependent variable or criterion variable."* (Baron & Kenny, 1986, p. 1174). Essentially, a moderator can be conceived as an interaction between an independent variable and a "third" factor that renders the relationship in terms of specification or condition (Baron & Kenny, 1986). Multicollinearity issues between interaction terms and respective components can be largely avoided by centering interaction variables (Aiken & West, 1991). Moderation can be distinguished from mediation effects. In a mediation model, the independent variable affects a third variable that, in turn, affects a dependent variable—contrary to the qualifying condition given by a moderation effect, mediation gives an explanation on "how" effects occur (Baron & Kenny, 1986).

Composites are more reliable than single-item variables, but require factor analysis to determine statistical reliability. Latent statistical constructs are formed by combining related variables in composite scores (Landis, Beal, & Tesluk, 2000). Composite measurement is statistically more reliable than single-item measurement (Gerbing & Anderson, 1988). For the statistical analysis in this thesis, already established constructs tested by previous researchers were used or adapted if possible. Exploratory factor analysis (EFA) was used to explore and extract the underlying dimensions (i.e. factors) of the observed variables without a pre-defined structure (Thompson, 2004). Confirmatory factor analysis (CFA) was used to verify the identified factors by using appropriate indicators of "model fit" (Thompson, 2004; Marsh, Balla, & McDonald, 1988).

2.4 Conclusion

This thesis uses a number of theories to approach the research questions raised in chapter 1. A conceptual research approach is used for chapter 3. A quantitative empirical methodology is used in chapters 4, 5, and 6, utilizing statistical techniques such as multiple regression complemented by moderation analysis. As a prerequisite for statistical analysis, a sample was generated for this thesis based on an electronic survey among European PE firms. In ***Table 2***, the chapters of this thesis are summarized regarding research objectives, theories, methodology, research design, and sample characteristics.

	Chapter 3 (Essay 1)	**Chapter 4 (Essay 2)**	**Chapter 5 (Essay 3)**	**Chapter 6 (Essay 4)**
Title	• Stepping into the buyer's shoes: looking at the value of family firms through the eyes of private equity investors	• Opening the black box: power in buyout negotiations and the moderating role of private equity specialization	• Bargaining power in family firm buyouts: does family influence make a difference?	• Sellers' affective deal commitment—buyout transactions as courtship
Research objective	• Investigate the role of the family in the family firm for value creation or value destruction in the post-buyout phase	• Identify sources of bargaining power in buyout negotiations	• Confirm sources of bargaining power in buyout negotiations for family firm buyouts • Investigate how sources of family heterogeneity affect bargaining power	• Determine the role of relationship factors in buyouts • Evaluate potential differences between family and non-family buyouts/sellers
Level of analysis	• Buyer/PE perspective	• Buyer/PE perspective	• Buyer/PE perspective	• Buyer/PE perspective
Research method	• Theoretical / conceptual	• Empirical / quantitative	• Empirical / quantitative	• Empirical / quantitative
Sample	• n/a (conceptual paper)	• 177 buyouts	• 82 buyouts	• 174 buyouts
Data collection	• n/a (conceptual paper)	• Cross-sectional data • Electronic survey	• Cross-sectional data • Electronic survey	• Cross-sectional data • Electronic survey
Methodology	• Theoretical development of a valuation model	• Multiple regression • Factor analysis • Moderation analysis	• Multiple regression • Factor analysis • Moderation analysis	• Multiple regression • Factor analysis • Moderation analysis
Theory	• ROA • SEW	• Bargaining power	• Bargaining Power • SEW	• Commitment-Trust • SEW

Variables *IV: Independent variable* *DV: Dependent variable* *M: Moderator*	• Family options • Non-family options • Mitigation measures	• IV: bidder competition, expertise, time pressure • DV: bargaining power • M: industry specialization, size specialization	• IV: bidder competition, expertise, time pressure • DV: bargaining power • M: family members in the business, trans-generational ownership dispersion	• IV: goal congruence, trust, PE firm reputation • DV: affective commitment • M: Family firm (ownership >50% & members in the business)

Table 2-2: Summary of research approaches per chapter

Source: Author

3 Stepping into the buyer's shoes: Looking at the value of family firms through the eyes of private equity[20]

3.1 Introduction

The quote *"Nowadays people know the price of everything and the value of nothing"* is attributed to Oscar Wilde. It could have well been spoken by family firm owners who sell their business to private equity (PE) investors. While it is relatively easy to put a price tag on products or services, it creates much more difficulty to do so when pricing a family business. Valuation techniques are used for expressing economic value of the family firm in monetary terms, i.e. establishing a basis for price negotiations (Granata & Chirico, 2010). Although the principles of corporate valuation are generally well known, it is unclear whether valuation for family firms should be any different from valuing non-family businesses (Granata & Chirico, 2010). Evidently, there is often disagreement between family firm buyers such as PE firms and family firm sellers on the appropriate price for the firm (Scholes et al., 2007).

Prior research has made great efforts to shed light on the valuation of family firms (Astrachan & Jaskiewicz, 2008; Zellweger & Astrachan, 2008; Granata & Chirico, 2010). In particular, the sellers' perspective has been emphasized (Zellweger & Astrachan, 2008; Niedermeyer et al., 2010; Zellweger et al., 2011), stressing that family firm owners' non-financial objectives play a role when selling the business (Lipman, 2001; Chrisman, Chua, & Zahra, 2003; Scholes et al., 2007; Scholes et al., 2008; Barron, Boehler, & Cook, 2010). A family's perception of price for the business is considered to be higher due to emotional value attached to the firm which family sellers intend to price in (Astrachan & Jaskiewicz, 2008; Zellweger & Astrachan, 2008; Zellweger et al., 2011).

In contrast to family sellers, PE firms' key interest is the economic or financial value of the firm, which refers to the ability to generate cash flow at present and in the future

[20] This chapter is based on Ahlers, O., Hack, A., & Kellermanns, F. W. (2012). "Stepping into the buyers' shoes": looking at the value of family firms through the eyes of private equity investors. Unpublished Working paper.

(Dawson, 2011; Damodaran, 2002; Makri, Hitt, & Lane, 2010). PE firms have often been described as relatively short-term and profit-focused investors who use high debt to finance deals (Dawson, 2011; Jensen, 1989). Also, there is empirical evidence that family firms are acquired at a discount due to PE investors' perceptions that such firms are less efficient, less professional, and less successful (Salvato et al., 2010; Granata & Chirico, 2010). This observed discount stands in contrast to research indicating that family firms experience superior economic performance and lower agency costs (Jensen & Meckling, 1976; Anderson & Reeb, 2003; Chrisman et al., 2004; Villalonga & Amit, 2006; Granata & Chirico, 2010) which suggests that they should receive higher valuations. It also contrasts with the existence of emotional value that family firm owners may want to price in when selling their business (Zellweger et al., 2011). Thus, the family firm valuation "puzzle" is still to be resolved.

We contribute to close this research gap and suggest a real options perspective to improve valuation for family firms. Thereby we emphasize the importance of incorporating a family firm buyers' perspective. The buyers' perspective is characterized by flexibilities to act in the post-buyout period independent of family firm considerations that are shaped by socioemotional wealth as a key valuation determinant at the time of buying.

Our study contributes to the literature in a number of areas. First, we focus on the PE buyer valuation of the family firm, a perspective that has been previously neglected in the family firm literature. We assume that the PE buyer treats the target family firm as a stand-alone investment, where the entire firm is sold and the family will exit the company soon after the sale. Second, we complement and challenge existing research on the value of family firms and apply real option analysis in a new (family firm) context. To the best of our knowledge, there is not yet a valuation approach that explicitly considers the influence of the family on family firm valuation. Third, by highlighting the differences between family and non-family firm valuation, we contribute to the overall theory of the family firm, as our paper may explain why family firms cease to exist and family influence is eliminated.

The rest of the paper is organized as follows. We first provide the theoretical foundations for our considerations and introduce the concept of a family firm buyout value. We continue by discussing how family exit could affect this value as an upside and/or downside risk, which can be mitigated. Finally, we discuss our findings and their implications for researchers and practitioners.

3.2 Theoretical background

We draw upon existing research on PE and family firms and use real options analysis as a theoretical lens to highlight distinctive real options and the abilities to generate them prevalent in family firms' resources and which require consideration in the process of PE valuation (Barney, 1991; Bowman & Hurry, 1993; Kogut & Kulatilaka, 2001).

3.2.1 Private equity & family firms

Research on the sale/acquisition of family firms and the distinct factors involved is gaining momentum (Dawson, 2011; Niedermeyer et al., 2010; Granata & Chirico, 2010; Chrisman, Chua, Steier et al., 2012; Wennberg, Wiklund, Hellerstedt et al., 2011). This is justified given the international significance of family firms (Anderson & Reeb, 2003; Morck & Yeung, 2003), along with increasingly frequent challenges to family succession that necessitate the sale of family businesses (Wright et al., 2001; Scholes et al., 2008), and significant macroeconomic implications of ownership transfer when this takes place (Calogirou et al., 2010).

The sale of the family firm is increasingly a succession route for family firms, often involving PE firms as buyers (Wennberg et al., 2011). Thus, a key source of buyout deals for PE firms are family-owned businesses facing ownership succession (Scholes et al., 2009; Scholes et al., 2010; Scholes et al., 2007; Scholes et al., 2008). PE firms, together with the incumbent or a new management team – and usually using debt as well as equity – buy out the current (family) owner (Meuleman et al., 2009).

Family firms take many specific forms (Chua et al., 2012; Astrachan et al., 2002) and we assume their distinctiveness originates in the desire for socioemotional wealth (SEW). SEW explains the distinctiveness of family firms and the variation among family firms by the sum of families' non-economic goals and affective needs which frame family firms' activities (Gómez-Mejía et al., 2007; Gómez-Mejía et al., 2010; Berrone et al., 2010; Zellweger et al., 2011). Typically, as a requirement to be classified as a family firm, we would consider firms with at least 50% of ownership concentrated among family members, with many of them active in the business (Eddleston et al., 2008).

Although often not being the family firms' initial preference, selling the family business to a PE firm is an option to secure firm survival if continuation of family ownership is no longer possible (de Massis, Chua, & Chrisman, 2008; Chrisman et al., 2012; Dehlen et al., 2012). The relationship between PE firms and family firms, however, can be problematic and conflict-prone (Blanco-Mazagatos, de Quevedo-Puente, & Castrillo, 2007; Tappeiner et al., 2012; Dawson, 2011). PE firms have often been thought of as relatively short-term and profit-driven investors who rely on high levels of debt financing (Dawson, 2011; Jensen, 1989); although it has been acknowledged that PE firms differ in terms of their investment style and the way they deal with investment targets (de Clercq & Sapienza, 2006; Cressy et al., 2007; Shepherd & Zacharakis, 2001; Norton & Tenenbaum, 1993). In contrast, family firms are usually known for pursuing long-term objectives and disregarding short-term profits – which provides them with "patient capital", and, moreover, could compromise financial goals, in pursuing non-financial goals motivated by SEW (Carney, 2005; Dreux, 1990; Sirmon & Hitt, 2003; Gómez-Mejía et al., 2007). PE buyers often disagree strongly with the seller on the appropriate value of the family firm (Scholes et al., 2007).

3.2.2 Real options analysis

With its foundations in financial options theory (Myers, 1977; Trigeorgis, 1996), real option analysis explains the value of flexibility in managerial decision making under uncertainty (Pindyck, 1988; Dixit & Pindyck, 1994; Trigeorgis, 1995) and how strategies emerge from firm resources and capabilities (Bowman & Hurry, 1993). A financial *call* option generates ex post returns when the stock price exceeds the predetermined exercise price, and a *put* option generates returns when the stock price falls below the exercise price (Trigeorgis, 1996; Hull, 2009). While financial options are created for financial transactions, real options involve real assets (Black & Scholes, 1973; Trigeorgis, 1995).

A real option can be defined as the *"right, but not the obligation, to take an action in the future"* (Amram & Kulatilaka, 1999, p. 5). When considering as a real option, the stock price of a financial option becomes the net present value (NPV) of the potential investment, when conducted today, volatility is the uncertainty of future cash flows, and the exercise price is the future cost of the follow-on investment (Howell, 2001). The underlying asset is the potential physical or intellectual investment, and the direction of the option holder's right is formed by the opportunity to invest (call) or to divest (put) (Howell, 2001). It is assumed that investments have follow-on opportunities and returns can be estimated with probabilities (Leiblein, 2003). Real options differ from financial options in their character, partly due to non-exclusiveness as a result of competition (Kester, 1984; Grenadier, 2002) as well as valuation difficulties such as asset specificity or option interactions (Krychowski & Quelin, 2010). In contrast to financial options' focus on time-deferred investments, real options theory emphasizes growth (Myers, 1977; Trigeorgis, 1996) and operational flexibility (Pindyck, 1988; Trigeorgis, 1996) applied in a variety of contexts such as technology-oriented firms (McGrath & Nerkar, 2004; Oriani & Sobrero, 2008), entrepreneurship (McGrath, 1999), joint ventures (Reuer & Tong, 2005; Shyam Kumar, 2005), and acquisitions or venture capital investments (Smith & Triantis, 1995; Hurry, Miller, & Bowman, 1992). We agree with

Myers' conclusion that *"Options are at the heart of the valuation problem in all but the most pedestrian corporate investments ... it is hard to think of an investment project that does not include important real options."* (Myers, 1996, p. 99). However, previous research has cautioned against a "laissez-faire" approach to applying real options analysis, and has encouraged the precise selection and framing of application situations (Folta, 1998; Adner & Levinthal, 2004). Nonetheless, in the context of family firm valuation in buyout situations, real options theory seems to be particularly appropriate and promising for a number of reasons.

Firstly, real option analysis has been frequently used to solve valuation problems; strongly suggesting that option value is an essential part of a firm's total value (McGrath et al., 2004). The discounted cash flow approach has been criticized by proponents of real option analysis for failing to capture key value drivers resulting from opportunities of managerial decision flexibilities in a competitive and uncertain environment (Trigeorgis, 1996; Copeland & Antikarov, 2001). Thus, in the real option perspective, the value of any firm has two components (Myers, 1977; Trigeorgis, 1995). One component is the existing value of the firm generated by its existing use of current assets (static component). The other component is the value that can be realized from (growth) opportunities of the firm, originating from the firm's resources and capabilities (dynamic component). Consequently, the value of a firm can be more appropriately captured by complementing the discounted cash flow value (static component) with the value of future flexibility or real options (dynamic component) resulting from (the potential new owner's) discretionary power over future firm investments (Myers, 1977; Trigeorgis, 1995). Thus, options can be viewed as an important component of firm value (Trigeorgis, 1993b; McGrath et al., 2004); if omitted, family firms may well be valued incorrectly.

Secondly, the option value of future strategic choices is likely to be distinctly different in the context of family firms compared to non-family firms and real option analysis can help us to account for this specificity. It has been emphasized in real options theory that identification of real options is dependent on firm structure, cognitive abilities and attitudes of organizational actors (Bowman & Hurry, 1993; McGrath et al., 2004). The prior-state of a real option is called a "shadow option" (Bowman & Hurry, 1993). Shadow options can only be turned into real options if they are recognized within the firm's resource and capabilities' base (McGrath et al., 2004). Family firms are supposed to be different from non-family firms in terms of structure and organizational actors and thus real option analysis could be used to account for this distinctiveness. Family firms, for example, try to maintain SEW, which includes but is not limited to the need to belong, the continuation of family values, the building of a family dynasty, the building and preservation of social capital, and the pursuit of non-economic goals (Gómez-Mejía et al., 2007; Berrone et al., 2010; Berrone et al., 2012). By doing so, and in contrast to non-family firms, the family vision and management could inhibit the family firm from realizing the full inherent economic potential due to non-willingness or inability to recognize and/or exercise certain real options embedded therein. Thus, family firms' distinctiveness provides new PE owners with a real options portfolio from which future strategic choices can be made differently, following real options logic. As such, real options could represent the new owner's ability to take alternative strategic courses of action after ownership transfer is conducted (McGrath et al., 2004). The new owner can benefit from exogenous uncertainty reduction as new information unfolds after deal closure, but can also contribute to reducing endogenous uncertainty by providing new expertise, abilities, and priorities to the business (Dixit & Pindyck, 1994; McGrath et al., 2004). In addition, PE investors could provide the firm with financial capital, allowing the buyout target, for example, to develop future technologies (Folta & Miller, 2002).

Thirdly, buyouts are accompanied by a high degree of uncertainty resulting from information asymmetries and complexity. Although some debate continues as to what a real option actually is, there is widespread agreement that situations of uncertainty and irreversibility represent generally fruitful terrain for the application of real options theory (Adner & Levinthal, 2004; McGrath et al., 2004). While due diligence is widely applied to reduce the amount of ex-ante uncertainty in buyouts, many acquisition investments fail to realize expected outcomes or realize returns significantly higher than expected (Harvey & Lusch, 1995). In both cases, valuation would have failed to capture the appropriate value of the firm. In the context of family firm buyouts, the uncertainty for potential buyers might be even higher than for non-family firms, because of the tacitness of family firms (Cabrera-Suárez et al., 2001; Lee & Rogoff, 1996) and additional complexity stemming from the interlink of family and business systems (Chrisman, Chua, & Litz, 2003). Accordingly, when valuing a family firm, PE buyers need to be aware of the existence of a unique resource base and capabilities intertwined with, influenced by, and dependent on the family (Habbershon & Williams, 1999; Habbershon et al., 2003; Sirmon & Hitt, 2003). In family firm valuation/acquisition situations, real option analysis can help to account for increased uncertainty resulting from complexity and tacitness. Furthermore, there is a high degree of investment irreversibility associated with the family firm buyout, for once a PE firm has acquired a business it cannot easily sell it (a typical PE holding period is around 3-7 years).

Lastly, Adner & Levinthal (2004) argued that if target markets and technical agendas are fixed, as opposed to being flexible, real options logic is an appropriate approach, rather than an analysis of path dependent investments. PE investments are typically made in mature and established industries, and given the holding period of PE firms, this type of investor will try to realize strategic and operational improvements within such boundaries. In fact, Adner & Levinthal (2004) mention specific criteria that they associate with firms following a real options logic such as strict action mandates, milestones with go/no-go procedures, and early abandonment of projects which are found in PE firms dealing with portfolio companies (Kaplan, 1989; Smith, 1990; Nikoskelainen & Wright, 2007; Wilson et al., 2012). To the contrary, family firms are reckoned to use SEW as a reference point for decision-making that can lead to an escalation of commitment and excessive risk-taking, rather than limiting downside risk (Gómez-Mejía et al., 2007; Gómez-Mejía et al., 2010; Berrone et al., 2012). This suggests that family firms themselves do not employ real options logic when managing and governing their business.

3.3 Family firm value

In this section, we will apply real option analysis to family firm valuation from a PE firms' perspective. When a PE firm decides to execute a due diligence for a family firm buyout target, relatively small investments are made when PE resources such as own investment professionals and contracted advisors (tax, legal) are committed to analyze the family firm buyout target systematically. After completion of the due diligence process we can conceptualize the acquisition of the family firm target as a call option (C) by using the model of Black & Scholes (1973) which is given by:

$$C = f(S, X, T, \sigma, r) \qquad (1)$$

S refers to the family firm target and represents the expected future cash flows from the existing business and the option value associated with the family business. ***X*** corresponds to the exercise price which is the expenditure needed to acquire the family business. T is the length of time (duration) that the buyout decision can be postponed until the option expires. σ is the uncertainty about the value of the family firm (***S***). ***r*** refers to the risk-free rate of return whose influence can be neglected for real option purposes (Folta & Miller, 2002).

In general, we argue that the change of ownership from the family firm owner to the PE firm changes the portfolio of real options due to the fact that former family-firm actions were motivated by considerations of socioemotional wealth. The new PE ownership is then provided with a new set of real options if being a non-family firm because socio-emotional wealth plays no or a different role.

We further incorporate family firm specific components into our analysis that lead to the generation or prevention of value and the mitigation of risk by the involvement of the family in the business. We propose that the dynamic component of valuation (real options) can be divided into two broad categories: those that are available to all firms with a comparable activity pattern and those that are more specific to family firms due to the central role of the family in firm performance (Dyer, 2003; Nordqvist, 2005; Bowman & Ambrosini, 2007; Astrachan, 2010). In the latter category, family exit affects family firm value by creating future flexibilities and inflexibilities to act for PE investors, i.e., real options gained and/or lost over non-family firms.

We argue that the option component in family firm valuation has three specific elements that need to be considered for valuation purposes: Non-family Options (NfO) as upside value, Family Options at Risk (FOaR) as downside value, and Mitigation Measures (MM), which could limit the effect of downside value. We refer to the outcome of this family firm specific valuation approach as Family Firm Acquisition Value (FFAV). This is essentially the economic value a family firm represents for a PE buyer in which the Non-family Firm Value (NfFV) is adjusted for both expected economic losses and gains from future real options due to family exit. We simplify and use the following formal equation to complement formula (1) and to structure our discussion in the remainder of this paper.

$$S = f(NfO, FOaR, NfFV, MM) \qquad (2)$$

Below, we discuss the individual components of the formula in more detail and identify the main components underlying the individual elements, before we develop propositions. We are aware that the application of this formula is difficult because real life situations often involve a collection of various options, both upward-potential enhancing calls and downward-protection put options present in combination. Their combined option value may differ from the sum of separate option values, i.e., they interact (Trigeorgis, 1993a). ***Figure 11*** provides a summary of these underlying elements outlined in the formula. We are also aware that we describe potential situations for existence of real options and each situation would require specification for the situation at hand. Thus, we provide typical situations on a generic level that could give rise to valuable real options and included in PE valuation of family firms.

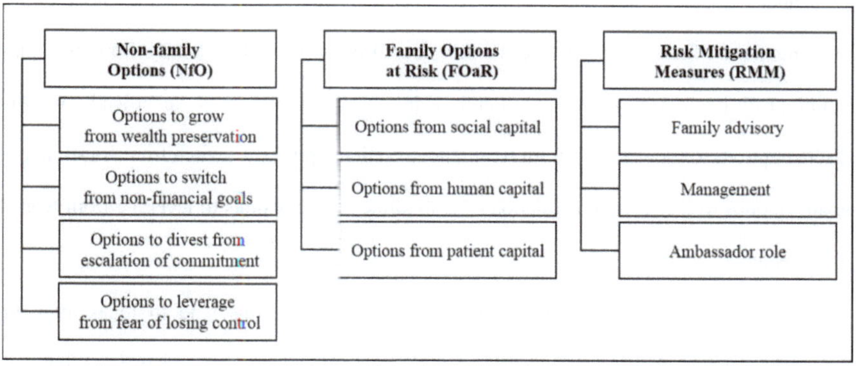

Figure 3-11: Real options for the new owner – NfO, FOaR, MM
Source: author

3.3.1 Non-family options

Opportunities for future resource enhancements in family firm buyouts form an important part of the investment decision (Lockett & Wright, 1999; Haspeslagh & Jemison, 1991; Lockett & Wright, 1999; Trigeorgis, 1995; Barkema & Schijven, 2008b; Makri et al., 2010). Family vision and management could inhibit the family firm from realizing the full economic potential inherent in familiness due to non-willingness or inability to recognize and/or exercise certain real options embedded therein. Indeed, recent research suggests that family firms try to maintain SEW, which includes but is not limited to the need to belong, the continuation of family values, the building of a family dynasty, the building and preservation of social capital, and the pursuit of non-economic goals (Gómez-Mejía et al., 2007). The latter entails the potential to decrease financial performance.

Because a PE buyer does not have to account for family system requirements (Lipman, 2001; Hellmann, 2002), family firms provide the non-family buyer with distinct real options allowing for economic value creation in the post-family era. We refer to the economic value of real options arising out of previous family ownership as NfO, which comprise different sequential real options depending on the real option to acquire the family firm. Based on the aforementioned focus on SEW, we identify four drivers of NfO in family firms that may inhibit profit maximization while the family is involved in the business. Specifically, we will discuss options to grow arising from wealth preservation, options to switch from non-financial goals, options to divest from escalation of commitment, and options to leverage from fear of losing control.

Options to grow from wealth preservation. Family firms tend to focus more on preserving wealth, which could constrain their inclination to invest and pursue company growth (Tagiuri & Davis, 1996; Carney, 2005; Astrachan, 2010). For example, some family members might want to invest for growth whereas others prefer dividend payouts, resulting in excessive risk aversion and hold-up (La Porta, Lopez-de-Silanes, & Shleifer, 1999; Schulze et al., 2003a, Schulze et al., 2003b; Gómez-Mejía, Wiseman, & Dykes, 2005; Danes, Stafford, Haynes et al., 2009). This can be reflected in a lower pace of international expansion and a focus on niche markets (Harris, Martinez, & Ward, 1994; Zahra, 2003; Gómez-Mejía et al., 2010).

Family firms as buyout targets, thus, are especially inclined to contain growth options for a potential PE buyer, as the desire to preserve wealth often restricts growth (Gómez-Mejía et al., 2007). Growth options encompass investment opportunities that entitle the buyer to pursue firm growth comparable to an American call option (Myers, 1977; Kester, 1984; Kulatilaka & Perotti, 1998). In family firms, buyers might find ample opportunities to grow by introducing related product segments, increasing geographic scope, and pursuing non-organic growth via mergers and acquisitions (Smith & Triantis, 1995; Tong, Reuer, & Peng, 2008; Scholes et al., 2009). PE firms are supposed to develop their investments strategically so that growth options can be realized (Nikoskelainen & Wright, 2007; Wilson et al., 2012).

Options to switch from non-financial goals. Family firms might not always structure their business operations efficiently, which originates from a combination of financial and non-financial goals (Tagiuri & Davis, 1992; Ward, 1997; Sharma, 2004; Zellweger, 2007). Indeed, Gómez-Mejía and colleagues (2001, 2003, 2007, 2010) argue that achieving non-financial goals is key to providing family firm owners with SEW. For example, family responsibilities might create less optimal staffing and biased incentive structures favoring family members (Dunn, 1995; Gómez-Mejía et al., 2001). Strong feelings of responsibility toward employees and personal ties to the local community could create obstacles to transferring manufacturing to low-cost countries (Lee & Rogoff, 1996; Dyer & Whetten, 2006). Long-term personal ties with suppliers might lead to uncompetitive sourcing prices. Consequently, economic rents of family firms may be captured by stakeholder groups or the family itself (Bowman & Ambrosini, 2007; Miller, Le Breton-Miller, & Scholnick, 2008).

The buyout of family firms thus offers real options to switch input and output factors, as well as switch firms' processes to improve overall efficiency. Switching options are change options that give the right, but not the obligation, to exchange one asset or process for another (Margrabe, 1978). If options to switch use are concerned, the option value is the cash flow of one mode of operation over another (Kulatilaka, 1993; Kogut & Kulatilaka, 1994; Kulatilaka, 1995). By executing diverse switching options, the buyer could emphasize efficiency and profit generation, thus improving financial performance. PE buyers are known to drive operational efficiency of their investments which indicates their use of switching options (Kaplan, 1989; Smith, 1990).

Options to divest from escalation of commitment. Family firms are typically less willing to employ important resource shedding to increase economic efficiency, often falling victim to escalation of commitment (Sirmon & Hitt, 2003; Brockner, 1992). Portfolio restructuring, i.e., the divestiture of non-performing businesses, might have been neglected in the past due to family legacy, nostalgia, emotional attachment, or managerial entrenchment (Denis, Denis, & Sarin, 1997; Sharma & Manikutty, 2005; Gómez-Mejía et al., 2007; Stavrou, Kassinis, & Filotheou, 2007). As a result, the opportunity costs of maintaining resources and leveraging inferior resources could negatively affect economic value creation in family firms (Mosakowski, 2002). Indeed, instead of exiting, family firms are even willing to risk their existence and wealth in order to maintain the business in the family and to preserve SEW (Gómez-Mejía et al., 2007).

With the buyout of a family firm, the PE buyer thus receives options to divest (or abandon) operations and assets. The option to divest exists if market price or salvage value of family firms' assets is higher than the future value it constitutes for the firm and is likely to be value-creating (Robichek & van Horne, 1967; Smith & Triantis, 1995). Divesture options can be formally expressed as American put options where the exercise price is the salvage value (Myers & Majd, 1990). As PE buyers will focus on financial objectives and strict performance criteria, they will not hesitate to execute abandonment options to secure appropriate returns from their investments (Nikoskelainen & Wright, 2007; Cumming et al., 2007; Kaplan & Schoar, 2005).

Options to leverage from fear of losing control. Because they tend to refrain from sharing equity with non-family investors to ensure control, family firms are less likely to use external financial sources (Daily & Dollinger, 1992; Anderson & Reeb, 2003). Indeed, family firms are willing to increase business risk in order to maintain family control and socioemotional wealth (Gómez-Mejía et al., 2007). New buyers might engage in a more optimal financial structure that could favorably shift relative value from outside creditors to proprietary capital financiers (Modigliani & Miller, 1958) because firm equity can be viewed as a call option on total firm value due to limited liability, with the exercise price equal to the amount of debt issued by outside creditors (Koch, 1999). When increasing risk of financing with higher leverage, the relative value of equity rises while the value of debt decreases (Black & Scholes, 1973; Koch, 1999). Buyout deals by PE firms are usually structured as leveraged deals, i.e. involve external debt so that options to leverage are a common instrument to increase the value of portfolio firms (Jensen, 1986, Jensen, 1989).

Overall, our arguments suggest that family influence and the desire to retain SEW in family firms may prohibit the generation and execution of economic value-creating real options (i.e., NfO). Accordingly, we propose:

Proposition 1: Buyers of family firms are able to realize a distinct set of real options (NfO) arising from previous family influence, thus allowing for subsequent enhancement of firm value.

3.3.2 Family options at risk

Options theory is primarily concerned with upside potential arising from opportunities of future flexibility (Trigeorgis, 1995). However, distinct future opportunities tied to the family might inevitably be lost due to family departure creating downside value effects. We refer to these real options originating in the unique resources available to family firms and its management as "Family Options." If the family exits the firm, these options are put at risk (FOaR). Next, we will discuss options arising from social capital, human capital, and patient capital, which have been discussed as key sources for family firm performance advantages (Sirmon & Hitt, 2003; Danes et al., 2009).

Options from social capital. Family firms are typically better equipped with social capital due to long-term orientation, a higher degree of freedom when selecting business partners, a personal and informal approach in transactions, and by applying suitable behavior driven by family principles (Miller et al., 2008; Pearson, Carr, & Shaw, 2008; Arregle, Hitt, Sirmon et al., 2007). Social capital is embedded in the family and in ties the firm has with its external stakeholders (Hoffman, Hoelscher, & Sorenson, 2006; Arregle et al., 2007; Pearson et al., 2008; Gedajlovic & Carney, 2010). By leveraging social capital, the family firm can facilitate transactions and create enhanced relationships with suppliers, customers, government, and support organizations (Hitt, Ireland, Camp et al., 2001; Bertrand & Schoar, 2006). Additionally, social capital could provide access to sources of competitive advantage such as information, technological knowledge, market access, and complementary resources (Hitt et al., 2001; Blyler & Coff, 2003). Social capital in family firms can also increase the firm's coherence and resilience (Arregle et al., 2007).

"Shadow options" represent future potential that, upon recognition, turns into real options (Bowman & Hurry, 1993). A higher propensity of social capital increases the amount of shadow options available to the family firm and allows firms to convert them into real options (McGrath, 1996). As a result, diverse real options can be created from stakeholder relationships such as options to grow, to switch, or to abandon (Trigeorgis, 1995). Although, each option needs further specification—in general social capital tied to the family could allow for superior performance and can be translated into substantial economic value for the family firm that could be lost to the new PE owner after family exit.

Options from human capital. Family firms could be equipped with superior human capital allowing for competitive advantage (Sirmon & Hitt, 2003). Human capital constitutes an intangible resource that encompasses employees' abilities, skills, and knowledge, which, in turn, could leverage other resources (Coleman, 1988; Hitt, Biermant L., Shimizu K. et al., 2001; Danes et al., 2009) and can be viewed as a proxy for productivity (Olson, Zuiker, Danes et al., 2003). Positive economic effects on firm performance could result from family and non-family members demonstrating higher motivation, loyalty, job tenure, and extraordinary commitment (Rosenblatt, 1985; Horton, 1986; Ward, 1987; Lansberg, 1999; Miller & Le Breton-Miller, 2005). Early exposure of family members to the business might equip them with deeper levels of extraordinary firm-specific and tacit knowledge (Sirmon & Hitt, 2003; Tokarczyk, Hansen, Green et al., 2007; DeNoble, Ehrlich, & Singh, 2007). Interaction between family and employees can be characterized by a high level of trust that is reflected in a positive firm culture (Miller et al., 2008; Arregle et al., 2007), which may lead to lower agency cost.

While social capital contributes to the availability of shadow options, committed human capital with high tacit and firm-specific knowledge positively affects the recognition of shadow options and the subsequent creation of real options (Bowman & Hurry, 1993). Additionally, the majority of real options cannot be exercised without the involvement of employees, management, and investments in (firm-specific) knowledge, skills, abilities, and relationships (Wang & Lim, 2008). Accordingly, family firms' high commitment of employees and management creates favorable incentives to conduct human capital investments, which increases real options values due to superior execution (Wang & Lim, 2008). Consequently, a potential PE buyer faces the risk of losing real options and superior option value due to family departure.

Options from patient capital. Family firms usually have a long-term orientation in their decision making, with extended investment horizons and lower cost of equity (Sirmon & Hitt, 2003; Carney, 2005; Zellweger, 2007). This is reflected by shareholders' provision of patient capital, which is not threatened by immediate disengagement (Dreux, 1990; Sirmon & Hitt, 2003). The long-term-oriented family firm with lower cost of equity will be able to undertake a larger pool of projects with more follow-on real options from which the most promising opportunities can be pursued as uncertainty unfolds (Zellweger, 2007).

As a result, family firms especially benefit from learning options, such as the option to defer or time to build, which enables management to wait and act upon resolution of uncertainty. Options to defer allow for later investments; time to build options refer to investments that can be abandoned before committing required investments (Majd & Pindyck, 1987; Dixit & Pindyck, 1994). Not surprisingly, patient capital is supposed to positively influence innovation capabilities in family firms (Kang, 1999; Zahra, Hayton, & Salvato, 2004; Miller & Le Breton-Miller, 2006). In contrast, PE buyers do not have patient capital, but will need to generate profits from their investment within a relatively short time period.

In summary, the presence of family influence may facilitate the generation and execution of value-creating real options for the family firm that potential buyers would be at risk of losing, thus limiting the potential for real-option creation.

Proposition 2: Buyers of family firms could lose economic value under new ownership due to a loss of family induced real options (FOaR).

3.3.3 Mitigation measures

We have stressed that family options are value-creating and at risk when the family departs. Having said this, we hasten to add that the loss of family options is not inevitable and can be mitigated. As initially stated, we assumed that the sale of the family business is complete. Now, we relax this assumption and outline "mitigation measures" (MM).

After the sale, continued family influence can be maintained to conserve the creation and value of real options (Granata & Chirico, 2010; Niedermeyer et al., 2010) by family members remaining in management positions, acting in advisory roles, or serving as ambassadors (Ehrhardt & Nowak, 2003; Steen & Welch, 2006). As a consequence, family capital and real options can be secured in the post-acquisition period (Sirmon & Hitt, 2003; Danes et al., 2009; Gedajlovic & Carney, 2010; Granata & Chirico, 2010).

This might coincide with the family firm seller's desire to be involved in the business post-acquisition as the sale of the family business can be difficult and accompanied by feelings of sorrow and regret (Pellegrin, 1999; Shepherd, 2009; Niedermeyer et al., 2010). A combination of family and non-family management could also have positive effects on firm performance (Villalonga & Amit, 2006; Dawson, 2011) and create a win-win situation, although former family management might be resistant to exercise NfO for strategic change (Scholes et al., 2007).

If advanced age of the family firm seller along with failed family succession is the reason for selling the business, continued family influence in the firm is only a temporary solution. However, such a transition period – comparable to family succession – can be used to transfer sources of real option creation capabilities such as relationships or tacit knowledge (Bresman, Birkinshaw, & Nobel, 1999; Cabrera-Suárez et al., 2001; Howorth et al., 2004). Accordingly, we suggest continued family influence as a potential MM.

Proposition 3: Buyers of family firms that secure family influence in the post-acquisition period could reduce the potential for family options at risk through mitigation measures.

3.4 Discussion

Based on our discussion, our analysis allows us to distinguish among three exemplary valuation cases that have implications for research and practice. ***Table 3*** summarizes these three fictive scenarios, which we will discuss in more detail below.

Cases	Description of exemplary Family Firm Acquisition Targets	Value of NFO	Value of FoAR	Value of MM	Value of Family Firm
No 1 **"Family Firm Performer"**	• The family firm is owned and largely managed by family members since two generations. The CEO and the Head of R&D originate from the owning families. • The family CEO's priority was to run the company professionally. He established an external advisory board to ensure that business interests always have priority over family interests. *(NFO, only limited potential)* • The family CEO has influential political connections which have secured government contracts in the past. *(FoAR, Options from social capital)* • Historically, the most important firm products were driven by the imaginative abilities and foresight of the R&D head . *(FoAR, Options from human capital)*	**Low**	**High**	**Not used**	**Lower compared to a similar non-family firm**
No 2 **"Family Firm Underper-former"**	• The family firm is owned and managed by two antagonised families. Family conflicts have plagued the family business and an unqualified family CEO missed many strategic business opportunities. *(FoAR, only limited potential)* • The families have prohibited shifting production to low cost countries due to reputational concerns. *(NFO, Options to grow from non-financial goals)* • The families have avoided the divesture of a highly unprofitable business unit since several years. *(NFO, Options to divest from escalation of commitment)* • The families decided not to invest in emerging markets like China and India because high investments would have been required. *(NFO, Options to grow from wealth preservation)*	**High**	**Low**	**Not used**	**Higher compared to a similar non-family firm**
No 3 **"Professio-nalized Family Firm"**	• Although the firm is still owned by the family, a professional external management has run the company operations independently since many years. *(NFO, only limited potential).* • The primary interest of the family is profit-maximization and the family is not involved in the business. *(FoAR, only limited potential)*	**Low**	**Low**	**Not used**	**Equal compared to a similar non-family firm**

Table 3-3: Exemplary valuation examples

Source: Author

First, *NfO* < *FOaR* (Case 1, Table 1) implies a loss of economic value in the post-acquisition period. If options are recognized, then potential PE buyers are justified in demanding an acquisition discount in comparison to non-family firms. Acknowledging the central role of the family for firm performance (Dyer, 2003; Nordqvist, 2005; Bowman & Ambrosini, 2007; Astrachan, 2010), the departure of the family after the business sale has negative implications for the creation and value of real options. Case 1 highlights in particular the role of family social and human capital options.

Second, *NfO* > *FOaR* (Case 2, Table 1) implies potentially excessive gains of economic value in the post-acquisition period which could be recognized by potential PE buyers, thus justifying an acquisition premium. Buyers of family firms could exploit previously untapped firm potential and drive economic value creation by exercising NfO to drive international growth (Astrachan, 2010), increase efficiency of business operations (e.g. production in low cost countries) (Wright, Ferris, Sarin et al., 1996), and restructure portfolios (Denis et al., 1997; Gómez-Mejía et al., 2007; Sharma & Manikutty, 2005).

Third, lack of significant NfO or FOaR (Case 3, Table 1) indicates that family firm acquisition prices should be in line with comparable prices for non-family firms. In other words, there is no difference between the values of family firms and non-family firms.

We argue, consistent with prior research, that SEW wealth has an important impact on family firm behavior. Research suggests that although family members attribute an emotional value to the firm (Astrachan & Jaskiewicz, 2008; Zellweger & Astrachan, 2008; Zellweger et al., 2011), for a seller, the translation of emotional value into economic value by realizing a higher selling price is a rather difficult task. However, we argue that few potential buyers of family firms would be willing to increase economic valuation by considering sellers' emotions.

Also, recent research on the sale of the family business highlights that family succession (internal succession route) and the sale of the family firm to external buyers (external succession route) have different implications for survival and future financial success of the business (Wennberg et al., 2011). Thus, buyers of family firms can be viewed as acquiring distinct real options which allow them to develop the business accordingly in the post-acquisition period. This finding underlines the need to incorporate family firm buyers' specific flexibilities to act in the post deal closure period as a key valuation determinant at the time of buying.

Overall, this paper contributes to the debate on the buyout and valuation of family firms in a number of ways (Scholes et al., 2009; Granata & Chirico, 2010; Dawson, 2011; Zellweger & Astrachan, 2008; Zellweger et al., 2011). First, we introduced a valuation approach by highlighting value-creating and value-decreasing real options arising out of family capital from the standpoint of an economically value-oriented buyer. Specifically, we explored how the family factor influences the resources of the family firm and contributes to real-option creation or prevention.

Second, we complement earlier research that assumes that family firms are perceived negatively by potential buyers and thus are acquired at a discount when sale multiples are concerned (Granata & Chirico, 2010). The acquisition discount is attributed to family firms being perceived as inefficient, unprofessional, and unsuccessful compared to non-family firms (Granata & Chirico, 2010). However, it should be mentioned that the observed acquisition discount in the study cited above occurs only for specific multiples within a particular industry and thus cannot necessarily be generalized. Indeed, the application of our valuation model leads to conclusions for an acquisition discount that differ from Granata and Chirico (2010). We argue that an acquisition discount occurs if $NfO < FOaR$ (Case 1, Table 1), since this would entail a loss of economic value due to a high-performing family leaving the firm. Consequently, it is not a false perception of family firms but rather the opposite: the buyer's recognition that superior performance depends on the family. Additionally, when $NfO >$

FOaR (Case 2, Table 1), any observed discount could be a sign of market failure, i.e., buyers fail to recognize NfO.

Third, while we focused on the buyer, our framework also informs the seller. Since the sale of the business is usually a singular event for the family firm CEO (Pellegrin, 1999), the seller is likely to be less informed and may want to price in SEW that the family is about to lose through the sale. Indeed, recent research shows that family firm CEOs would sell the firm to family members for 30% less than to non-family members (Zellweger et al., 2011). If sellers of family firms are able to better rationalize and communicate their pricing ideas, they are likely to improve their negotiation position with potential PE investors when applying real options reasoning.

3.5 Limitations and future research

We are aware that the application of real option analysis imposes several challenges in practice. First of all, valuing real options can be complex. Unlike financial options with clearly defined parameters and contracts, real options are part of the business. Valuation difficulties might arise from asset specificity (Henderson & Hobson, 2002; McGrath et al., 2004; McGrath & Nerkar, 2004), option interaction (Trigeorgis, 1993a, Trigeorgis, 1993b), uncertain expiration dates (Adner & Levinthal, 2004), and implicitness and invisibility (Kogut & Kulatilaka, 2001). Also, multiple sources of risk need to be included in modelling (Copeland & Keenan, 1998). Family options identification can be especially challenging in light of information availability due to tacitness and limited company information when (private) family firms are concerned (Cabrera-Suárez et al., 2001; Capron & Shen, 2007). Although real options theory offers different valuation models, mathematical complexity and restrictive assumptions have raised the bar for practitioners' usage despite ongoing interest by researchers (Philippe, 2005). Thus, any practical application of our model would imply to focus on real options that significantly influence value creation post-sale.

Our valuation framework also needs some degree of adjustment to different buyer types. Depending on the type of buyer, the real options framework might appear different. Especially the extent to which certain types of buyers could make use of particular real options could deviate. Family firm buyers for example might be less inclined or able to exercise NfO when acquiring other family firms, but might be naturally equipped with means to mitigate FOaR. Also, it has to be mentioned that the execution of NfO could require additional investments.

In line with other researchers, our paper further emphasizes the need for future research in the context of family firm buyouts (Howorth et al., 2004; Niedermeyer et al., 2010; Granata & Chirico, 2010). Given the fact that family firms face considerable challenges involving family succession (Sharma et al., 2003), selling the family firm could be a promising way to secure survival (Wright et al., 2001). By looking at inherent real options, the buyout route might be rewarding for buyers of family firms. It might be of particular interest to empirically investigate whether real options are used as reasoning or valuation tools when family firms are concerned and how family firm valuation is affected by NfO and FOaR, i.e., how strong these effects are relative to each other and on an aggregated level in comparison to non-family firms. We recommend further empirical investigation of how factors of family influence such as ownership and management structure, company objectives, company size, and generations involved in the firm influence family firm valuation.

The buyout of a family firm is a process; valuation is only one important element. Valuation is usually followed by price negotiations, investment decisions, and post-acquisition measures (Pablo, Sitkin, & Jemison, 1996; Shepherd et al., 2003; Anand & Singh, 1997; Barkema & Schijven, 2008b; Saoriniborra, 2008). Thus, several nearly untapped research opportunities arise. As far as the negotiation process is concerned, little is known about its characteristics, specific behavior, and power of family firm sellers and buyers. Further, a better understanding of investment criteria applied by buyers of family firms and perceptions on the attractiveness of family firms as acquisition targets could be of benefit when considering a sale.

In addition to considerations of economic value, many non-financial factors can also lead to a family firm being acquired at a discount. The seller could, for example, intentionally sell the business at an emotionally induced discount because of personal ties (e.g., former management as buyer) or positive feelings toward buyers' intentions to continue a firm's strategic direction (Kensinger, Martin, & William Petty, 2000; Thomas, 2002; Scholes et al., 2007; Scholes et al., 2008). Family firm sellers could also be at a bargaining disadvantage due to a potential lack of deal experience or transaction knowledge, time pressure, and a limited number of bidders resulting from market intransparency for trading of private firms (Pellegrin, 1999; Steen & Welch, 2006; Capron & Shen, 2007; Kim et al., 2005; Saoriniborra, 2008). Future research will need to further investigate the exact composition of valuation discounts, which are likely to be a combination of reduced real options and factors alluded to here.

Firms and investors often struggle to realize anticipated synergies or upside potential in the post-acquisition period (Haspeslagh & Jemison, 1991; Barkema & Schijven, 2008b; Barkema & Schijven, 2008a). If family firms are sold to non-family buyers, the post-acquisition process might require substantial strategic change (Scholes et al., 2009). Thus, how family firms perform in the post-acquisition period and whether their performance is in line with pre-acquisition buyer expectations offers promise for future research.

It is also important that new models for real options valuation are detailed that allow for easier implementation while offering acceptable accuracy. Also, real option analysis must point out behavioral aspects inherent in family firms to gain acceptance and unfold explanatory power. Undoubtedly, because the application of real options theory to family firms entails many avenues of research, further work is required to extend our understanding of this relationship. By applying real options in the context of family firm valuation, we have taken a first step.

In conclusion, our paper, grounded in insights from SEW research and utilizing a real options approach, provides a theoretical explanation for potential discounts and premiums when a family firm is sold to an external buyer. We hope that our paper adds to discussion about the sale of family businesses (Granata & Chirico, 2010; Dawson, 2011; Niedermeyer et al., 2010), sparks future research, and informs practice.

4 Opening the black box: Power in buyout negotiations and the moderating role of private equity specialization[21]

4.1 Introduction

Buyouts are the main investment route for private equity (PE) firms and negotiations are required to reach an agreement with current owners as to how to form a new corporate entity (Meuleman et al., 2009). The negotiation of buyouts is extraordinary complex, given the number of financial, tax, and legal issues which need to be resolved between the negotiating parties (Reed et al., 2007; Cumming & Johan, 2009). Previous research has emphasized the importance of negotiations as a critical phase of the investment process (Tyebjee & Bruno, 1984), to the extent that *"success or failure of the future business is determined"* by them (Birley, 1984, p. 32).

Surprisingly, we know very little about buyout negotiations. Previous literature was primarily concerned with PE performance issues (Cumming et al., 2007; Wilson et al., 2012) and investment decision-making (Arora & Chakraborty, 2012; Dawson, 2011; Shepherd et al., 2003; Zacharakis & Meyer, 2000). It has also been acknowledged that PE firms increasingly develop specialization (strategies) to gain competitive advantage over peers in a mature marketplace (Cressy et al., 2007). The important negotiation phase, however, has been largely bypassed in previous research (apart from Scholes et al., 2007). In particular, there is no research on how well PE firms perform in negotiations compared with their counterparts and why. Further, it remains unclear if and what forms of specialization play a role in the negotiation stage (Cressy et al., 2007; Gompers, Kovner, Lerner et al., 2008; Gottschalg & Wright, 2008).

We address this research gap by utilizing bargaining power theory. Power is a key factor in negotiations (Greenhalgh, Neslin, & Gilkey, 1985; Dreu & van Kleef, 2004) and

[21] This chapter is based on Ahlers, O., Hack, A., Kellermanns, F. W., & Wright, M. (2013). Opening the black box: power in buyout negotiations and the moderating role of private equity specialization. Unpublished Working paper.

decisively influences who is able to claim more value from an agreement (Argyris & Liebeskind, 1999; Nair, Narasimhan, & Bendoly, 2011; Overbeck, Neale, & Govan, 2010). Negotiation power arises from different factors, specific to the individual negotiation situation, so as such, no universally applicable framework of power in negotiations exists (Astley & Sachdeva, 1984; Leap & Grigsby, 1986). Thus, the research on buyout negotiations calls for insights about how power is created.

With this paper, we hope to make a number of contributions. First, we add to the literature on bargaining power theory which has not been applied to the specific context of buyouts. In particular, we hypothesize and empirically test bargaining power sources in buyout transactions from a PE/buyer perspective. Secondly, we add to the literature on PE-backed buyouts and strategic entrepreneurship. PE-backed buyouts are regarded as a successful form of entrepreneurship, supposedly outperforming other forms of entrepreneurship (Wright et al., 2001). We investigate whether and how this also holds true for the negotiation stage. Thirdly, we contribute to a growing body of research that recognizes the heterogeneity of PE firms by examining how different forms of PE firm specialization can provide competitive advantage in negotiations. To accomplish our objectives, we use a survey-based, hand-collected data set of 177 PE-backed buyouts across Europe from 2008–2011. The majority of our respondents are distinguished individuals occupying managing director or investment director positions in PE firms.

In the remainder of the paper, we first provide the theoretical foundations for our considerations and briefly summarize the existing literature on bargaining power. We continue by formulating hypotheses regarding the sources of bargaining power and the moderating effects of different PE firm specializations. This is followed by a description of the sample made, as well as the variables and constructs we have used in our statistical analysis. We then present and discuss our empirical results. Finally, we consider limitations of our study and outline opportunities for future research.

4.2 Theoretical background: power in negotiations[22]

Negotiation is *"... the deliberate interaction of two or more complex social units which are attempting to define or redefine the terms of their interdependence"* (Walton & McKersie, 1965, p. 35). Power is a key factor in negotiations (Greenhalgh et al., 1985; Dreu & van Kleef, 2004) and can be broadly defined as the potential to influence others (Kelley & Thibaut, 1978; Bacharach & Lawler, 1981; Dreu & van Kleef, 2004). Sometimes negotiation power in business contexts is limited to the ability to determine a price (Lindblom, 1948). However, we follow Kim et al. (2005, p. 799-800) who define power in negotiations more broadly as *"... the underlying capacity of negotiators to obtain benefits from their agreement"*.

As power is individually perceived, objective features are cognitively determined using available information, subjective assessments, values, and comparisons based on "shadows of the future" (i.e., expectations) and "shadows of the past" (i.e., history) (Cyert & March, 1963; Bacharach & Lawler, 1976; Leap & Grigsby, 1986; Wolfe & McGinn, 2005; Dawson, 2011). Differences in power distribution are manifested in negotiation outcomes: powerful negotiators are likely to claim more value from the agreement, while being proactive rather than reactive (Argyris & Liebeskind, 1999; Nair et al., 2011; Overbeck et al., 2010). Evaluating power distribution in negotiations is also important for determining appropriate negotiation tactics (Bacharach & Lawler, 1981; Kim et al., 2005). Additionally, power imbalances in the negotiation relationship lead to a higher occurence of conflict escalation and lower propensity towards reaching integrative outcomes (de Dreu, 1995; de Dreu, Giebels, & van de Vliet, 1998; Wolfe & McGinn, 2005).

The overall efficacy of power (sources) largely depends on each specific situation, and hence no universally applicable framework of power in negotiations exists (Astley & Sachdeva, 1984; Leap & Grigsby, 1986). Although it has been established by previous

[22] See for this section chapter 2.1.3.

research that negotiations, and in particular bargaining power, is an important determinant in interorganizational transactions such as joint-ventures and corporate mergers (Inkpen & Beamish, 1997; Lee, Chen, & Kao, 1998; Varaiya, 1987; Yan & Gray, 2001b), we know surprisingly little, in this respect, about buyout negotiations. Relating to prior research on interorganizational transactions, we use the distinction between "context-based" and "resource-based" bargaining power sources which determine the interdependence of the negotiation parties (Yan & Gray, 1994, Yan & Gray, 2001a, Yan & Gray, 2001b). Thus, our work is theoretically grounded in the relational concept of bargaining power which assumes that power exists as a social relationship property and not the property of an actor (Emerson, 1962).

"Context-based" bargaining power highlights the context-dependency of the relationship between the bargaining parties (Yan & Gray, 2001b). It specifically argues that A's negotiation power rises when B's dependence on the negotiation relationship increases (Emerson, 1962; Blau, 1964; Wolfe & McGinn, 2005). Put differently, the party that has more alternatives to choose from could threaten to exit the current negotiation and select one of its alternatives which manifests bargaining power (Fisher, 1981). "Resource-based bargaining power" is the second derivative of power-dependence theory and assumes that power in interorganizational relationships can derive from the possession of critical tangible or intangible resources employed in a relationship (Pfeffer & Nowak, 1976; Aldrich, 1977; Pfeffer & Salancik, 1978; Yan & Gray, 2001b).

In the context of interorganizational relationships we have identified and hypothesized three sources of bargaining power which we posit to be relevant for buyout transactions (Yan & Gray, 1994, Yan & Gray, 2001a, Yan & Gray, 2001b). We identify bidder competition as source of "context-dependent" bargaining power, expertise as a source of "resource-based bargaining power" and time pressure as a "hybrid", i.e. containing both context-dependent and resource-based characteristics.

4.3 Derivation of hypotheses

In this section we derive a set of hypotheses on bargaining power in buyout negotiations. We start by outlining the factors that create bargaining power and then hypothesize on the moderating effect of PE firm specialization.

4.3.1 Bidder competition

In power-dependence theory, emphasis is given to context-dependency of negotiators (Emerson, 1962; Blau, 1964; Wolfe & McGinn, 2005). Dependence is derived from the number of alternatives party A has in a negotiation relationship with B: the more alternatives available to A, the higher the respective negotiation power, provided that B's alternatives remain unchanged (Bacharach & Lawler, 1980; Leap & Grigsby, 1986). Consequently, increasing the number of alternatives a party can establish to substitute the current negotiation relationship leverages the party's negotiation power due to dependency reduction (Bacharach & Lawler, 1984).

Put differently, a selling party with a higher number of potential buyers willing to bid for the firm (alternatives) could threaten to exit the current negotiation, while simultaneously engaging the next best alternative party to reach a negotiated agreement ("BATNA") (Fisher, 1981). In order to be regarded as an "alternative", a certain minimum quality standard needs to be fulfilled (Yan & Gray, 2001b). The seller will feel less inclined to make concessions during negotiations where there is a substantial number of quality alternatives available. Additionally, if one negotiating party is assuming attractive BATNAs available to the other negotiation party, its perceived value attributed to the current deal is likely to increase due to potential scarcity value (Cialdini, 1984; Kim & Fragale, 2005).

In joint-ventures, more alternatives for one party can be utilized as "context-based" bargaining power to achieve greater control (Yan & Gray, 1994, Yan & Gray, 2001a, Yan & Gray, 2001b). In the context of public acquisitions, it was shown that higher buyer competition is also reflected in higher acquisition premiums (Varaiya, 1987). However, buyout transactions usually take place in less information-efficient private takeover markets and thus buyer competition cannot be taken for granted, but rather exists due to professional search for exchange partners (Fama, 1991; Wright, Thompson, & Robbie, 1992; Capron & Shen, 2007; Shen & Reuer, 2005; Scholes et al., 2007). Selling or purchasing privately held targets is thus often problematic due to greater information asymmetries and higher difficulty to identify exchange partners (Scholes et al., 2007). In summary, we hypothesize as follows:

Hypothesis 1: The higher the bidder competition, the lower the buying PE firm's perceived bargaining power in buyouts will be.

4.3.2 Expertise advantage

Superior expertise has been emphasized as important source of power in (inter-organizational) negotiations (French & Raven, 1959; Inkpen & Beamish, 1997; Raven, 1993; Coff, 1999). Sometimes authors subsume "information" and "expertise" under the concept of "knowledge" (Patchen, 1974; Bacharach & Lawler, 1980). While informational power in negotiations is usually tied to the negotiator's efforts and ability to accumulate and organize information, power generated from expertise requires a higher level of education, skill, accomplishment, and experience in a certain domain allowing for informational sense-making (Lewicki, Saunders, & Barry, 2010). As a result, experts are associated with authority, credibility, and superior status (French & Raven, 1959; Cronkhite & Liska, 1976).

If one negotiating party possesses superior expertise, it can be used to manipulate the other party's assumptions, beliefs, and choices (Pfeffer, 1981; Coff, 1999). Thus, power from expertise can also be viewed as being manipulative or persuasive in nature. Unsurprisingly, much of the practitioner-oriented negotiation literature concerned advantage achieved through expertise development in pre-negotiation preparations to favorably influence the negotiations in one's own interest (Fisher, 1981; Leap & Grigsby, 1986). In sum, the power negotiator A can generate in negotiations is significantly shaped by B's perception that A possesses certain expertise (French & Raven, 1959; Kim et al., 2005). Evidence from joint ventures indicates that "resource-based" bargaining power such as expertise can be used to negotiate greater control in joint venture deals (Yan & Gray, 2001b, Yan & Gray, 2001a).

In the context of buyouts, superior expertise can be of critical importance to successfully negotiate a deal (Petty, Bygrave, & Shulman, 1994; Scholes et al., 2007). The negotiation of buyouts is extraordinary complex given the number of financial, taxation, and legal issues that need to be resolved often involving a range of specialist advisors (Reed et al., 2007; Cumming & Johan, 2009). Buyout transactions also involve great uncertainty, complexity, and the risk of exploitation due to limited transparency on the appropriate price, as transactions usually occur in less efficient private markets (Fama, 1991; Capron & Shen, 2007; Shen & Reuer, 2005; Olekalns & Smith, 2009). This is reflected in the often observed disagreement between buyers and sellers on the appropriate transaction price (Scholes et al., 2007).

As buyers, PE firms could possess higher transaction relevant expertise derived from education and experience, compared to the selling side (Admati & Pfleiderer, 1994; Wright & Robbie, 1996; Manigart, de Waele, Wright et al., 2002; Scholes et al., 2008).[23] The expertise advantage could comprise, among other aspects, the valuation of the buyout target, assessments on synergies which could be realized under new ownership, and the process or technical details of the deal (tax, law, covenants etc). Thus, PE firms could possess an expertise advantage in sale negotiations and use it to challenge and reduce seller's price perception while structuring a buyout deal in their interest. Sellers in turn might be able to counter buyers' negotiating power if comparable expertise can be utilized as a result of their own experience, education, inside information, and/or the support of professional sale

[23] This excludes cases of secondary buyouts, where the selling side can also be a PE firm.

advisors (Petty et al., 1994; Westhead & Howorth, 2007; Howorth et al., 2004). We conclude as follows:

Hypothesis 2: The higher the expertise advantage relevant for the buyout deal, the higher the buying PE firm's perceived negotiation power will be.

4.3.3 Sellers' time pressure

Time plays an important role in negotiations and time pressure can be defined as desire or need to close the negotiation process (Smith, Pruitt, & Carnevale, 1982; Druckman, 1994; Saoriniborra, 2008). Time pressure can be either internally imposed or externally induced (Saoriniborra, 2008) and is often associated with acquisition processes (Newburry & Zeira, 1997, Zeira & Newburry, 1999). In joint ventures, urgency of cooperation is identified as a source of negotiation power because it increases the need to cooperate (Inkpen & Beamish, 1997). The negotiation party suffering from time pressure is equipped with weaker negotiation power, as pressure creates the necessity to close the deal though circumstances may be unfavorable (Pruitt, 1969; Rubin & Brown, 1975; Cohen, 1980; Stuhlmacher, Gillespie, & Champagne, 1998). Necessary processes for value creation in negotiations, such as information collection and trust-building also benefit from the absence of time pressure (Walton & McKersie, 1965; Adler, 1997; Stuhlmacher & Champagne, 2000; Li & Labig, 2001; Saoriniborra, 2008).

We consider time pressure as a hybrid of resource-dependency and context-dependency sources of bargaining power (Yan & Gray, 2001a, Yan & Gray, 2001b). When it has merely a resource-dependent character, higher time availability allows the seller to prepare for the complex buyout sale so that exit objectives can be realized. This process can be considered as resource-building. While on the one hand, detailed information about the current and expected future state of the firm needs to be compiled for potential buyers in the buyout process (due diligence requirements) which is in any case time- and cost-consuming, the seller is also advised to prepare the organization for the sale in a much broader sense (DeTienne, 2010). Organizational processes, routines, leadership structures, decision-making, and (accounting) systems need to be designed transparently and independent from individuals leaving the firm post-sale so that ownership transfer is possible without creating harm to firm performance—a process which might take several years (Haveman, 1993; Minor, 2003; Haveman & Khaire, 2004; Schmohl, 2009).

If we consider time pressure as rather being context-dependent, time availability allows the seller to favorably decide on the optimal timing to exit. A variety of factors have been identified which influence the conditions of buyout markets, such as the availability of firm investment opportunities (supply side), provision of capital to finance transactions (demand side), and possibilities to realize gains from investments which are in turn shaped by country-specific industry and market characteristics (Wright et al., 1992; Cumming et al., 2007). Thus, buyout markets fluctuate and temporary overfunding on the supply side might create pressure to invest and positively influence negotiation power of the seller (Wright, Renneboog, Simons et al., 2006). We thus hypothesize that:

Hypothesis 3: The higher the time pressure on the buyout seller, the higher the buying PE firm's perceived negotiation power will be.

4.3.4 Private equity firm specialization and moderation

Superior performance of PE-backed buyouts has been explained by the "Jensen hypothesis", which posits that PE firms can establish superior governance structures to realize economic efficiencies for their portfolio companies (Jensen, 1986, Jensen, 1989). In particular, managers of buyout firms are disciplined in their use of free cash flows, due to regular repayment of debt typically put on the balance sheet of the buyout target (financial leverage). Additionally, PE firms continuously monitor the performance of their portfolio companies and initiate measures to improve operational performance (Kaplan, 1989; Smith, 1990), but also add value to their portfolio firms via strategic advice often focused on growth initiatives (Nikoskelainen & Wright, 2007; Wilson et al., 2012). However, rising competition in a growing PE industry has forced PE firms to develop strategies of specialization to differentiate their value proposition and to realize competitive advantage over peers (Cressy et al., 2007). "Narrowing the target" has already been part of Porter's famous "generic strategies" and long ago has been recognized as a source of competitive advantage (Porter, 1985). For example, Skinner (1974) argued that limiting the breadth of a firm's activities improves operational performance. Similarly, PE firms use specialization to optimize their investment activities when identifying, selecting, and developing their buyout portfolio companies (de Clercq & Dimov, 2008; Lossen, 2007; Norton & Tenenbaum, 1993; Ruhnka & Young, 1991).

Forms of specialization might vary depending on the investment style of the PE firm. Prior research, but primarily for VC firms, suggested forms of PE specialization such as geography, technologies, or the development stage of investments (Bygrave, 1987, Bygrave, 1988; Lossen, 2007; de Clercq & Dimov, 2008). Industry specialization, however, has been most studied, where specialization here refers to the selected range of industries a PE firm prefers to invest in (de Clercq & Dimov, 2008; Cressy et al., 2007; Gompers et al., 2008; Knill, 2009). PE firms' industry specialization is recognized as being the main future source of PE firms' value creation in buyouts, marginalizing the role of financial leverage and multiple arbitrage (Kaplan & Schoar, 2005; Kaplan, 2007; Kaplan & Strömberg, 2009, Kaplan & Strömberg, 2009; Heel & Kehoe, 2005). Industry specialized PE firms might be able to optimize their investment activities when identifying, selecting, and developing their buyout portfolio companies—realizing superior returns and limiting company risk at the expense of industry diversification (Cressy et al., 2007; de Clercq & Dimov, 2008; Norton & Tenenbaum, 1993; Ruhnka & Young, 1991). Industry-specialized investments firms are also able to make investments during market booms, without performance reductions

(Gompers et al., 2008). Industry specialization is associated with shorter investment durations (time between investment and exit) suggesting that higher expertise is provided to portfolio companies when PE firms specialize (Knill, 2009). It is yet unclear whether it is possible to disentangle the relative importance of (industry) specialization from different stages of the investment process such as investment selection, negotiations and value creation in buyout firms (Gompers et al., 2008). It remains to be further explored whether there are other forms of specialization relevant for PE-backed buyouts and whether they are important for negotiations.

A key form of PE firm specialization that has been apparently neglected in prior research is specialization on the company size of buyout investment targets. This is surprising because a size specialization is often disclosed or explicitly stated by PE firms or their respective funds (EVCA, 2011). Specialization in size can refer to the number of employees, revenues or market capitalization of the buyout target depending on the specific definition employed by the PE firm. In general, a size distinction is often made between small, mid, or large cap investments (EVCA, 2011). The key difference between industry and size specialization can be thought of graphically as "vertical" vs. "horizontal"; industry specialization defines a vertical segment of the buyout market whereas size specialization defines a horizontal segment.

Specializations in size and industry are likely to be similar in their effects on bargaining power during the negotiation stage of buyouts. Specialization might affect situations of bidder competition which we hypothesize to provide bargaining power. Specialized PE firms become insiders, equipped with superior networks and associated benefits about deal targets in their area of deal specialization—be it industry or size—an advantage over those PE firms without specialization. In particular, specialized PE firms will be able to develop valuable networks with relevant stakeholders, i.e. social capital that can be beneficial for buyout negotiations (Batjargal & Liu, 2004; de Clercq & Dimov, 2008). This will provide them with important information about attractive deal opportunities, as buyout markets are less information-efficient (Lossen, 2007; Wright et al., 1992; Capron & Shen, 2007). In addition, specialized PE firms can focus their resources on the most attractive deal opportunities and prepare thoroughly for the bidding competition (Mosakowski, 1993).

Part of PE networks can also be potential sellers with whom relationships can be developed directly over time—which leads to an accumulation of knowledge about each other (Granovetter, 1973; Coleman, 1988; Adler & Kwon, 2002). Assuming other criteria are satisfied, sellers of buyout targets will favor PE firms with whom they have developed relationships as exchange partners or those PE firms which have been referred to them by third parties (Batjargal & Liu, 2004). These ties become important when PE firms compete with others for buyout targets. Additionally, specialized PE firms might be also better able to target sellers' needs, achieve goal congruence, and thus, become preferred exchange partners (de Clercq & Sapienza, 2006). As a result, specialized PE firms will have a competitive edge even in situations of bidding competition and benefit from higher bargaining power. We hypothesize:

Hypothesis 4a: Industry specialization of buying PE firms moderates the perceived bargaining power derived from bidder competition. Specifically, the strength of the negative relationship between bidder competition and PE's perceived bargaining power will be weaker.

Hypothesis 5a: Size specialization of buying PE firms moderates the perceived bargaining power derived from bidder competition. Specifically, the strength of the negative relationship between bidder competition and PE's perceived bargaining power will be weaker.

In addition to bidder competition, specialization of industry and size should be able to complement expertise that specialized PE firms can utilize in negotiations as bargaining power by providing access to additional information and enhanced confidence of expertise assessments. Valuation (and synergy) expertise can be used by PE firms to derive a corridor for the estimated value of the buyout business, i.e. the PE firm's willingness to pay. Specialized PE firms will be able to identify additional potential for value creation in the buyout target due to previous governance of similar buyout targets and various interactions which provided valuable insights and lessons (Sapienza & Korsgaard, 1996; Busenitz, Fiet, & Moesel, 2004). Additionally, risks associated with the buyout target can be identified because of specialized knowledge. In particular, specialized PE firms will have more confidence in their estimates, narrowing its spread (Shepherd & Zacharakis, 2001; Fiet, 1995), and thus, are able to decrease perceived uncertainty associated with their projections. Access to competent managers that can be recruited as a result of specialization will give them additional confidence that their projections will be implemented successfully once the deal is closed (Hellmann, 2002). We hypothesize:

Hypothesis 4b: Industry specialization of buying PE firms moderates the perceived bargaining power derived from a PE firm's expertise advantage. Specifically, the strength of the positive relationship between expertise advantage and PE firm's perceived bargaining power is stronger.

Hypothesis 5b: Size specialization of buying PE firms moderates the perceived bargaining power derived from a PE firm's expertise advantage. Specifically, the strength of the positive relationship between expertise advantage and their perceived bargaining power is stronger.

Specialized PE firms could also benefit from higher bargaining power when buyout targets are under time pressure to quickly reach an agreement. Superior information from prior experience and networks might provide them with more opportunities to identify such deals compared to non-specialized firms. More importantly, specialized firms are likely to benefit from standardization of executed deals. If the specialized PE firms continuously engage in the same type of deals, they can speed up due diligence, valuation, and decision-making to close the deal quickly. These capabilities allow specialized PE firms to execute deals quickly without compromising risk assessment of the deal so that time pressure of potential deal targets can be fully exploited. Thus, we hypothesize as follows:

Hypothesis 4c: Industry specialization of buying PE firms moderates the perceived bargaining power derived from seller's time pressure. Specifically, the strength of the positive relationship between seller's time pressure and a PE firm's perceived bargaining power is stronger.

Hypothesis 5c: Size specialization of buying PE firms moderates the perceived bargaining power derived from seller's time pressure. Specifically, the strength of the positive relationship between seller's time pressure and a PE firm's perceived bargaining power is stronger.

Figure 12 summarizes and provides an overview of our research model and hypotheses.

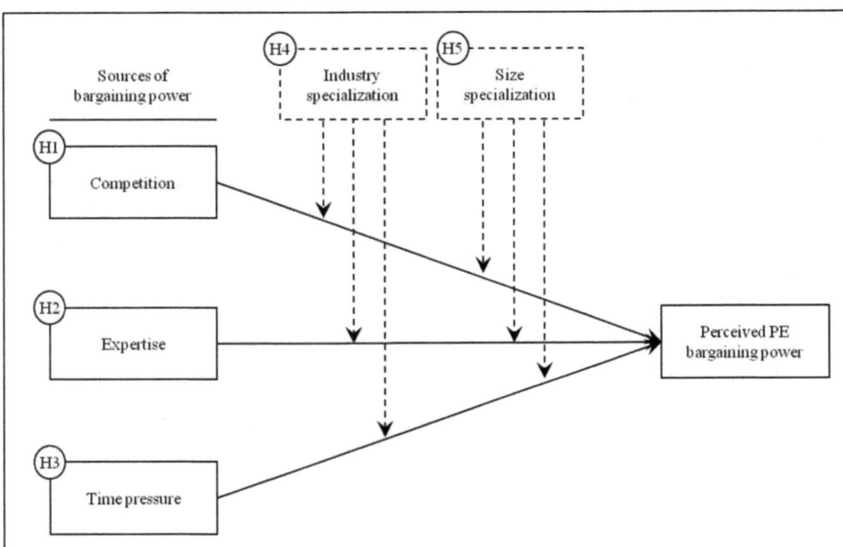

Figure 4-12: Research model – perceived PE bargaining power
Source: Author

4.4 Research design

4.4.1 Sample

For our sample, we identified 856 PE firms located across Europe based on information obtained from membership directories of national and European PE industry associations, as well as an Internet search. We eliminated 348 firms if their focus of operations was on early stage/venture capital investments, they did not complete a single transaction, or they no longer existed. As a result, our total sample consists of 508 individual PE firms.

For each firm, we generated multiple personal contact details of senior investment professionals by utilizing membership directories of PE associations complemented by internet research (company websites). The respondent was supposed to answer the survey based on one particular buyout deal. Thus, we relied on a key informant approach (Kumar, Stern, & Anderson, 1993), assuming that one PE manager could credibly give information on one particular deal given that firms work in small deal teams with similar perceptions, attitudes, and qualifications of team members. Along with the questionnaire, we sent out a short introduction explaining the study's purpose and ensuring confidential and anonymous processing of all questionnaires. Respondents were asked to select a randomly chosen buyout in which (1) their firm represented the buying side in negotiations; (2) they, as individuals, have been actively involved in negotiations; and (3) negotiations took place during the last three years.

Between September 2011 and March 2012, we mailed the questionnaire and received 188 responses, each representing information on one particular buyout deal from one respondent per PE firm. Thus, our response rate was 37%. Eleven questionnaires could not be used due to incompleteness and were removed from the sample. Most respondents were partners or managing directors (43%), while 44% occupied investment director positions, and

13% were classified as investment associates. The majority of respondents came from Germany (27%), Italy (14%), France (10%), U.K. (9%), and Spain (6%).

In order to assess a potential non-response bias, we used ANOVA to test for differences between early and late respondents. Later respondents can be considered as being similar to non-respondents when data for non-respondents is unavailable (Kanuk & Berenson, 1975; Armstrong & Overton, 1977). Depending on the time when responses were received, the sample was split into early and late respondents and no statistically significant differences were observed. We further tested for common method bias (Podsakoff, MacKenzie, Lee et al., 2003; Podsakoff, 1986). After entering independent, moderator, and control variables into a factor analysis, we extracted 9 factors with eigenvalues > 1.0, which accounted for 74% of the variance. We found that the first factor accounted for 12% of the variance and the remaining factors accounted for 59% of the variance. No individual factor accounted for the majority of the variance explained, and thus we assume common method bias is not a concern in our study.

We also checked our data for multicollinearity. We found only moderate levels of correlation among the variables and calculated variance inflation factors (VIF) (all < 2.239), tolerance (all > .447), and condition index (all < 3.067). All indicators are away from suggested warning levels (Field, 2009; Hair, 1987). Thus, multicollinearity is not a concern.

4.4.2 Model and measures

The constructs and items were all measured on a five-point Likert scale with endpoints labelled "strongly disagree" (1) and "strongly agree" (5) except for the items relating to "competition" which were labelled "low" (1) and "high" (5). All construct items and the corresponding alphas (all $\alpha > .70$) are listed in the Appendix. We also conducted a confirmatory factor analysis which showed good fit with χ^2 (58, n=177) = 108.3) ($p < .001$), a comparative fit index (CFI) of .939, an incremental index of fit (IFI) of .941, a Tucker-Lewis

Index (TLI) of .918, a root mean square error of approximation (RMSEA) of .070 (Hu & Bentler, 1999).

Dependent variable. We developed five items to measure perceived bargaining power in buyout transactions based on Mjoen and Tallmann (1997). We covered two time-related dimensions when measuring bargaining power, referring to both potential bargaining power and realized bargaining power. We could have used one or the other, but intended to capture both dimensions to ensure potential bargaining power matched realized bargaining power. By doing so, we ensured that bargaining power is a more reliable construct, which proved to be effective. Contrary to other works on bargaining power in joint ventures, we did not use the level of control achieved in the deal as a substitute or reflection of realized bargaining power (Yan & Gray, 2001a), as majority control (>50% stake) is almost always achieved in buyouts. The alpha of the composite is .78.

Independent variables. Two items were used to measure *bidder competition*—adapted to the context of buyouts from Yan and Gray (2001) who used the items in the context of joint ventures. We used two items to cover "bidder interest" as well as "submission of official offers". Bidder interest is likely to contribute to the perceived level of bargaining power, which is why we felt inclusion was necessary. Furthermore, we could have asked for a specific number of bidders. However, we were interested in how bidding competition was perceived to be consistent with our dependent variable "perceived bargaining power", and thus, it seemed indicative to measure competition also on a five-point Likert scale with the endpoints labelled "low" (1) and "high" (5). Moreover, we did not specifically measure alternatives to invest for PE firms, as PE firms continuously generate investment alternatives as part of their daily business. Including such an item in our scale might have been misleading. The alpha of the composite is .79.

Four items, inspired from Raven (1998) and Stahelski (1989), were used to measure *PE firms' expertise advantage*. The items covered general competence and deal-specific expertise related to valuation, synergies, and the technical aspects of the buyout process. We had to omit one item that was related to general competence in order to reach a sufficient alpha, suggesting that specific forms of expertise related to the transaction itself matter the most. The composite's alpha is .70. The *seller's time pressure* was measured by adapting three items from Stuhlmacher (2000). The alpha of the composite is .87.

Control variables. The robustness of our findings was ensured by including a number of control variables. Firstly, we controlled for industry of the buyout target with five dummy codes (consumer, IT, healthcare, manufacturing, and other industries). This was required because some industries might be more or less attractive, and thus are systematically associated with higher or lower levels of bargaining power. "Manufacturing" was the reference category omitted.

Secondly, we controlled for the year in which the buyout took place. Buyout markets are cyclical and market climate varies accordingly which might affect bargaining power (Scholes et al., 2009). "2011" was the omitted reference category. Thirdly, we controlled for PE firms' funds under management (FUM) because larger PE firms could have resource advantages that give them superior bargaining power. Fourth, we further controlled for the "age" of the PE firm because more experienced PE firms could be equipped with higher bargaining power. Fifth, we controlled for the deal size because smaller or larger deals could be associated with different levels of bargaining power. We used the logarithm of PE firms' FUM, age, and transaction value which was necessary to achieve normal distribution for these items.

Moderating variables. We tested two different moderating variables. Instead of utilizing historic deal information (Scholes et al., 2009; Cressy et al., 2007), we asked respondents directly to what extent their PE firm specialized in the industry and/or size of the buyout target. We consider direct measurement superior to data that tries to capture portfolio composition of buyout funds (Cressy et al., 2007). This data might be misleading as industry classifications differ, potential non-reflection or time-lagged reflection of changing PE specializations, and biased data for smaller PE firms who have achieved a lower number of transactions.

4.5 Data analysis and results

Means, standard deviations and correlations for all variables are shown in ***Table 4***. ***Table 4*** shows some significant correlations of the three independent variables with the dependent variable perceived bargaining power. Thus, these correlations provide some preliminary evidence that bidder competition, expertise advantage, and seller's time pressure are positively associated with perceived bargaining power.

Variable	*Mean*	*SD*	*1*	*2*	*3*	*4*	*5*	*6*	*7*	*8*	*9*	*10*	*11*	*12*	*13*	*14*	*15*	*16*	*17*	*18*
1. Consumer	0.28	0.45	1																	
2. Industry	0.37	0.48	-.478**	1																
3. IT	0.12	0.32	-.230**	-.280**	1															
4. Healthcare	0.10	0.30	-.211**	-.256**	-.123	1														
5. Other	0.13	0.34	-.242**	-.294**	-.142	-.130	1													
6. 2011	0.49	0.50	-.108	.033	.098	-.028	.028	1												
7. 2010	0.29	0.45	.100	-.071	-.041	-.008	.014	-.618**	1											
8. 2009	0.08	0.27	-.044	.037	-.043	.040	.011	-.285**	-.186*	1										
9. 2008	0.15	0.36	.059	.015	-.054	.019	-.065	-.403**	-.264**	-.122	1									
10. PE firm FUM[1]	6.63	1.74	.125	-.295**	.151*	.026	.087	.026	.085	-.108	-.063	1								
11. PE firm Age[1]	2.77	0.60	.064	-.111	.126	-.087	.031	.084	-.067	-.095	.040	.423**	1							
12. Transact. Value[1]	4.45	1.52	.209**	-.214**	-.031	-.036	.089	.007	-.005	.020	-.019	.629**	.259**	1						
13. Competition	3.08	1.12	.043	-.141	.037	.119	.003	.060	.037	.014	-.144	.187*	.030	.216**	1					
14. Expertise	3.16	0.80	.007	.127	-.119	-.056	-.027	.107	-.028	-.139	-.009	-.248**	-.092	-.250**	-.143	1				
15. Time Pressure	2.70	1.09	.017	.088	-.118	-.021	-.017	.041	.029	.024	-.114	.022	-.006	.054	.062	.010	1			
16. Special Industry	3.41	1.26	-.103	-.121	.062	.180*	.089	.109	.031	-.011	-.185*	.057	.144	.097	.111	.045	.052	1		
17. Special Size	4.00	0.99	-.140	.119	.035	.000	-.017	.092	-.038	-.021	-.065	-.038	.075	.002	.082	.190*	.078	.153*	1	
18. Bargain. Power	3.22	0.70	-.038	.083	-.072	-.128	.116	.078	-.041	.053	-.098	-.071	-.151*	-.030	-.183*	.312**	.281**	.061	.092	1

N= 177; **. p < .01 ; *. p < .05; [1] logarithmized

Table 4-4: Correlation matrix, means, and standard deviations

Source: Author

To test our hypothesis, we used hierarchical regression analysis. Multicollinearity issues between interaction terms and respective components were largely avoided by centering interaction variables (Aiken & West, 1991). Results are presented in ***Table 5***.

	Model 1	*Model 2*	*Model 3*	*Model 4*
Step 1: Control				
Consumer	-.048	-.027	-.020	-.041
IT	-.083	.010	.002	-.005
Healthcare	-.153[†]	-.091	-.105	-.100
Other	.071	.102	.096	.089
2010	-.079	-.056	-.057	-.054
2009	.012	.064	.066	.023
2008	-.104	-.074	-.061	-.034
PE FUM[1]	.018	.064	.076	.074
PE Age[1]	-.158[†]	-.164*	-.180*	-.164*
Transaction Value[1]	-.048	-.027	-.020	-.041
Step 2: Independent				
Competition		-.175*	-.182*	-.181*
Expertise		.306***	.293***	.308***
Time Pressure		.276***	.271***	.232**
Step 3: Moderators				
Specialization Industry			.065	.049
Specialization Size			.030	.051
Step 4: Interaction Terms				
Industry x Competition				-.207**
Industry x Expertise				-.112
Industry x Time Press.				.021
Size x Competition				.168*
Size x Expertise				.179*
Size x Time Pressure				.167*
Change in R^2	.072	.188***	.005	.103**
R^2	.072	.260	.265	.368
Adjusted R^2	.017	.201	.196	.283
F	1.295	4.406***	3.867***	4.301***

Notes: Beta weights are reported for the final stage in each model; n = 177; *** $p < 0.001$; ** $p < 0.01$; * $p < 0.05$; [†] $p < 0.1$; [a] Regression coefficients are reported as betas. [1] Logarithmized.

Table 4-5: Results of regression analysis

Source: Author

The control variables were entered into model 1. Only two variables show weak significance: "healthcare" and "age of the PE firm" ($p < .10$). In order to test hypotheses 1, 2, and 3 we entered all independent variables in the second model. A significant change in R^2 was observed ($\Delta R^2 = 0.19$, $p < .001$) and competition ($\beta = - .18$, $p < .005$), expertise, ($\beta = .31$, $p < .001$), and time pressure, ($\beta = .28$, $p < .001$) were found to have a significant effect on perceived bargaining power. Thus, we can confirm hypothesis 1, 2, and 3.

In order to test the hypothesized moderation effects, we first entered the moderators' industry and size specialization in model 3. Model 4 represents the interaction effects of PE industry specialization and size specialization. For model 3, no significant change in R^2 was observed ($\Delta R^2 = .05$). For model 4, the interaction of industry specialization and competition is significant, but, contrary to our hypothesis, negative ($\beta = - .21$, $p < .001$). The other interaction terms of industry specialization with expertise and time pressure are not significant. Thus, we can reject hypothesis 4 a, b, and c. Model 4 further demonstrates, a significant interaction was found between size specialization and the independent variables competition ($\beta = .17$, $p < .05$), expertise ($\beta = .18$, $p < .05$), and time pressure ($\beta = .17$, $p < .05$). The change in R^2 was significant ($\Delta R^2 = .10$, $p < .01$). We further examined whether the slopes of the interaction effects significantly differ from zero (Aiken & West, 1991). We could confirm high significance for simple slope testing of size specialization when expertise and time pressure are concerned. For competition we can confirm significance of slope tests for low levels of size specialization. Thus, we can confirm hypothesis 5. To facilitate the interpretation of the moderation effects, the significant interactions were plotted in ***Figures 13, 14*** and ***15***.

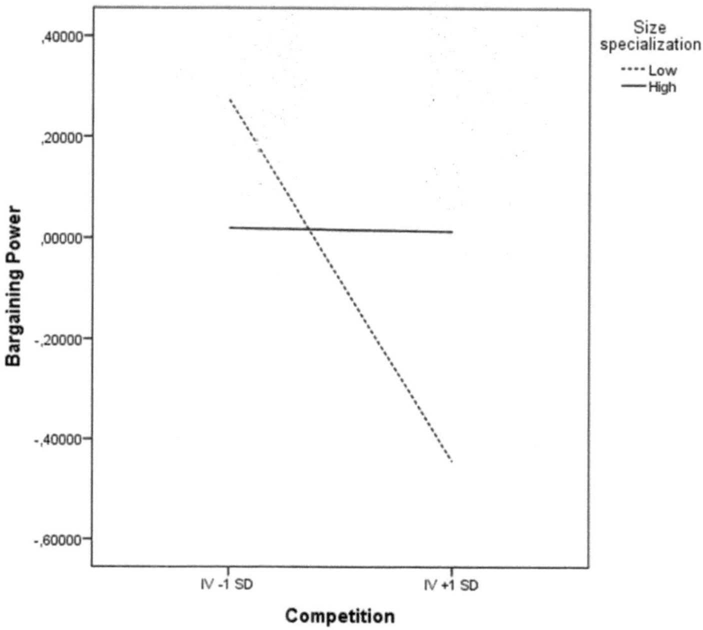

Figure 4-13: Interaction between FE firm size specialization and competition
Source: Author

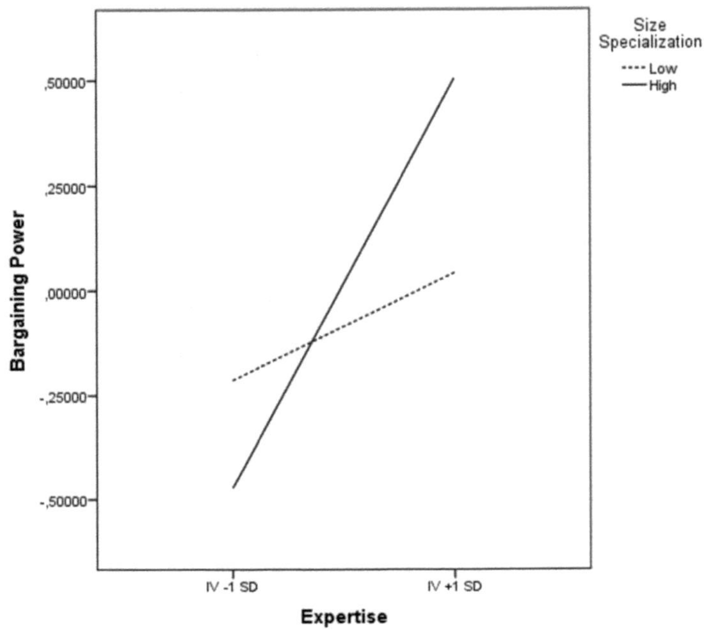

Figure 4-14: Interaction between PE firm size specialization and expertise
Source: Author

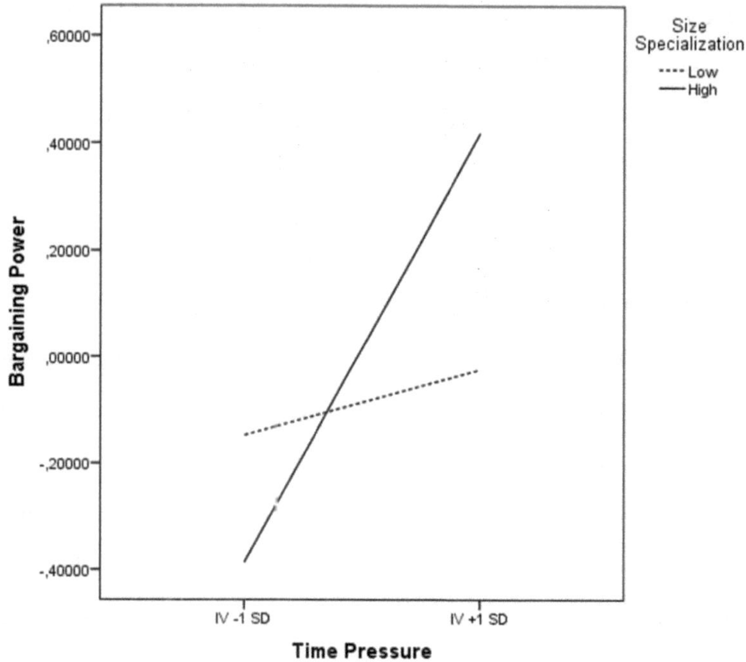

Figure 4-15: Interaction between PE firm size specialization and time pressure
Source: Author

Figure 13 shows the interaction between size specialization of PE firms and bidder competition. Size specialization moderates the effect of bidder competition on PE firms' perceived bargaining power. PE firms with a high size specialization show higher levels of perceived bargaining power in situations of bidder competition.

Figure 14 shows the interaction between size specialization of PE firms and expertise advantage. Size specialization moderates the effect of expertise advantage on PE firms' perceived bargaining power. PE firms with a high size specialization show higher levels of perceived bargaining power when exhibiting their expertise advantage.

Figure 15 shows the interaction between size specialization of PE firms and time pressure. Size specialization moderates the effect of seller's time pressure on PE firms' perceived bargaining power. PE firms with a high size specialization show higher levels of perceived bargaining power when sellers' are under time pressure.

4.6 Discussion and conclusion

Prior research has largely neglected the negotiation stage of buyouts. Bargaining power in buyout negotiations, in particular, has not yet been studied. Additionally, research insights into the effects of PE firm specialization are limited to stages of buyouts other than the negotiation stage, and have been focused on industry specialization. This paper has helped to close this research gap. We have highlighted different factors that provide PE firms with negotiation power such as bidder competition, expertise advantage, and seller's time pressure. Moreover, we have demonstrated whether or not, and if so, how selected forms of PE firm specialization affect power in buyout negotiations. We have shown that positive effects on bargaining power derived from specialization arise if PE firms specialize on deal size. On the contrary, industry specialization has shown negligible or adverse effects on bargaining power. PE size specialization and its effects on performance, to the best of our knowledge, have not been studied before.

Our research indicates that PE firms are equipped with higher bargaining power in buyout negotiations, where factors of competition, expertise advantage, and seller's time pressure play to their advantage. For bidder competition, we could conclude that higher bidder competition for a buyout target leads to lower bargaining power of PE firms. The seller of the buyout firm will feel less inclined to make concessions during negotiations if the number and quality of alternative bidders available are substantial (Fisher, 1981). Put differently, PE firms which are able to identify buyout targets with lower bidder competition are equipped with higher bargaining power, which should in turn result in favorable negotiation outcomes. In a perfectly information-efficient market, bidder competition can be taken for granted (Fama, 1991), but buyouts usually take place in private takeover markets with greater information asymmetries and difficulty in identifying exchange partners (Scholes et al., 2007). Thus, the role of bidder competition becomes prominent because of the context of imperfect markets, and our research further highlights the importance of PE firms' deal searching activities.

Expertise (advantage) was also highlighted as a source of bargaining power. Power generated from expertise requires education, skills, and accomplishment in a domain allowing for informational sense-making (Lewicki et al., 2010). We have evaluated expertise related particularly to valuation, synergies, and process-related aspects of buyout deals which we hypothesized to be critical for a number of reasons. Firstly, there is a great deal of uncertainty and information asymmetries making future cash flow projections and "upside potential" for the buyout target difficult. Unsurprisingly, there is often disagreement between buyers and sellers on the appropriate transaction price (Scholes et al., 2007). Secondly, buyout transactions are complex and involve a number of financial, tax, and legal issues that need to be resolved between the negotiation parties (Reed et al., 2007; Cumming & Johan, 2009). Consequently, the more a PE firm possesses transaction-relevant expertise and the less the selling side has, the greater the bargaining position of the PE firm (Admati & Pfleiderer, 1994; Wright & Robbie, 1996; Manigart et al., 2002; Scholes et al., 2008). Thus, our findings further highlight the importance and role as a source of bargaining power which expertise plays in the pre-buyout stage.

Additionally, we have demonstrated that if the selling side in buyout deals suffers from time pressure, PE firms consequently gain higher levels of bargaining power. Time availability allows the seller to favorably decide on the optimal timing to exit in volatile markets and to prepare an organization for the transfer of ownership (DeTienne, 2010; Wright et al., 2006). Similarly to what has been said before, PE firms' deal searching activities seem to be critical in the pre-buyout stage in identifying buyout targets in less efficient market situations, which becomes a source of bargaining power in negotiations.

Moreover, our research indicates that not all forms of specialization seem to be equally successful for bargaining power in negotiations—a perspective previously neglected. Our hypothesis has been that industry and size should play out similarly in terms of their moderating effects on bargaining power. However, and contrary to our expectations, we can only confirm that size specialization enables PE firms to increase bargaining power from bidder competition, expertise advantage, and seller's time pressure. Industry specialization—although it might give competitive advantages in later stages of the investment process (Cressy et al., 2007; Lossen, 2007; de Clercq & Dimov, 2008)—has no beneficial effect on bargaining power during the negotiation stage of buyouts. There might be several reasons why PE size specialization is more effective during negotiations than industry specialization explaining our statistical observations.

Firstly, size specialization might be more effective in situations of bidder competition (***Figure 13***). Size specialization allows PE firms to generate more attractive deal opportunities across a range of industries. A horizontal size specialization delineates a segment of the buyout market across industries, which means that no potentially attractive industries or targets are excluded out of principle, even while the firm specializes. PE firms with a size specialization might also experience fewer obstacles to invest in industries which suddenly become more attractive for investment. Thus, the deal flow from which attractive buyout targets can be selected might be more attractive for size specialized PE firms compared to industry specialized ones. Consequently, size-specialized PE firms can increase the number of deal alternatives they can establish to substitute the current negotiation relationship which leverages the party's negotiation power due to dependency reduction (Bacharach & Lawler, 1984). Thus, due to a superior deal flow, size specialized PE firms have more alternatives to invest in, which means they are under less pressure to engage in the current deal.

In a similar vein, size specialized PE firms could create and benefit from horizontal networks. In these networks, certain sizes of firms such as SMEs face similar problems and challenges such as ownership succession (Sharma et al., 1997; Davis & Harveston, 1998; Dyck, Mauws, Starke et al., 2002; de Massis et al., 2008). Family firm owners (a majority of SMEs are family owned), often show a higher emotional attachment to their business (Zellweger et al., 2011; Zellweger & Astrachan, 2008), and thus require a more personal approach from the PE firm. By developing horizontal networks, size specialized PE firms could develop a better understanding for the needs and requirements (financial and non-financial) of similar business types and their owners, that can be addressed appropriately in negotiations to give a competitive edge over other PE bidders. Having dealt with similar businesses of the same size and similar problems could give size specialized PE firms more credibility, trust, and an understanding of seller needs. As a result, these PE firms could prevail in situations of bidder competition.

Secondly, size specialization could be more effective for realizing expertise advantage (***Figure 14***). With expertise advantage we refer to the technical side of the deal—valuation, synergies, and deal process. This expertise, we have hypothesized, can be enhanced by size and industry specialization. It seems, however, that only size knowledge is beneficial for negotiations. The reason might be that size-specific knowledge is less apparent and debated while industry-specific knowledge, in contrast, becomes explicit and accessible "rules of the industry" discussed in research reports or by industry experts. Depending on a business' size classification, the characteristics of the business could significantly vary—even within the same industry, thus creating value creation opportunities for PE firms. For example, SMEs differ between themselves, and especially in comparison with larger firms in many ways, including their internationalization approach (Etemad & Wright, 2003), innovation capabilities (Lindgren, 2012), access to capital (Kouser, Durani, Hussain et al., 2012), HR practices (Schmelter, Mauer, Boersch et al., 2010), strong personalization and owner-centric decision-making (Gómez-Mejía et al., 2007), as well as strategy (Hagen, Zucchella, Cerchiello et al., 2012). Thus, size specialized PE firms will be able to identify additional potential for value creation and risk reduction complementing PE firm's (traditional) valuation and knowledge of synergies (expertise advantage) more than industry specialized firms.

Additionally, it appears that size specialized firms will have greater confidence in their valuation estimates due to previous successful governance of similar buyout targets and access to competent managers (Sapienza & Korsgaard, 1996; Busenitz et al., 2004). It will require different kinds of management capabilities, i.e. managers, to realize synergies post-acquisition, which depend on the size of the business. A PE firm's access through horizontal networks as a result of size specialization will give them recruitment access to competent managers, resulting in additional confidence that their projections will be implemented successfully once the deal is closed (Hellmann, 2002).

Thirdly, size specialization could be beneficial for exploiting time pressure targets (***Figure 15***). It seems that size specialization allows speeding up due diligence, valuation, and investment decision-making to close the deal quickly, to a greater extent than industry specialization does. While the required industry knowledge to assess risks and opportunities can be accessed quickly, the size dimension may require more sustained efforts.

Our research also has practical implications for PE firms, as well as for sellers of buyout firms. PE firms might acknowledge sources of bargaining power and search for deals in which these factors can be maximized. PE firms might also reconsider the role of specialization for their activities. In particular, PE firms could consider specialization effects for different stages of the investment process and by doing so develop superior specializations over the course of the investment process and consequently achieve competitive advantage.

The selling side of the buyout deal is advised to limit situations in which they have lower bargaining power to fulfill their exit objectives. Long-term preparation of the sale and external advice are ways to overcome bargaining power disadvantages and to realize deal priorities (DeTienne, 2010; Petty et al., 1994; Westhead & Howorth, 2007; Howorth et al., 2004). By doing so, sellers could search more actively for various potential exchange partners, match the expertise of the buying PE side, and execute deals at the optimum point of time.

4.7 Limitations and guidance for future research

A number of limitations need to be considered when reviewing the findings above. Firstly, we only surveyed one side of the buyout deal—the PE/buying side. The selling side and its perceptions of bargaining power were not surveyed due to confidentiality restrictions. However, as PE firms regularly engage in this kind of transactions, the PE side of the buyout deal surely provides a reliable source of information. Additionally, our sample mainly contains responses of managing and investment directors, who typically have profound deal experience, increasing further the response validity of the key informant approach (Kumar et al., 1993).

Secondly, we have not investigated specific bargaining tactics (Leap & Grigsby, 1986; Dreu & van Kleef, 2004; Kim & Fragale, 2005). However, the tactics that can be employed to make use of bargaining power or to compensate for a lack of bargaining power might play an important role (Bacharach & Lawler, 1981; Kim & Fragale, 2005). These tactics are beyond the scope of this paper. Future research should be concerned with tactics in the context of buyouts building upon different situations of bargaining power.

Thirdly, the effect of PE specialization and its interplay on different stages of the investment process needs further investigation. We have investigated the negotiation stage of the deal process and illustrated the benefits of size specialization. However, while we have showed that size specialization is important for the negotiation phase of the deal, it might have a different degree of importance for the operational and strategic development of the buyout company, i.e. other forms of specialization are more important. Size specialization has not yet been tested in these situations, so we encourage future research to validate the role of size specialization in other than negotiation stages of the investment process.

Fourth, it could be promising to analyze whether the structure of co-investing, where multiple PE firms invest in a buyout, is driven by different kind of specializations. It was found that higher risk investments trigger co-investment of VC firms (Bygrave, 1987, Bygrave, 1988), as interconnectedness among firms is driven by an uncertain environment (Pfeffer & Salancik, 1978). Similarly, for private equity, it could be the case that when co-investing occurs (which we have excluded from our research), different kinds of PE firms pool different kind of specializations to reduce investment uncertainty. Further research might provide further insights in that respect.

Fifth, the geographic scope of our research is limited to major European countries. It is unclear whether our findings are also valid for other geographic areas such as the U.S., Asia or emerging economies (Leeds & Sunderland, 2003; Wright, Lockett, & Pruthi, 2002). However, given that PE firms are highly internationalized and deal teams usually cross geographic boundaries (Cumming & Walz, 2009), we have reason to believe that validity of our results also extends to regions outside Europe.

5 Bargaining power in family firm buyouts: Does family influence make a difference?[24]

5.1 Introduction

With a previous paper[25] we have started to explore the neglected topic of buyout negotiations. This paper aims to refine and to extend our previous findings to the context of family firm buyouts. Management buyouts have to be negotiated between buyer and vendor, which is highly complex in light of financial, tax, and legal issues that require consideration (Reed et al., 2007; Cumming & Johan, 2009). Power is important in negotiations (Greenhalgh et al., 1985; Dreu & van Kleef, 2004) and conceived as potential to influence the other negotiating party (Kelley & Thibaut, 1978; Bacharach & Lawler, 1981; Dreu & van Kleef, 2004). Powerful negotiators often succeed in negotiations because they have the ability to capture more benefits from an agreement (Argyris & Liebeskind, 1999; Nair et al., 2011; Overbeck et al., 2010). Previous research acknowledged the importance of bargaining power for joint ventures and mergers (Inkpen & Beamish, 1997; Lee et al., 1998; Varaiya, 1987), but has not yet touched upon buyout negotiations with family firm seller involvement.

Family-owned businesses are a key source of buyout deals for PE firms, which is not surprising given the significance of family firms when it comes to unlisted companies (Anderson & Reeb, 2003; Morck & Yeung, 2003) and difficulties to secure succession specific to this type of firm (Kets de Vries, 1993; Lee et al., 2003; DeTienne, 2010). Although often not the family sellers' initial preference, selling the family business in a buyout is a means to ensure firm survival if perpetuation of family ownership is not an option (de Massis et al., 2008; Chrisman et al., 2012; Dehlen et al., 2012). The relationship between PE firms and family firms, however, is not without tensions (Blanco-Mazagatos et al., 2007; Tappeiner et al., 2012; Dawson, 2011). Family firm owners often assume a higher value of the business

[24] This chapter is based on Ahlers, O., Hack, A., & Kellermanns, F. W. (2013). Bargaining Power in Family Firm Buyouts: Does Family Influence Make a Difference?. Unpublished Working paper.
[25] See chapter 4 of this thesis.

than justified by cash-flow-based valuations due to emotional attachment (Astrachan & Jaskiewicz, 2008; Zellweger & Astrachan, 2008; Zellweger et al., 2011). Additionally, family sellers could have non-financial objectives associated with the business sale, unlike those of non-family firms (Graebner & Eisenhardt, 2004; Howorth, 2001; Shepherd, 2009; López-Gracia 2007, Poutziouris, 2001; Niedermeyer et al., 2010; Steen & Welch, 2006; Mickelson & Worley, 2003). According to socioemotional wealth theory (SEW), the sum of non-financial goals that shape family firms' actions is what distinguishes this form of entrepreneurship (Gómez-Mejía et al., 2007; Gómez-Mejía et al., 2010; Berrone et al., 2010; Zellweger et al., 2011).

PE firms might negatively perceive family firms as being old-fashioned and under-performing (Granata & Chirico, 2010). However, family firms exist with a great deal of variation (Chua et al., 2012) and researchers have called for further efforts to establish how SEW is affected by forms of family influence and when it is beneficial for the performance of family businesses (Berrone et al., 2012). Thus, a more specific objective of this paper is to investigate different features of family influence, its consequences for SEW embodiment, and how in turn bargaining power of PE firms is affected in buyout negotiations.

We hope to make some contributions to existing research: firstly, we add to the literature on PE and family firm buyouts by investigating bargaining power in family buyout negotiations. Specifically, we try to confirm sources of bargaining power established in a previous paper[26] for the specific setting of family buyouts. We investigate whether and how family firm characteristics moderate sources of PE firms' bargaining power, such as bidder competition, expertise advantage, and sellers' time pressure, and attribute differences to varying degrees of SEW. Thus, we provide further evidence needed to establish the existence of SEW and how it shapes family firm behavior. Lastly, our paper also has considerable practical implications. It specifically illuminates how PE buyers and family firm sellers could

[26] See chapter 4

improve their negotiation power by becoming aware of its sources and of how SEW has consequences for negotiation power. To reach our objectives, we use a survey-based, hand-collected subsample of 82 PE-backed buyouts from across Europe in the period 2008–2011 that involved family firms. The majority of our respondents are distinguished individuals occupying managing director or investment director positions in PE firms.

The remainder of the paper is organized as follows: We first provide the theoretical background for our considerations and summarize prior research on PE, family firms, and SEW. As a next step, we formulate hypotheses regarding the sources of bargaining power in family buyouts and the moderating effects of family firm influence. We continue by describing the sample, the variables, as well as constructs used in our statistics. We continue with a presentation and discussion of our empirical results. Finally, we acknowledge any limitations and discuss avenues for future research.

5.2 Theoretical background

5.2.1 Private equity, family firms, and SEW

PE firms provide finance for unquoted firms and in return are compensated with equity stakes (Dawson, 2011). PE firms' main investment destination are buyouts in which PE firms acquire a business, usually involving the new or incumbent management team, from the current owner by using debt and often a high degree of debt financing (Meuleman et al., 2009). Prior research often highlighted PE firms' superior performance achievements in portfolio firms (Boucly et al., 2011; Brown et al., 2009; Cumming et al., 2007; Amess, 2002; Gottschalg & Wright, 2008; Cressy et al., 2007), and PE firms' ability to provide their investors with high returns (Nikoskelainen & Wright, 2007; Cumming et al., 2007; Kaplan & Schoar, 2005).

Family firms constitute a dominant type of corporate ownership (Anderson & Reeb, 2003; Morck & Yeung, 2003) and increasingly face difficulties in securing intra-family succession, which can lead to the sale of the family business to PE firms (Scholes et al., 2008; Calogirou et al., 2010). Family firms are distinct from non-family firms, due to family members' impact on strategy, objectives and the creation of the firms' resources and capabilities (Sharma, 2004; Habbershon et al., 2003; Chrisman et al., 2003). Recent research suggests that family firms aspire to realize socioemotional wealth (SEW), a kind of wealth which comprises affective needs such as family control, harmony, belonging, and the continuation of the family dynasty (Gómez-Mejía et al., 2010; Gómez-Mejía et al., 2007; Gómez-Mejía et al., 2001; Berrone et al., 2010).

Relationships between PE firms and family firms have some conflict potential (Blanco-Mazagatos et al., 2007; Tappeiner et al., 2012). PE firms have often been described as short-term investors motivated solely to maximize profits (Dawson, 2011; Jensen, 1989) and family firms often strive for long-term objectives, motivated by SEW, which could compromise financial goals (Carney, 2005; Dreux, 1990; Sirmon & Hitt, 2003; Gómez-Mejía et al., 2007). For family firm sellers, the firm ownership is associated with a strong emotional attachment, because the family firm represents far more than a source of financial gains (Zellweger & Astrachan, 2008; Astrachan & Jaskiewicz, 2008). Consequently, the sale of the family business in a buyout is emotionally difficult for family owners (Shepherd, 2009; Pellegrin, 1999; Niedermeyer et al., 2010). When succession is required to transfer control, the external sale is less desirable or even considered a failure by family CEOs, because it means the end of a family dynasty (Pellegrin, 1999; Niedermeyer et al., 2010). Even after the sale SEW plays a role, as family sellers might continue to identify with their former business and exhibit feelings of responsibility for employees and stakeholders (Lee & Rogoff, 1996; Dyer & Whetten, 2006; Mickelson & Worley, 2003).

5.3 Derivation of hypotheses[27]

In this section we capitalize on insights from our previous paper regarding sources of bargaining power in buyouts and specifically focus on the moderating effects of family firm sellers.

5.3.1 Sources of bargaining power

Negotiations occur all the time and can be defined as *"... the deliberate interaction of two or more complex social units which are attempting to define or redefine the terms of their interdependence"* (Walton & McKersie, 1965, p. 35). The concept of power is of key importance for negotiations and can be broadly defined as the potential to influence others (Kelley & Thibaut, 1978; Bacharach & Lawler, 1981; Greenhalgh et al., 1985; Dreu & van Kleef, 2004). Differences in power distribution are reflected in negotiation outcomes: powerful negotiators are those that receive more value from agreements (Argyris & Liebeskind, 1999; Nair et al., 2011; Overbeck et al., 2010).

The overall efficacy of power (sources) is dependent on context and the specific situation at hand (Astley & Sachdeva, 1984; Leap & Grigsby, 1986). Relating to prior research on interorganizational transactions, we use the distinction between "context-based" and "resource-based" bargaining power sources which establish interdependence between negotiators (Yan & Gray, 2001b, Yan & Gray, 2001a). Thus, this paper assumes the relational concept of bargaining, i.e. power becomes a social relationship property (Emerson, 1962). "Context-based" bargaining power emphasizes the context-dependent character of the relationship between negotiators (Yan & Gray, 2001b) arguing that A's negotiation power increases as B's dependence on the negotiation relationship increases (Emerson, 1962; Wolfe & McGinn, 2005). "Resource-based bargaining power" assumes that power is created from the possession of important resources employed in a relationship (Pfeffer & Nowak, 1976;

[27] Compare chapter 4.

Aldrich, 1977; Pfeffer & Salancik, 1978; Yan & Gray, 2001b). In our previous paper, we have argued that "context-dependent" bargaining power in buyouts is created from "bidder competition", "resource-based bargaining power" from "expertise advantage", and "time pressure" is a "hybrid", simultaneously possessing context-dependent and resource-based characteristics.

Bidder competition. Rising bidder competition in management buyouts leads to lower bargaining power of PE firms vis-à-vis the vendor. Increasing the number of alternatives the vendor can establish that could replace the PE firm in the negotiation relationship, leverages the vendor's negotiation power due to dependency reduction (Bacharach & Lawler, 1984). Put differently, the vendor with more buyers willing to bid for the firm ("alternatives") could threaten to exit the current negotiation, while simultaneously engaging the next best alternative to reach a negotiated agreement ("BATNA") (Fisher, 1981). The seller will feel less inclined to make concessions during negotiations when there are enough alternatives available. In less information-efficient buyout markets bidder competition is not guaranteed, but rather arises through the search for exchange partners (Fama, 1991; Wright et al., 1992; Capron & Shen, 2007; Shen & Reuer, 2005; Scholes et al., 2007). Selling or purchasing privately held targets such as family firms in buyouts is often problematic due to greater information asymmetries and higher difficulty in identifying exchange partners (Scholes et al., 2007). Thus, we hypothesize:

Hypothesis 1: The higher the bidder competition in family firm buyouts, the lower the buying PE firm's perceived bargaining power in buyouts will be.

Expertise. In the context of family firm buyouts, superior expertise can be of critical importance to successfully negotiate a deal (Petty et al., 1994; Scholes et al., 2007). Buyout transactions typically occur in a setting of information asymmetry which gives rise to the risk of exploitation due to price uncertainty in less efficient private takeover markets (Fama, 1991;

Capron & Shen, 2007; Shen & Reuer, 2005; Olekalns & Smith, 2009). This is reflected in the often-observed disagreement on the pricing of buyout deals between negotiating parties (Scholes et al., 2007). Moreover, buyout deals are complex to negotiate comprising financial, taxation, and legal issues that need to be decided (Reed et al., 2007; Cumming & Johan, 2009).

If one negotiating party has greater expertise, it can be used to manipulate the other party's arguments, assumptions, beliefs, and choices (Pfeffer, 1981; Coff, 1999). PE firms likely possess higher transaction specific expertise compared to the family seller for whom the sale is a singular event (Admati & Pfleiderer, 1994; Wright & Robbie, 1996; Manigart et al., 2002; Scholes et al., 2008; Niedermeyer et al., 2010).[28] The expertise advantage of PE firms for example could comprise expertise on valuation, synergies, and the technical knowledge of deal-making. Thus, PE firms might use an expertise advantage to challenge family firm seller's price perception while structuring a buyout deal to their advantage. We conclude as follows:

Hypothesis 2: ***The higher the expertise advantage relevant for the family firm buyout deal, the higher the buying PE firm's perceived negotiation power will be.***

Time pressure. Time pressure can be defined as desire or need to close the negotiation process (Smith et al., 1982; Druckman, 1994; Saoriniborra, 2008). The negotiation party suffering from time pressure is equipped with weaker negotiation power, as pressure creates the necessity to close the deal though circumstances may sub-optimal (Pruitt, 1969; Rubin & Brown, 1975; Cohen, 1980; Stuhlmacher et al., 1998). Higher time availability not only allows the seller to decide on the optimal timing to exit when markets are developing favorably, but also to prepare for the complex buyout sale so that exit objectives can be realized.

[28] This excludes cases of secondary buyouts, where the selling side can also be a PE firm.

Although succession is ideally conducted in a long-term and carefully planned process (Sharma et al., 1997; Cabrera-Suárez et al., 2001; Sharma et al., 2003), family firms often postpone succession planning due to family CEOs' sense of immortality, reluctance to give up power, generational or intra-family conflicts or a unwillingness to treat family members unequally (Sharma et al., 1997; Davis & Harveston, 1998; Dyck et al., 2002; de Massis et al., 2008). As a result, incumbent family owners generally do not leave the business before adverse circumstances (e.g. advanced age, critical health conditions, conflicts) force them to do so (Lansberg, 1988; Sharma et al., 2001; de Massis et al., 2008; Wennberg, Wiklund, DeTienne et al., 2010). Thus, family firms often suffer from escalation of commitment (Staw, 1981; Brockner, 1992; Sharma & Irving, 2005). We thus hypothesize that:

Hypothesis 3: The higher the time pressure on the family firm seller in the buyout, the higher the buying PE firm's perceived negotiation power will be.

5.3.2 Family firms and moderation effects

The specific embodiment and impact that SEW has for family firms' decision-making is dependent on family influence (Berrone et al., 2012). Family influence can be conveyed in many diverse ways (Chua et al., 2012; Astrachan et al., 2002). We focus our analysis on two features of family influence: "number of family members in the business" and "generational ownership dispersion" (Ling & Kellermanns, 2010; Kellermanns, Eddleston, Sarathy et al., 2012). In sum, we assume the more family members are involved in the business, the more the families' decision-making is affected by SEW. The more ownership is dispersed across generations in charge of the business, the more SEW loses importance as a reference point in decision-making. Further, we hypothesize that the varying degree of SEW embodiment depending on family influence has specific consequences for PE firms' bargaining power.

5.3.2.1 Family influence 1: generational ownership dispersion

The aim of transgenerational control is reckoned to be a strong motive and characteristic of family firms (Zellweger et al., 2011; Ling & Kellermanns, 2010). As a result, the lifecycle of the family firm can move from generation to generation if the business survives and the family secures family control over the business. The specific generation(s) in charge of the family business is viewed as a determining factor for explaining family firms' specific SEW embodiment (Gómez-Mejía, Cruz, Berrone et al., 2011b; Ling & Kellermanns, 2010; Berrone et al., 2012). In particular, generational ownership dispersion, which refers to the number of family generations that dominate ownership of the business, is reckoned to be a key influencing factor of family firms' decision-making (Kellermanns et al., 2012; Gersick, 1997; Ling & Kellermanns, 2010; Sonfield & Lussier, 2004; McConaughy & Phillips, 1999).

Prior research has conceptualized stylized structures of ownership concentration. According to Gómez-Mejía et al. (2007), families move episodically through three stages. In the first stage, ownership and management is controlled by the first or founding generation, whereas in the second stage this role is occupied by the extended family and its members. In the third generation, the role of the even further extended family is complemented by non-family management (Gómez-Mejía et al., 2007). Similarly, Gersick et al. (1997) conceptualize the development stages of the family firm from a stage of founders' unitary control to a stage with "sibling partnerships" with shared control, and ultimately to a stage of further dispersed control in the "cousin consortium". Thus, as the family firm ensures family succession, ownership is transferred from parents, to children, and ultimately to relatives (Kellermanns et al., 2012).

The more generational ownership is dispersed, the more SEW loses prominence as a reference point for decision-making. As ownership of family firms shifts towards later generations, a rising number of fractional owners almost inevitably distances each individual from the family business and SEW becomes less of a concern. Extraordinary commitment, the need for family control, emotional attachment, and identification with the family business as key dimensions of SEW might have had highest priority for the founding generation – interestingly, the generation that has also been associated with higher performance (Jayaraman, Khorana, Nelling et al., 2000; Villalonga & Amit, 2006; Gómez-Mejía et al., 2007; Sraer & Thesmar, 2007; Eddleston & Kellermanns, 2007). Later generations may lose interest in the business or feel obliged to join the family business (Freudenberger, Freedheim, & Kurtz, 1989; Schulze et al., 2001), experience the family firm as a burden or decide not to leave the business, based on calculative reasoning (Kellermanns et al., 2012). At the same time, later generations could have also developed more professional management structures which deprioritize SEW (McConaughy & Phillips, 1999). As a result, dimensions of SEW can lose importance to the extent that SEW becomes negatively "valenced" (Berrone et al., 2012; Kellermanns et al., 2012).

5.3.2.2 Family influence 2: number of family members in the business

Another source of family influence is the number of family members which actively participate in the business. Family members can occupy different roles in the family business and thus constitute a strategic asset (Sirmon & Hitt, 2003). In particular, family members participate in the management of the family firm, in governance roles or most prominently as family CEO (Klein et al., 2005). While the direct participation in management roles might strengthen the influence of the family on the business, indirect influence through governance roles might be weaker compared to direct influence, but could also matter considerably (Klein et al., 2005).

Participation of family members in the business has often been linked to agency costs, so therefore having more family members in the business reduces agency costs (Jensen & Meckling, 1976; Fama & Jensen, 1983). Accordingly, when family members work together, there is a lower potential for interest conflict, which leads to lower control costs and less need for financial incentives to ensure interest alignment (Chrisman et al., 2004). Thus, the more family members are involved in the business, the more the business is characterized by personal and implicit relationships as opposed to contract-based arrangements (James, 1999). However, with the introduction of new family members to the business, new agency problems may arise (La Porta et al., 1999; Schulze et al., 2003a, Schulze et al., 2003b; Gómez-Mejía et al., 2005; Eddleston & Kellermanns, 2007). What agency-theory considers a problem is what SEW theory highlights as being rational from a family members' perspective. Playing an active role in the business allows the family to control the business, and thus, satisfies the need for control as a key dimension of SEW (Berrone et al., 2012; Schulze et al., 2003b). Moreover, having more family members in the business also implies that the family firm becomes a central part of the life of the family and vice versa. As a result, the more family members participate in the family business, the more likely that identification with the family business increases, while emotional attachment becomes more pronounced (Berrone et al., 2012). Thus, having more family members active in the family business implies that SEW has a higher priority.

5.3.2.3 Moderating effects of family influence on sources of bargaining power

The varying degree of SEW embodiment depending on aspects of family influence has consequences for PE firms' bargaining power. The more family members are part of the business, the more the firm is present in the life of the family and the more important SEW becomes for family firms' actions (Berrone et al., 2012). Additionally, the more ownership is dispersed across generations, the less prominent is SEW as a reference point for decision-making. Further, a change in importance of SEW for family sellers in turn affects bargaining power of PE buyers. In general, we hypothesize a rise in SEW importance as a result of stronger family influence increases PE firms' bargaining power derived from bidder competition and expertise advantage, and the opposite is the case for sellers' time pressure.

Accordingly, due to the varying extent and importance of SEW for family firms' decision-making, factors of bargaining power are likely to be moderated by aspects of family influence.

Bidder competition. The varying importance of SEW will guide family sellers in situations of rising bidder competition. If family firms were purely rationally motivated actors, they would maximize their bargaining power by exploiting bidder competition to their advantage. However, family sellers assume an active and influential role when they sell their business (Graebner & Eisenhardt, 2004). Moreover, family sellers can have distinct SEW-motivated preferences that go beyond concerns to maximize sale price, in that they allow for future identification with the business (Carlock & Ward, 2001; Zellweger et al., 2011; Graebner & Eisenhardt, 2004; Steen & Welch, 2006; Petty et al., 1994). For example, a PE buyer's hypothetical plans to significantly restructure the family-firm business after the buyout could imply a sacrifice or change of company relationships, culture, philosophy, and traditions which would likely contradict family seller wishes where SEW is of high concern (Steen & Welch, 2006; Mickelson & Worley, 2003). Potential buyers with such plans are likely to be disregarded by highly SEW-influenced family sellers. Thus, family sellers with a high desire for SEW will likely increase the requirements for PE buyers to be eligible to acquire the firm. On the other hand, if buyers can fulfil the high SEW-influenced standards demanded by family sellers, family sellers in turn are likely to be highly committed towards such PE firms. Put differently, although multiple PE bidders compete for the firm, preferred PE bidders that can satisfy family sellers in terms of SEW will be preferred transaction partners and will suffer less from a loss of bargaining power under rising bidder competition. Thus, we hypothesize as follows:

Hypothesis 4a: Ownership dispersion across family generations moderates the perceived bargaining power of PE buyers derived from bidder competition. Specifically, the strength of the negative relationship between bidder competition and PE firms' perceived bargaining power is stronger.

Hypothesis 4b: The number of family members in the business moderates the perceived bargaining power of PE buyers derived from bidder competition. Specifically, the strength of the negative relationship between bidder competition and PE firms' perceived bargaining power is weaker.

Expertise advantage. Similar to bidder competition, the more SEW is a concern for family firms, the more PE firms' expertise advantage should translate into higher bargaining power. A key dimension of SEW is binding social ties, i.e. a family firm's collection of social relationships (Miller, Lee, Chang et al., 2009; Cruz, Justo, & de Castro, 2012; Miller & Le Breton-Miller, 2005). Family firms extend family ties to non-family stakeholders and the more family firms are affected by considerations of SEW, the more interactions with business partners are based on trust, reciprocity, and closeness (Berrone et al., 2012). If family sellers move away from full control of the business it becomes critical that they can trust and perceive the buying side to be competent in continuing their "lifetime achievement" (Tappeiner et al., 2012; Niedermeyer et al., 2010; Graebner & Eisenhardt, 2004). This has two consequences: PE firms with an expertise advantage will enjoy more credibility and trust the more SEW is a concern and will be challenged less vigorously by family sellers with a high desire for SEW. Thus, we propose the following hypotheses:

Hypothesis 5a: Ownership dispersion across family generations moderates the perceived bargaining power of PE buyers derived from expertise advantage. Specifically, the strength of the positive relationship between expertise advantage and PE firms' perceived bargaining power will be weaker.

Hypothesis 5b: The number of family members in the business moderates the perceived bargaining power of PE buyers derived from expertise advantage. Specifically, the strength of the positive relationship between expertise advantage and PE firms' perceived bargaining power will be stronger.

Sellers' time pressure. Higher SEW can also be detrimental for PE firms' bargaining power when it comes to sellers' time pressure. Family firms are reckoned to be associated with survivability capital—the collective resources that family members are willing to loan, contribute, or share for the benefit of the family business (Sirmon & Hitt, 2003; Horton, 1986; Dreux, 1990). This survivability capital is greater the larger the role SEW plays in the motivation of the family. For example, the family could provide financial capital to ensure liquidity of the business regardless of the risks associated with capital provision. In principle, the more SEW is a concern for the family, the more family members should contribute to ensure the family firms' survivability and the more situations of time pressure can be sustained.

We hypothesize:

Hypothesis 6a: Ownership dispersion across family generations moderates the perceived bargaining power of PE buyers derived from family sellers' time pressure. Specifically, the strength of the positive relationship between family sellers' time pressure and PE firms' perceived bargaining power will be stronger.

Hypothesis 6b: The number of family members in the business moderates the perceived bargaining power of PE buyers' derived from family sellers' time pressure. Specifically, the strength of the positive relationship between family sellers' time pressure and PE firms' perceived bargaining power will be weaker.

Figure 16 summarizes and provides an overview of our research model and hypotheses.

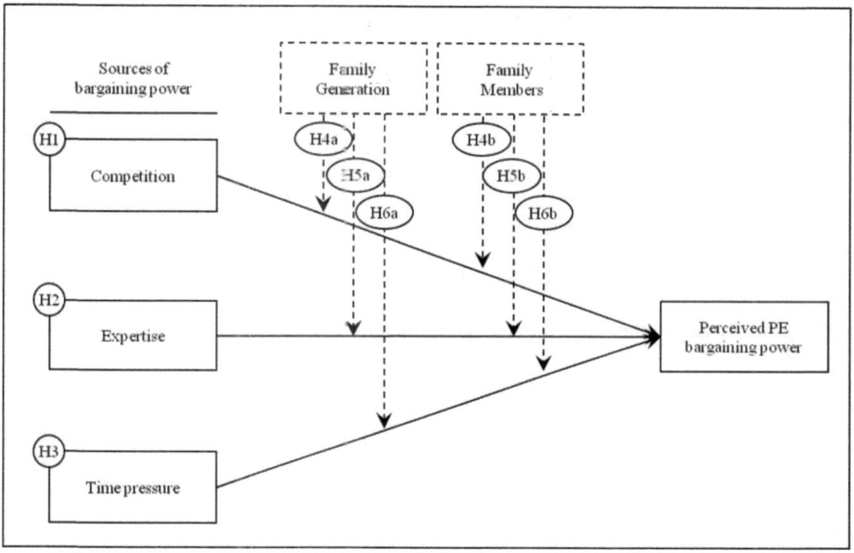

Figure 5-16: Research model for PE perceived bargaining power
Source: Author

5.4 Research design[29]

5.4.1 Sample

Membership directories of PE industry associations and internet search helped us to identify 856 PE firms across Europe. 348 identified firms were excluded from from the initial search result if their investment focus was on venture capital, or they had not completed a single transaction, or operations had already stopped. Thus, the remaining sample comprised 508 individual PE firms. Between September 2011 and March 2012, we sent the questionnaire to senior investment professionals at the respective firms and received 188 responses, each providing information on one particular buyout deal per PE firm. Thus, our response rate was 37%. As a next step, a subsample was created which contains 82 family firm buyouts deals.

[29] Compare to chapter 4.4

"Family firm sellers" were classified as those selling firms with an ownership level of at least 50% and at least one family member acting in management or governance roles (Eddleston & Kellermanns, 2007).

With our survey, we followed a key informant approach (Kumar, Stern, & Anderson, 1993), assuming that one PE manager could credibly give information on one particular deal as PE deal teams involve few people with similar background and attitudes. We qualified respondents by asking them to fill in the questionnaire for a randomly selected buyout which took place no longer than three years ago, and within which the PE manager represented the PE firm in negotiations with the selling side. Respondents assume partner or managing director roles (44%), investment director positions (47%), or investment associate job titles (9%). Respondents originated primarily from Germany (27%), Italy (15%), France (11%), UK (8%), and Spain (8%).

Potential issues of statistical multicollinearity, non-response bias, and common method bias were investigated. However, variance inflation factors (VIF) (all < 3.146), tolerance (all > .318), and condition index (all < 4.075) calculations all indicated no reason for concern about multicollinearity (Field, 2009; Hair, 1987). Further, ANOVA helped us to check for differences between early and late respondents to rule out a potential non-response bias (Kanuk & Berenson, 1975; Armstrong & Overton, 1977). However, we could not find any statistically significant differences between early and late survey participants. To test for common method bias (Podsakoff et al., 2003; Podsakoff, 1986), independent, moderator, and control variables were included into a factor analysis and eight factors with eigenvalues > 1.0 were selected which accounted for 82% of the variance. The first factor was responsible for 14% of the variance and the other factors accounted for 68% of the variance. Thus, we could rule out common method bias because no individual factor accounted for the majority of the variance.

5.4.2 Model and measures[30]

For measurement of constructs and items we used a five-point Likert scale with the endpoints defined as "strongly disagree" (1) and "strongly agree" (5) except for the items relating to "competition". We have listed all construct items and the corresponding alphas (all $\alpha > .70$) in the appendix. Our confirmatory factor analysis indicated a good fit with χ^2 (58, n=82) = 80.21) ($p < .01$), a comparative fit index (CFI) of .971, incremental index of fit (IFI) of .948, Tucker-Lewis Index (TLI) of .926, and a root mean square error of approximation (RMSEA) of .068 (Hu & Bentler, 1999).

Dependent variable. For the construct *bargaining power* in buyout transactions, we adapted five items based on Mjoen and Tallmann (1997). The composite's alpha is .78.

Independent variables. Inspired by Yan and Gray (2001) from the context of joint ventures, two items were used to measure *bidder competition*. One item covers "bidder interest" and one refers to "submission of official offers". We were interested in how bidding competition was perceived which is why we included both items and measured a five-point Likert scale with the endpoints defined as "low" (1) and "high" (5). The alpha of the composite is .80. The construct *PE firms' expertise advantage* was based on the work of Raven (1998) and Stahelski (1989). Items of the construct comprise general competence and deal-specific expertise related to valuation, synergies, and the technical aspects of buyouts. One item was omitted to accomplish a sufficient alpha. The remaining three items contribute to a composite's alpha of .70. Measurement of *sellers' time pressure* was based on adaptation of three items from Stuhlmacher (2000). The alpha of the composite is .83.

Control variables. We used multiple control variables. First, four dummy codes (consumer, manufacturing, IT, and other industries) ensured control for industries of the buyout target because attractiveness of industries could vary with implications for bargaining power. The omitted reference category was "manufacturing". Second, the size of PE firms'

[30] Compare chapter 4.4

funds under management (FUM) was included as control variable because larger PE firms could have befitted from translating resource advantages into higher bargaining power. Third, the buyout year was included as control variable because buyout markets fluctuate and potentially affect bargaining power (Scholes et al., 2009). "2011" was omitted as the reference category. Fourth, the "age" of the PE firm was a control variable as greater experience could lead to higher bargaining power. Fifth, we controlled for the "transaction value" because deal size could affect bargaining power. It was necessary to logarithmize PE firms' FUM, age, and transaction value to achieve a normal distribution of these variables.

Moderating variable. "Generational ownership dispersion" ("family generation") refers to those who control the ownership of the family firm and answers could be "1st generation" (founding), "2nd generation" or "3rd generation" which we coded accordingly from 1 to 3 (Ling & Kellermanns, 2010). In our sample, family generations were distributed as follows: 59% were classified as 1st generation, 30% as 2nd generation, and 11 % as 3rd generation.

The number of family members in the business ("family members") comprises the number of family members that actively participate in the family business. We coded the number of family members as "1" (1 member in the business), "2" (2–3 members in the business), and "3" (4 or more members in the business). We counted 34% of firms with one family member in the business, 46% with 2–3 members, and 20% with 4 or more family members in the business.

5.5 Data analysis and results

A summary of means, standard deviations and correlations for all variables is displayed in ***Table 6***. The three independent variables correlate significantly with the dependent variable of perceived bargaining power. The correlations indicate preliminary evidence that bidder competition, expertise advantage, and sellers' time pressure are associated with perceived bargaining power in family firm buyouts.

Variable	*Mean*	*SD*	*1*	*2*	*3*	*4*	*5*	*6*	*7*	*8*	*9*	*10*	*11*	*12*	*13*	*14*	*15*
1. Consumer	.25	.43	1														
2. Manufacturing	.40	.49	-.463**	1													
3. IT	.11	.32	-.202	-.286**	1												
4. Other	.25	.43	-.328**	-.463**	-.202	1											
5. 2011	.47	.50	-.137	-.001	.061	.093	1										
6. 2010	.30	.46	.130	.029	-.057	-.121	-.610**	1									
7. 2009	.07	.26	.057	-.036	-.100	.057	-.266*	-.184	1								
8. 2008	.16	.37	-.016	-.009	.059	-.016	-.411**	-.284*	-.124	1							
9. Transact. Value[1]	3.89	1.40	.189	-.063	-.182	.016	.020	.018	.030	-.071	1						
10. Age[1]	2.72	.58	-.041	-.061	.141	.007	.104	.028	-.022	-.160	.230*	1					
11. Competition	2.94	1.10	.039	-.215	.074	.150	.172	.009	-.032	-.222*	.238*	.002	1				
12. Expertise	3.26	.80	.171	.094	-.255*	-.092	-.101	.115	-.220*	.151	-.271*	-.145	-.188	1			
13. Time Pressure	2.26	.98	.025	.024	-.120	.035	.209	-.019	-.252*	-.081	.117	.087	.028	.075	1		
14. Generation	1.49	.67	-.080	.007	-.202	.219*	.120	-.277*	.214	.029	-.048	-.041	.133	-.053	.032	1	
15. Family member	1.86	.74	-.096	-.022	-.039	.149	.172	-.244*	-.019	.084	.370**	.052	.112	-.216	.172	.365**	1
16. Bargain. Power	3.18	.71	-.018	-.010	-.238*	.203	.000	-.008	-.018	.023	.082	-.066	-.346**	.311**	.328**	-.141	.065

*. Correlation is significant at the 0.05 level (2-tailed) **. Correlation is significant at the 0.01 level (2-tailed). [1] Logarithmized.

Table 5-6: Correlation matrix, means, and standard deviations

Source: Author

Hierarchical regression analysis was used to test the hypothesis outlined above. By centering the interaction variables we could largely avoid multicollinearity problems when testing for interactions (Aiken & West, 1991). Results are displayed in ***Table 7.***

	Model 1	*Model 2*	*Model 3*	*Model 4*
Step 1: Control				
Consumer	-.017	-.030	-.032	.089
IT	-.196	.045	-.007	-.102
Other	.161	.274*	.286**	.367***
2010	.002	-.008	-.036	-.039
2009	-.045	.088	.128	.072
2008	.028	-.087	-.082	-.034
Transaction Value[1]	.062	.267*	.201 †	.118
PE Age[1]	-.051	-.125	-.114	-.089
Step 2: Independent				
Competition		-.414***	-.375***	-.419***
Expertise		.339**	.338**	.230*
Time Pressure		.305**	.305**	.266**
Step 3: Moderators				
Family Generation			-.213	-.209
Family Members			.092	.186
Step 4: Interaction Terms				
Generation x Competition				-.270*
Generation x Expertise				.299**
Generation x Time Pressure				-.064
Members x Competition				.303**
Members x Expertise				.225*
Members x Time Pressure				.007
Change in R^2	.089	.332***	.031	.181***
R^2	.089	.421	.452	.633
Adjusted R^2	-.012	.329	.346	.518
F	.885	4.565***	4.251***	5.528***

Notes: Beta weights are reported for the final stage in each model; n = 82; *** $p < 0.001$; ** $p < 0.01$; * $p < 0.05$; † $p < 0.1$

[a] Regression coefficients are reported as betas.
[1] Logarithmized.

Table 5-7: Results of regression analysis
Source: Author

None of the control variables which were entered into model 1 showed significance. To test hypotheses 1–3 we included all independent variables into model 2. We could identify a significant R^2 change ($\Delta R^2 = 0.33$, $p < 0.001$) and competition ($\beta = -0.41$, $p < 0.001$), expertise, ($\beta = 0.34$, $p < 0.01$), and time pressure, ($\beta = 0.31$, $p < 0.01$) significantly affect perceived bargaining power. As a result, statistical confirmation of hypothesis 1, 2, and 3 is given.

The moderators "family generation" and "family members" were included into model 3 and 4 to test for interaction. For model 3 (only moderating variables), the observed change in R^2 was not significant ($\Delta R^2 = 0.03$). For model 4, the interaction of family generation and competition was found to be negatively significant ($\beta = -0.27$, $p < 0.05$). The other interaction term of family generation with expertise was found to be positively significant ($\beta = 0.30$, $p < 0.01$) which, however, is contradictory to our hypothesis. The interaction of family generation and time pressure is statistically insignificant. Thus, we can confirm hypothesis 4a, but need to reject 5a and 6a.

Additionally, model 4 demonstrates family members and the independent variables competition ($\beta = 0.30$, $p < 0.01$) and expertise ($\beta = 0.23$, $p < 0.05$) to be significantly interacting. On the contrary, the variable "family members" does not interact with time pressure. Consequently, we are able to confirm hypotheses 4b and 5b. However, hypothesis 6b is rejected. The R^2 change in model 4 is significant ($\Delta R^2 = 0.18$, $p < 0.001$). We visualized the significant moderation effects in ***Figures 17, 18,*** and ***19*** to allow for easier interpretation.

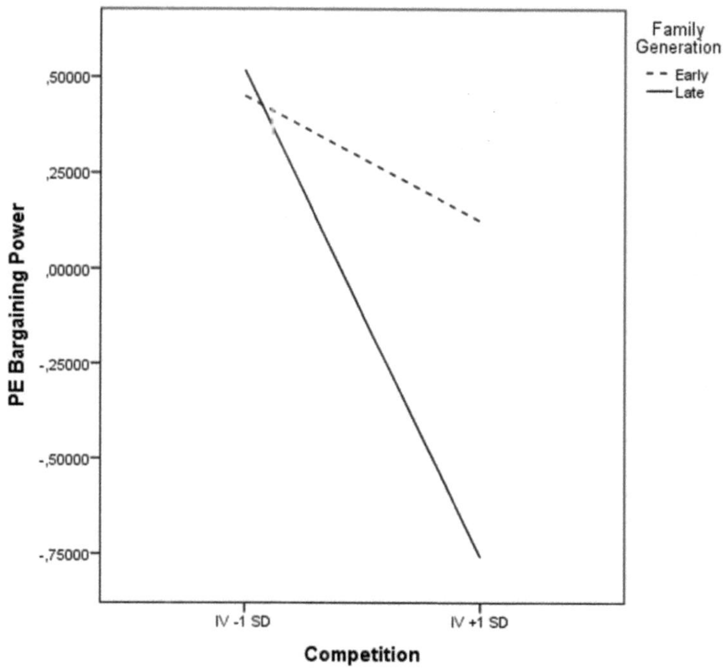

Figure 5-17: Interaction between bidder competition and family generation
Source: Author

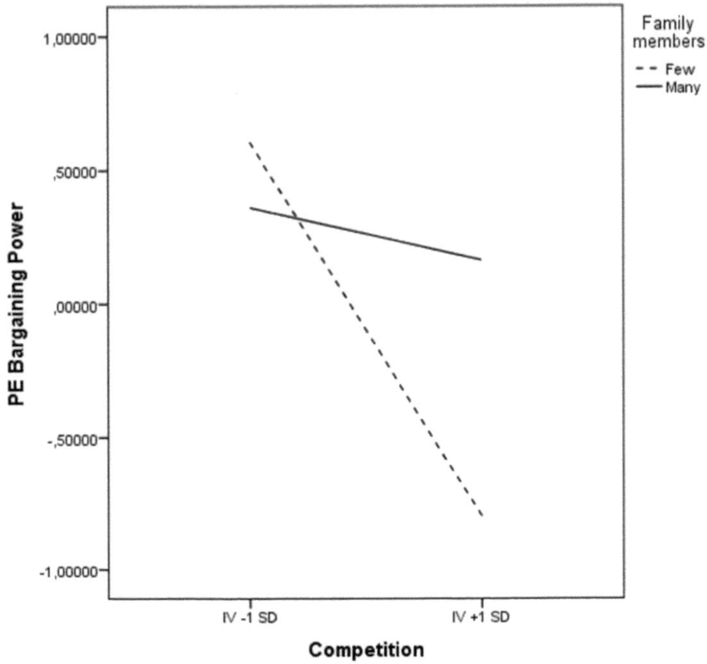

Figure 5-18: Interaction between bidder competition and number of family members
Source: Author

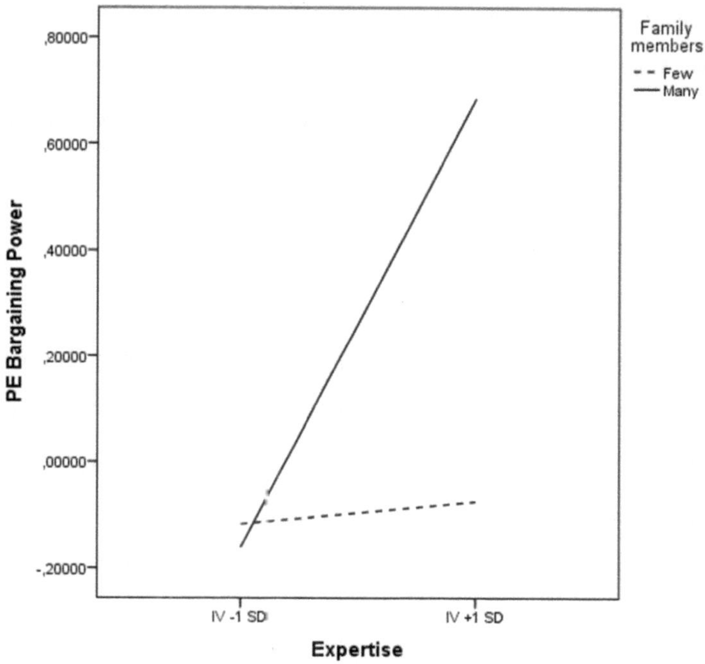

Figure 5-19: Interaction between expertise and number of family members
Source: Author

Figure 17 illustrates the interaction of family generation and bidder competition. More precisely, bidder competition's effect on PE firms' perceived bargaining power is moderated by family generation. Bidder competition's negative effect on PE firms' perceived bargaining power is stronger the more the family firm is controlled by later generations.

Figure 18 illustrates the interaction of the number of family members and bidder competition. More precisely, bidder competition's effect on PE firms' perceived bargaining power is moderated by the number of family members. Bidder competition's negative effect on PE firms' perceived bargaining power is weaker the more family members are involved in the family firm.

Figure 19 illustrates the interaction of the number of family members and expertise advantage. More precisely, expertise advantage's effect on PE firms' perceived bargaining power is moderated by the number of family members. Expertise advantage's positive effect on PE firms' perceived bargaining power is stronger the more family members are involved in the family firm.

5.6 Discussion and conclusion

This paper has helped to close the research gap on negotiations in family firm buyouts. We have confirmed sources that provide PE firms with higher or lower negotiation power, such as bidder competition, expertise advantage, and sellers' time pressure outlined in an earlier paper for the specific case of family firm buyouts. Moreover, we have demonstrated whether and how family influence affects SEW and in turn PE firms' bargaining power in buyout negotiations.

PE firms generate bargaining power in buyout negotiations based on factors of bidder competition, expertise advantage, and sellers' time pressure. Higher bidder competition for a family firm reduces PE firms' bargaining power. The family seller will tend to avoid concessions in negotiations if other bidders provide acceptable alternatives to the current negotiation partner (Fisher, 1981). PE firms which are able to identify buyout targets with lower bidder competition benefit from higher bargaining power and should be able to succeed in claiming a higher outcome value of negotiations. Expertise advantage contributes to higher bargaining power for PE firms because buyouts are extremely complex (Reed et al., 2007; Cumming & Johan, 2009; Scholes et al., 2008). PE firms will often benefit from special transaction-relevant skills that the family firm lacks as the sale usually occurs once-in-a lifetime of the family entrepreneur (Admati & Pfleiderer, 1994; Wright & Robbie, 1996; Manigart et al., 2002). Additionally, PE firms gain higher levels of bargaining power from time pressure. Family firms often postpone succession of the business and thus lack time availability to decide on optimal exit timing and to prepare the sale which can be exploited by PE firms (DeTienne, 2010; Wright et al., 2006).

Moreover, our research indicates that different forms of family influence on the selling side have different impacts on PE buyers' bargaining power. Generational ownership dispersion, as a form of family influence, is associated with a lower impact of SEW on decision-making of family sellers. In contrast, we have argued that a rising number of family members active in the business is associated with a higher impact of SEW (Berrone et al., 2012). Sellers' SEW prioritization in turn has consequences for PE buyers' sources of bargaining power. For bidder competition, we have confirmed our hypothesis that higher ownership dispersion moderates the effect of bidder competition on bargaining power. Specifically, the strength of the negative relationship between bidder competition and PE firms' perceived bargaining power becomes stronger because lower SEW drives exploitation of bidder competition to PE buyers' disadvantage. To the contrary, more active family members in the business emphasize non-financial goals associated with the sale, which lets preferred PE bidders favourably sustain situations of higher bidder competition, i.e. PE firms can enjoy higher bargaining power.

Furthermore, we have confirmed our hypothesis that the number of family members in the business moderates the effect of expertise advantage on bargaining power. Specifically, the strength of the positive relationship between PE firms' expertise advantage and PE firms' perceived bargaining power becomes stronger. We attribute the increase of PE buyers' bargaining power to a stronger emphasis of SEW associated with a higher number of family firm members active in the business. Thus, relational aspects of trust, reciprocity, and closeness import for SEW provision can lead to lower efforts to challenge PE firms' expertise advantage and simultaneously higher positive valuation of competent buyers by family sellers. We have further hypothesized that the positive relationship between PE firms' expertise advantage and PE firms' perceived bargaining power becomes weaker when generational ownership dispersion is concerned. Although the relationship is significant, similar to that of the number of family members in the business, we found a positive moderation on expertise advantage by generational ownership dispersion. Thus, the hypothesized effects of family influence on time pressure could not be confirmed. However, the moderating effect is weaker than that of "family members in the business". Neither the number of family members in the business nor generational ownership dispersion were found to significantly moderate the effect of time pressure on PE firms' bargaining power although beta values indicate a moderating effect as hypothesized.

Our research also has practical implications for PE firms, but also simultaneously for family sellers. PE firms might acknowledge sources of bargaining power and search for deals in which these factors can be maximized. PE firms might also reconsider the role of family influence for their activities. In particular, PE firms could account for and incorporate factors of SEW as part of their deal sourcing strategies when dealing with family firm buyout targets. Family sellers are advised to limit situations which lower bargaining power. Long-term preparation of the sale and external advice might be beneficial to overcome bargaining power disadvantages (DeTienne, 2010; Petty et al., 1994; Westhead & Howorth, 2007; Howorth et al., 2004). By doing so, sellers could search more actively for various potential exchange partners, match the expertise of the buying PE side, and execute deals at the right time. Furthermore, family firms might be advised to be careful when SEW affects decision-making to their bargaining power disadvantage.

5.7 Limitations and guidance for future research

Our research has limitations that need to be acknowledged. Firstly, we only incorporated the perspective of the PE firm which represents the buying side. The family firm sellers' perspective was only indirectly covered through the PE respondents. It is highly difficult to directly survey the family sellers given confidentiality restrictions and anonymity of private sellers. On the contrary, PE firms usually have experience from multiple transactions and thus likely providing us with reliable information. Moreover, our respondents were on top of the PE firm's hierarchy (mostly managing and investment directors) which indicates a high degree of response validity.

Secondly, consideration was not given to bargaining tactics that might render the value of perceived bargaining power (Leap & Grigsby, 1986; Dreu & van Kleef, 2004; Kim & Fragale, 2005). Bargaining tactics can be used to increase an already strong bargaining power or to compensate for low bargaining power (Bacharach & Lawler, 1981; Kim & Fragale, 2005). Bargaining tactics are beyond the scope of this paper, but might be addressed in future research.

Thirdly, our sample size is rather small. Our research refers to a subsample of only 82 family firm buyout deals. However, in the context of buyout deals lower sample sizes are common given the difficulties for getting data on highly confidential transactions and time restrictions of busy PE managers. Furthermore, we raised the bar for firms in buyout deals to be considered as family firms (at least 50% ownership had to be held by a single family or multiple families). By doing so, we minimized the risk of including firms without credible family firm characteristics.

Fourth, our sample includes respondents from the major European countries. It requires future investigation to verify the validity of our findings to other buyout markets such as the U.S. or Asia (Leeds & Sunderland, 2003; Wright et al., 2002).

6 Seller's affective deal commitment – Buyout transactions as courtship[31]

6.1 Introduction

Private equity (PE) backed buyouts are often considered a superior form of entrepreneurship, in which PE firms increase efficiency and effectiveness as well as realize strategic growth (Harris, Siegel, & Wright, 2005; Wright et al., 2001; Meuleman et al., 2009). While much of the research in that domain has focused on how successful PE firms and buyouts are performing (Cumming et al., 2007; Boucly et al., 2011; Brown et al., 2009; Cumming et al., 2007; Amess, 2002; Amess, 2003; Gottschalg & Wright, 2008; Cressy et al., 2007; Wilson et al., 2012; Nikoskelainen & Wright, 2007; Cumming et al., 2007; Kaplan & Schoar, 2005)–Arthurs and Busenitz (2003) have called for new theoretical approaches to advance our understanding about the *relationship* between PE firms and their acquisition targets. In particular, the authors assume factors such as "goal congruence" and "trust" to be a promising route for future research (Arthurs & Busenitz, 2003). This paper takes up that call and aims to investigate "the soft" side of buyout deal-making.

While some advancements in understanding of the role of relational factors in PE buyouts have been made (de Clercq & Sapienza, 2006; Howorth et al., 2004), we still know very little in this respect. In particular, we have limited knowledge about a key construct in exchange relationships: commitment. In particular, the affective form of commitment, which goes beyond "cold" cost-benefit calculations and results in preferences for certain exchange partners (Meyer, Becker, & Vandenberghe, 2004) has not been investigated in buyout deals.

Some research progress on the relational side of deals has been made when family firm sellers are concerned – they are often sellers in buyouts (Scholes et al., 2007; Niedermeyer et al., 2010; DeTienne, 2010; Dawson, 2011; Chrisman et al., 2012). Family firms prioritize non-financial goals that help to fulfil their need for socio-emotional wealth

[31] This chapter is based on Ahlers, O., Hack, A., & Kellermanns, F. W. (2013). Sellers' affective deal commitment – Buyout transactions as courtship. Unpublished Working paper.

(SEW) which guides family firm behavior (Gómez-Mejía et al., 2007; Berrone et al., 2010; Zellweger et al., 2011). It has been shown that due to SEW-motivated sellers make conscious selection decisions about PE firms as transaction partners, in which the relationship or affective dimension plays a key role (Tappeiner et al., 2012). In this regard, family sellers could constitute a class of buyout sellers for whom the relationship with a potential buyer is even more important than for non-family sellers. Thus, family sellers certainly deserve particular attention when researching the relationship side of buyout deals.

With this paper, we aim for a number of contributions. First, we add to the literature on PE and buyouts by investigating the role of commitment when it comes to the closure of buyout deals. In particular, we hypothesize and empirically test antecedents of sellers' affective deal commitment in buyouts, i.e. by assuming the sellers' perspective. By doing so, we shed light on the neglected role of relational factors in the context of PE and buyouts. Secondly, we add to the growing body of literature on family firms. We investigate whether family firms differ from non-family firms as sellers in buyout transactions. Specifically, we investigate whether and how family firm characteristics moderate sources of deal commitment. Thus, we provide further insights into the sale of family businesses. The sale of a family business is an important alternative to secure family firm survival when internal family succession is not feasible (Wennberg et al., 2010; Wright et al., 2001; Scholes et al., 2008). To reach our objectives, we use a survey-based, hand-collected data set of 174 PE-backed buyouts across Europe from 2008–11. Respondents to our survey are high-profile individuals who mostly occupy managing director or investment director positions in PE firms. Thus, we explicitly ask PE managers representing the buying side for their perception of the selling side.

We proceed by firstly outlining the theoretical background for our considerations. In doing so, we briefly summarize the existing literature on private equity, courtship, and commitment. Secondly, hypotheses regarding antecedents of affective commitment in buyouts and the moderating effects of family firm sellers are developed. Thirdly, we describe the sample, the variables and constructs of our statistical analysis and present our empirical results. Lastly, we discuss our findings and acknowledge limitations of our study while pointing to avenues of future research.

6.2 Theoretical background

We use a courtship perspective and commitment theory to complement existing literature on PE, buyouts, and family firms, by exploring the role of relational factors for deal closure.

6.2.1 Private equity

PE firms provide unquoted firms with financing and in return receive equity stakes; referred to as a *buyout* when a controlling stake is acquired (Dawson, 2011; Gilligan & Wright, 2008; Meuleman et al., 2009). PE firms are heterogeneous when it comes to their specific investment strategy (Gupta & Sapienza, 1992; Norton & Tenenbaum, 1993; Cressy et al., 2007), but all focus on later-stage businesses investments which distinguishes them from venture capital (VC) firms who invest in early-stage businesses (Cumming & Johan, 2009). However, the PE and VC literature is often closely related, as both type of investors possess many similarities (Jain & Kini, 1995).

Previous research on PE strongly focused on financial performance (Cumming et al., 2007). It is largely established that PE-backed buyouts increase the performance of buyout firms (Boucly et al., 2011; Brown et al., 2009; Cumming et al., 2007; Amess, 2002; Gottschalg & Wright, 2008; Cressy et al., 2007; Wilson et al., 2012) and investors of buyout funds benefit from high returns (Nikoskelainen & Wright, 2007; Cumming et al., 2007; Kaplan & Schoar, 2005). However, competition among PE firms is rising and it is becoming increasingly difficult for PE firms to secure attractive buyout deals (Cressy et al., 2007).

6.2.2 Courtship

Graebner & Eisenhardt (2004) have called for telling the "seller's side of the story" in research dealing with acquisitions. According to the "classic" research paradigm, only the buyers' perspective matters in acquisitions—while the selling side is portrayed as an *"unimportant, unsuccessful, and reluctant"* victim (Graebner & Eisenhardt, 2004, p. 367). Contrary to the classic research paradigm, Graebner & Eisenhardt (2004) conceive acquisition as "courtship", i.e. sellers assume an active and influential role in transactions. The authors argue that an acquisition is a process in which mutual agreement and decision-making of both buyers and sellers has to be established. Sellers (especially entrepreneurial ones) consciously decide not only about the timing, but also to whom the business is sold. Sellers are assumed to base their sale decision upon a number of factors that go beyond financials, such as social and emotional criteria (Graebner & Eisenhardt, 2004). Factors that matter for sellers are in line with a long-term perspective that takes into account strategic hurdles and synergistic potentials for the business. Additionally, the selling decision is highly based on the relationship with particular buyers. In particular, factors contributing to organizational rapport such as common goals, trust, and commitment are of key importance.

6.2.3 Commitment

Definitions of commitment vary and commitment can occur on different levels such as between individuals, between individuals and organizations, and between organizations (Becker, 1960; Anderson & Weitz, 1992; Beamish & Banks, 1987; Cullen et al., 1995). We follow Meyer & Herscovitch (2001, p. 301) who define commitment as *"force that binds an individual to a course of action that is of relevance to a particular target"*. Commitment is a special form of motivation that lets individuals and organizations stick to *"actions and decisions that have relatively long-term implications"* (Meyer et al., 2004, p. 994). In particular, commitment refers to joint values, goals, and actions in a relationship leading to the intention of relationship continuation and deployment of resources (Mäkelä & Maula, 2006; Beamish, 1984; Mowday et al., 1982). Commitment can result in preferences for dealing with existing partners (Gounaris, 2005) and a propensity for relation continuity although alternatives exist (Anderson & Weitz, 1992; Morgan & Hunt, 1994; Ghemawat, 1991). Ghemawat (1991) emphasized "irreversibility" as a key feature of commitment, i.e. it is a decision with consequences in the form of a "lock-in" to subsequent actions and "lock-out" of alternatives.

Commitment has a great deal of importance in a variety of business relationships (Dwyer et al., 1987; Lund, 1985; Scheer & Stern, 1992). For example, commitment has been associated with stronger cooperation and a desire for mutual profitability (Anderson & Weitz, 1992), greater access to market intelligence and loyalty, and being important for successful long-term relationships (Gundlach et al., 1995). Commitment is conceptually differentiated into two main forms, based on the specific motivation: affective and calculative commitment (Becker, 1960; Mowday et al., 1979; Mathieu & Zajac, 1990). The former type of commitment is more emotional and the latter is more economic or rational in nature (Allen & Meyer, 1990; Bansal et al., 2004; Fullerton, 2003). Affective commitment can be considered being more positive and calculative commitment rather negative (Geyskens, Steenkamp, Scheer et al., 1996). Previous research highlighted the need to differentiate between different forms of commitment so that underlying motivations and antecedents can be distinguished (Geyskens et al., 1998).

Affective commitment's motivation is associated with a variety of feelings about the relationship with an exchange partner. These feelings include, among others, emotional attachment (Konovsky & Cropanzano, 1991; Somers, 2010), loyalty and belongingness (Allen & Meyer, 1990; Jaros, Jermier, Koehler et al., 1993; Iverson & Buttigieg, 1999), reciprocity and mutual attraction (Gouldner, 1960; Anderson & Weitz, 1992), enjoyment and positive feelings (Bergman, 2006; Meyer et al., 2004), high identification and trust (Grant, Dutton, &

Rosso, 2008; Morgan & Hunt, 1994), and a desire to continue the relationship despite the existence of alternatives (Lawler & Yoon, 1993). Affectively committed actors are inclined to favor certain exchange partners for (repeated) buying decisions, and thus, affective commitment translates into specific actions (Allen & John P. Meyer, 1990; Gundlach et al., 1995).

On the contrary, motivation for calculative commitment originates in rationality. A calculative commitment is followed-up if the calculation of costs and benefits is the reason for engaging, staying or departing in a certain relation (Meyer & Allen, 1991, Allen & Meyer, 1996). More precisely, calculative commitment stems from an analysis of anticipated termination, switching, and sunk costs as well as attractive alternatives available independent of the non-economic relationship value itself (Meyer & Allen, 1991; Bendapudi & Berry, 1997). In this sense, calculative commitment can be viewed as being the result of maximizing a perceived current return independently of long-term and non-financial considerations.

Commitment has been studied in the context of PE/buyouts, but most research has been focused on venture capital firms (VCs). When using involvement as a proxy for commitment, VCs vary in the extent to which they provide their portfolio firms with strategic and operational advice or valuable network contacts (Sapienza, 1992), which is attributed to individual preferences or tastes of VC managers (MacMillan, Kulow, & Khoylian, 1989). Gifford (1997), to the contrary, explains the degree of involvement with VC managers' attempt to optimize overall portfolio outcomes which drives personal time allocation (Gifford, 1997). Mäkelä and Maula (2006) argue that VC investors' commitment towards their portfolio companies is driven by expectations fulfillment and moderated by factors of geographic distance, embeddedness, and financial importance of the portfolio firm. Independent of antecedents of portfolio managers' involvement, the more VC managers are committed to the relationship with portfolio firms, the more they are able to enhance their performance (Sapienza, 1992). According to the study by Busenitz et al. (1997), deep commitment/fairness enhances information exchange due to increased acceptance of VCs' advice by portfolio firms (Busenitz, Moesel, Fiet et al., 1997). It was also shown that VCs' commitment towards portfolio companies affects VCs' perception of portfolio companies' performance—the higher the commitment the higher the perceived performance (de Clercq & Sapienza, 2006). Thus, when commitment translates into performance perceptions, commitment influences important investment decisions, even more so as these decisions take place in situations of high uncertainty (de Clercq & Sapienza, 2006).

In the existing research literature a number of gaps can be discerned. Firstly, the selling side perspective has been neglected. We know very little if, how, and why the selling side might be committed or about the consequences for sellers' decision-making. We also need to distinguish between different forms of sellers such as family vs. non-family firms. This is particularly relevant for the deal closure stage of buyouts. Secondly, we need to precisely differentiate between different forms of commitment—at the very least between calculative and affective commitment. Put succinctly, can buyouts be classified as *courtship* rather than *takeover*?

6.3 Derivation of hypotheses

In this section we derive a set of hypotheses regarding sellers' affective commitment in buyout negotiations. We start by outlining antecedents which could determine sellers' affective commitment, such as trust, goal congruence, and PE firm reputation. Afterwards, we hypothesize about the moderating effect of family sellers on these variables.

6.3.1 Trust

Trust likely plays a role for sellers in buyout deals. The concept of trust has its origins in social psychology theory (Blau, 1964; Pruitt, 1981; Rotter, 1967; Larzelere & Huston, 1980) and its role has been described as a critical element for relationships and economic exchange

(Wilson, 1995; Ring, 1996). In general, trust can be conceived as the belief about the intent of an exchange partner—be it an individual, a group, or an organization (Pirson & Malhotra, 2011). The individual perspective, however, is supposed to be the originating force of trust generation (Zaheer, McEvily, & Perrone, 1998). Definitions of trust rest upon dimensions of reliability, honesty, benevolence or similar constructs (Schurr & Ozanne, 1985; Anderson & Weitz, 1989; Anderson & Narus, 1990; Moorman, Zaltman, & Deshpande, 1992; Scholes et al., 2007; Morgan & Hunt, 1994; Ganesan, 1994; Kumar, Scheer, & Steenkamp, 1995; Geyskens et al., 1996). For example, Morgan and Hunt (1994, p. 24) define trust as *"existing when one party has confidence in an exchange partner's reliability and integrity"* and Anderson and Weitz (1989, p. 312) as *"one party's belief that its needs will be fulfilled in the future by actions undertaken by the other party"*. In the current study, trust is defined as the belief that a PE firm will be perceived as being honest, fair, and reliable while taking the needs and requirements of the selling side into account (Anderson & Weitz, 1989; Anderson & Narus, 1990; Dwyer et al., 1987; Leonidou, Barnes, & Talias, 2006; Morgan & Hunt, 1994). Trust is the outcome of previous interactions and/or expectations about the future (Poppo et al., 2008), but its creation is difficult and, once created, trust is vulnerable (Heide & John, 1992).

Trust is considered as an essential determinant of the performance of exchange relationships (Blau, 1964). Trust infuses relationships with stability by transforming uncertainty into predictability (Doney & Cannon, 1997; Zaltman & Moorman, 1988), and thus, limits concerns about opportunism (Gulati, 1995; Hill, 1990; Parkhe, 1993; Nooteboom, 1996; Nooteboom, Berger, & Noorderhaven, 1997; Zaheer & Venkatraman, 1995). As a consequence, trust requires less monitoring and facilitates risk-taking, fruitful communication as well as knowledge exchange (Morgan & Hunt, 1994; Zaheer et al., 1998; de Clercq & Sapienza, 2006). In particular, trust becomes important when economic transactions occur under conditions of high risk and complexity such as in buyouts (Sitkin & Pablo, 1992; Pablo et al., 1996; Currall & Judge, 1995). For example, VC firms prefer to pair with trusted other VC firms for identification of investment opportunities and rely on them to monitor portfolio firms (Sorenson & Stuart, 2001).

Trust is known for its effect on affective commitment. The relationship between trust and commitment has been widely established (Andaleeb, 1996; Anderson & Schalk, 1998; Eastlick, Lotz, & Warrington, 2006; Achrol, 1991; de Ruyter, Moorman, & Lemmink, 2001; Morgan & Hunt, 1994; Lohtia, Bello, Yamada et al., 2005). For example, it has been demonstrated that the more vendors are attributed with trust, the more committed buyers are in return (Ganesan, 1994). This is not surprising given that higher trust actors are biased in a sense that they maintain positive attitude, motivation, and identification toward their exchange partners while discounting negative attributions (Holmes & Rempel, 1989). Additionally, perceived performance is facilitated by trust in buyouts (de Clercq & Sapienza, 2006; Sapienza & Korsgaard, 1996). Actors with a high level of trust will de-prioritize calculative reasons while being willing to make concessions, and commit resources to the relationship (de Ruyter et al., 2001; Bendapudi & Berry, 1997; Geyskens et al., 1996). Put differently, commitment comprises a certain degree of vulnerability and in turn sellers in buyouts will prefer trustworthy partners to avoid exploitation (Mayer et al., 1995). We hypothesize:

Hypothesis 1: The higher the perceived sellers' trust in the acquiring PE firm, the higher the level of sellers' affective commitment in buyouts will be.

6.3.2 Goal congruence

We refer to goal congruence as the extent to which buying and selling sides share similar goals regarding important elements of the buyout deal agreement (Nahapiet & Ghoshal, 1998; Morgan & Hunt, 1994). Goal congruence goes beyond pure economic motivations of interactions and is instead concerned with aspects of future relationship evolvement (Davis et al., 1997). Goal congruence between buying and selling side in buyout transactions is not a given; there is rather a great potential for goal divergence (Sapienza & Gupta, 1994; Arthurs & Busenitz, 2003). However, it has been established by prior research that the role of shared goals and values is important for the reciprocal commitment of exchange partners—the more common goals are shared, the more each side is likely to be committed to the other exchange partner (Hunt & Morgan, 1994; Vancouver & Schmitt, 1991; Vancouver, Milisap, & Peters, 1994; Reichers, 1986; Vroom, 1960).

Goal congruence is supposed to have positive effects on the effective interaction between different parties, due to a higher willingness for information and knowledge sharing activities and less motivation for opportunistic behavior (Jap, 1999; Larsson, Bengtsson, Henriksson et al., 1998; Gifford, 1997; Cable & Shane, 1997; Busenitz et al., 1997; Telser, 1980). Additionally, higher goal congruence is associated with more cooperative bargaining solutions (Apfelbaum, 1974; Cable & Shane, 1997), less conflict and higher relationship stability (Larsson et al., 1998; Jap & Anderson, 2003; Luo, 2006). In the context of PE, high goal congruence requires less frequency of contact between investor and investee (Sapienza & Gupta, 1994), and positively affects perceptions of performance (de Clercq & Sapienza, 2006).

If the seller's objectives cannot be met by buyers, i.e. goal congruence cannot be established, negotiations to close deals might fail (Graebner & Eisenhardt, 2004). Sellers' objectives are known to be diverse in nature and go beyond financials especially when affective commitment is concerned (Petty et al., 1994; Allen & Meyer, 1990). We identify the degree of control, seller's business involvement post-sale, the degree of leverage, and the future strategy of the business as being important, primarily non-financial sale objectives for sellers (Petty et al., 1994; Tappeiner et al., 2012; Graebner & Eisenhardt, 2004).

Motivations of the seller to initiate a buyout can be diverse and comprise personal, social, business or industry related reasons that have consequences for the need for future control (Le Breton-Miller, Miller, & Steier, 2004). For example, the seller could have an interest to completely exit the business due to advanced age, poor health, declining interest, or to allow for strategic renewal of the business (Petty et al., 1994; Busenitz & Barney, 1997; Bleackley & Hay M., 1994; Graebner & Eisenhardt, 2004). Alternatively, the seller might only want to partially exit, i.e. retain an ownership stake or a role in the business, but at the same time allow for knowledge infusion or realization of strategic opportunities by PE firms (Bleackley & Hay M., 1994; Nikoskelainen & Wright, 2007; Wilson et al., 2012). Thus, the degree of control, and also the related future involvement of the seller in management, advisory, or governance roles of the business should matter considerably (Petty et al., 1994).

Additionally, PE firms have often been described as relatively short-term-oriented investors who use a considerable amount of debt to finance transactions (Jensen, 1986, Jensen, 1989). Leverage is used to discipline managers of buyout firms in their use of free cash flows due to pressure from regular repayment of imposed debt. However, the more leverage is increased the more it limits management's flexibility or enforces short-term-oriented actions with potentially negative long-term implications for the vitality of the buyout business (Wright, Hoskisson, Busenitz et al., 2000). Along with goal congruence regarding the future strategy of the business, the seller is likely to consider the degree of leverage that is imposed on the buyout business. We propose:

Hypothesis 2: The higher the perceived seller's goal congruence with the acquiring PE firm, the higher the level of seller's affective commitment will be.

6.3.3 PE reputation

Reputation can be defined as expectations about a company's ability to provide future value based on past performance (Philippe & Durand, 2011; Podolny, 2005; Jensen & Roy, 2008; Benjamin & Podolny, 1999; Washington & Zajac, 2005; Weigelt & Camerer, 1988). Reputation is cognitively constructed and attributed to a company when stakeholders monitor, evaluate, and interpret the company's activities based on available information (Basdeo,

Smith, Grimm et al., 2006; Fombrun & Shanley, 1990; Heil & Robertson, 1991; Rindova, Pollock, & Hayward, 2006; Milgrom & Roberts, 1982; Fombrun & Shanley, 1990). An excellent reputation can be seen as a strategic asset which can differentiate a company from others in the marketplace (Allen, 1984; Rhee & Valdez, 2009). In particular, it could help to overcome information asymmetries by indicating customers' favorable purchase decisions (Kreps & Wilson, 1982; Shapiro, 1983). Reputation is however fragile and if a firm's reputation diminishes, stakeholders may reduce commitment towards it. As a consequence, a decreasing quality of reputation makes it more difficult for firms to maintain existing exchange relationships and to gain new ones (Wilson & Grimlund, 1990).

Prior research has recognized the importance of past performance for future performance in the context of PE. Investors will be able to generate a higher fund inflow for future funds the more previous funds have succeeded in the past (Norton, 1995; Gompers & Lerner, 2001; Dimov, Shepherd, & Sutcliffe, 2007). Thus, the proxy used for an investor's reputation is the volume or number of funds raised in previous periods (Janney & Folta, 2006; Hsu, 2004; Balboa & Martí, 2007). Reputation represents a valuable asset both for the ability to raise future funding, but also because PE firms will benefit from more favorable financing conditions when leveraging their transactions (Demiroglu & James, 2010). Unsurprisingly, it has been shown that PE reputation is positively related to superior investment selection and long-term performance (Krishnan, Ivanov, Masulis et al., 2011). PE firms also undertake efforts to promote reputation (Balboa & Martí, 2007) and to protect it by limiting the risk of investment activities, since reputation has to be continuously justified (Dimov et al., 2007). Reputable investment firms already have a strong legitimacy in the market which explains why they are preferred syndication partners by other investors (Manigart, Lockett, Meuleman et al., 2006; Lerner, 1994; Stuart, Hoang, & Hybels, 1999).

The importance of reputation could extend to the selling side of buyout transactions. In VC transactions it was shown that entrepreneurs are willing to accept lower valuations, leading to higher dilution, when dealing with high reputation VCs and/or if VCs' expertise is beneficial for the future development of the buyout target (Seppa, 2002; Hsu, 2006, Hsu, 2004). Further, visibility of high-reputation VCs might provide entrepreneurs with legitimacy towards stakeholders (e.g. suppliers, customers) which provide future business opportunities and talented managers (Gompers, 1996; Black & Gilson, 1998), as well as attract subsequent financing (Janney & Folta, 2006). Additionally, entrepreneurs feel more inclined to follow advice of reputable investors (Busenitz et al., 1997; Hsu, 2004, Hsu, 2006).

In a similar vein, reputation was perceived to be one of the key criteria for sellers to select PE firms as exchange partners in buyouts (Schmohl, 2009). Selecting a partner with a good reputation will provide the selling side with more certainty that the firm's development post-buyout will be positive due to previous performance of the PE firm (Dimov et al., 2007). Further, PE firms with better reputations are associated with a lower likelihood for opportunistic actions, given the PE firms consciously try to maintain and gain future legitimacy (Raub & Weesie, 1990). Thus, reputation can help to overcome challenges of information asymmetry for sellers in less information-efficient investment markets, considering that the sale of a business is often a once-in-a-lifetime event for an entrepreneur or CEO (Akerlof, 1970; Capron & Shen, 2007; Pellegrin, 1999). PE reputation is likely based on expertise and specialization, which should also provide sellers with a value-add for their former business once a deal is closed (Gompers, 1996; Cressy et al., 2007). We hypothesize as follows:

H3: The higher the perceived seller's reputation of the acquiring PE firm, the higher the level the seller's affective commitment will be.

6.3.4 Family firms and moderation effects

A particular type of seller in buyout transactions is the family firm. Family firms constitute a dominant type of corporate ownership (Anderson & Reeb, 2003; Morck & Yeung,

2003) and increasingly face difficulties to secure intra-family succession, which can lead to the sale of the family business (Scholes et al., 2008; Calogirou et al., 2010). Family firms differ from non-family firms in that family members influence mission, strategy, business objectives and shape resources and capabilities (Sharma, 2004; Habbershon et al., 2003; Chrisman et al., 2003). The relationship between PE firms and family firms has some potential for conflict (Blanco-Mazagatos et al., 2007; Tappeiner et al., 2012). Also, business philosophies of PE firms are reckoned to be very different from family firms. PE firms are rather short-term and profit-focused investors who use considerable leverage to finance deals (Dawson, 2011; Jensen, 1989). On the contrary, family firms usually employ a long-term perspective on the business and often compromise on financial objectives (Carney, 2005; Dreux, 1990; Sirmon & Hitt, 2003).

Prior research suggests that family firms aim for realization of socioemotional wealth (SEW) which comprises multiple factors such as ensuring control of the family business, securing binding ties to family members and family harmony, and continuing a family dynasty among others (Gómez-Mejía et al., 2010; Gómez-Mejía et al., 2007; Gómez-Mejía et al., 2001; Berrone et al., 2010). According to SEW, the distinctiveness of family firms is due to SEW, which represents the collection of families' non-economic goals and affective needs guiding family firms' actions (Gómez-Mejía et al., 2007; Gómez-Mejía et al., 2010; Berrone et al., 2010; Zellweger et al., 2011). Family sellers need for SEW will likely influence the aforementioned hypothesized antecedents of affective commitment.

6.3.4.1 Family influence on trust

Trust could play a more dominant role for family firm sellers when they engage with PE firms in buyout transactions compared to non-family sellers. Family firms are often referred to as "high trust" organizations which reflects families' need for SEW provision (Jones, 1983; Gómez-Mejía et al., 2001). Trust-infused behavior both internally and externally characterizes family firms in comparison with non-family firms. In particular, the internal work relationship between family members is associated with high trust because family members usually know each other for a long time, share many experiences and personal characteristics as well as intimacy (Davis et al., 2010; Carney, 2005; Kets de Vries, 1993; Lane & Bachmann, 1996; Stewart, 2003). Additionally, the interaction between family members and non-family employees often shows a high degree of trust, because family firms are regarded as acting more responsibly as employers, even in difficult economic circumstances (Damodaran, 2002; Danes, Haberman, & McTavish, 2005; Lee, 2006). Family firms also have a preference for informal agreements with exchange partners, which is enabled by relationships based on trust (Corbetta & Salvato, 2004). Trust can also contribute to higher levels of social capital in family firms, in terms of superior relationships with suppliers, customers, politicians and support organizations which provide competitive advantage (Bertrand & Schoar, 2006; Blyler & Coff, 2003; Gelman & Hill, 2007; Portes, 1998; Gedajlovic & Carney, 2010). As a result, family firms might benefit from high trust relationships in the form of lower control costs, faster decision-making, and more effective information sharing (Davis et al., 1997; Daily & Dollinger, 1992; Eddleston, Otondo & Kellermanns, 2008).

The need of trust for affective commitment might be even higher for family firms when dealing with PE firms in buyout situations. For family firm sellers, the company ownership is associated with strong emotional attachment that goes far beyond the firm being a tradable asset (Zellweger & Astrachan, 2008; Astrachan & Jaskiewicz, 2008). The sale of the family business can be difficult and accompanied by feelings of sorrow and regret, or even perceived as defeat (Shepherd, 2009; Pellegrin, 1999; Niedermeyer et al., 2010). In such a situation, the role of trust is likely to become critical for family sellers. If they depart from full control of the business, it becomes critical that they can trust whom they sell their "lifetime achievement". Indeed, family firms look for PE firms as exchange partners whom they trust and they could (intentionally) limit their search for transaction partners, despite the fact that a higher amount of bidders could maximize the selling price (Tappeiner et al., 2012). To quote one family entrepreneur in the case study analysis of Tappeiner et al., (2012, p. 47), *"We did not look at any other PE houses. We only knew them and we trusted the people."*

Additionally, prior research has argued that family sellers initially want to price-in SEW the family gives up due to departure from ownership of the businenss (Zellweger et al., 2011; Zellweger & Astrachan, 2008). When family sellers sell their business, they cannot exhibit family control and adopt a SEW-influenced reference point so that only a higher price can convince them to sell the business (Zellweger et al., 2011). However, family firms are not traded at above-market prices for comparable non-family firms, but rather at a discount (Salvato et al., 2010). Thus, in real world market transactions, SEW is not factored in financially. To compensate for a loss of SEW, family sellers might require non-financial, affective compensation for their loss of SEW in order to show deal commitment. The role of affective compensation for a loss of SEW could be played by trust. We hypothesize as follows:

Hypothesis 4: Family sellers moderate the role of trust for affective deal commitment. Specifically, the strength of the positive relationship between trust and deal commitment is stronger.

6.3.4.2 Family influence on goal congruence

Family sellers might also put more emphasis on goal congruence for affective commitment compared to non-family firms, as a result of their need to earn SEW after the buyout sale is signed (Graebner & Eisenhardt, 2004; Niedermeyer et al., 2010; Gómez-Mejía et al., 2007; Berrone et al., 2010). The family sellers' own identity is ultimately connected to the identity of the firm (Cruz et al., 2012). Through identification of family (members) with the business, the family firm functions as an extension and defining aspect of their sense of self (Zellweger, Eddleston, & Kellermanns, 2010; Dyer & Whetten, 2006). As such, the family firm is a catalyst of social prestige, recognition, and reputation, and by doing so creates SEW (Chrisman et al., 2004; Westhead et al., 2001; Berrone et al., 2010). Even after the sale, family sellers still identify with the business and exhibit feelings of responsibility for employees and stakeholders, especially if the firm operates under the family's name (Lee & Rogoff, 1996; Dyer & Whetten, 2006; Mickelson & Worley, 2003). Whether or not SEW can still be generated after the sale depends to a large extent on how the goals of PE and family sellers are congruent with each other.

We have already outlined factors of deal goal congruence such as degree of control, degree of leverage, seller's involvement after the deal, and the future strategy, which we hypothesize to be important in buyout deals (Petty et al., 1994; Tappeiner et al., 2012; Graebner & Eisenhardt, 2004). We hypothesize that family sellers will place a greater emphasis on factors of goal congruence so that their future desire for SEW can be met. Family sellers require goal congruence regarding the degree of leverage which is used by private equity buyers to finance a deal. The higher the leverage, the higher the risk of bankruptcy and the more restrained the opportunities are to invest in the long run. An important dimension of SEW in family firms originates in the personal need for identification which can be defined as individuals' self-conception and perceived dimensions of belonging (Gómez-Mejía et al., 2007). If the survivability of the business and its prosperity is potentially at risk due to high leverage, ongoing identification with the business to generate SEW will not be possible.

Family sellers might further require goal congruence regarding a potential involvement of themselves or family members once the buyout sale is completed. From ongoing involvement in the business post-sale, family members might be further able to realize SEW even after the business has been sold (Ehrhardt & Nowak, 2003; Steen & Welch, 2006; Gómez-Mejía et al., 2007; Berrone et al., 2010). Potential opportunities for ongoing involvement might include having family members in management positions, acting in advisory roles, or serving as ambassadors (Steen & Welch, 2006).

Another issue for which goal congruence could be required is the degree of control, i.e. the ownership stake, which the PE firm and management team acquire. Families' degree of control has been directly associated with SEW (Gómez-Mejía et al., 2007; Zellweger et al., 2011). As a consequence, family firm owners may fear sharing control with outsiders (Poutziouris, 2001; Howorth, 2001; Romano & Tanewski, 2001). Although less preferable for family sellers, selling the family business can be a viable option to secure firm survival if, for example, perpetuation of family ownership is unfeasible (de Massis et al., 2008; Chrisman et al., 2012). However, while some family firms might be willing to give away full ownership where family succession is not possible, some family firms might want to retain a minority or larger share which directly gives them access to SEW. In any case, the control issue will usually have a great importance for family sellers compared to non-family sellers. We conclude:

Hypothesis 5: Family sellers moderate the role of goal congruence for affective deal commitment. Specifically, the strength of the positive relationship between goal congruence and deal commitment is stronger.

6.3.4.3 Family influence on reputation

Above, we have mentioned that reputation could be a key criterion for affective deal commitment in buyouts. The role of PE firm reputation is even more relevant for family sellers. Family sellers compared to non-family sellers will incorporate a SEW-influenced reference point when engaging with potential PE firms. Family firm sellers have need for reputation and prestige that provides them with SEW (Chrisman et al., 2004; Westhead et al., 2001; Berrone et al., 2010). Previous performance of reputable PE firms is likely to be based on expertise and specialization, which should provide a value-add to the former family business post-acquisition (Gompers, 1996; Black & Gilson, 1998; Cressy et al., 2007). Reputable PE firms will be less inclined to engage in unpopular activities, such as restructuring or opportunistic actions that might damage their own reputation (Raub & Weesie, 1990). If family sellers partner with reputable or prominent PE firms, legitimacy can also be bestowed on the exchange partner, even more so if the partner is exclusive (Podolny, 2005; Baum & Oliver, 1991; Janney & Folta, 2006). In order to generate as much reputation from the sale as possible, at the moment when the sale is announced and going forward, a reputable PE firm's legitimacy shines upon sellers and lets them enjoy endorsement by family stakeholders (Baum & Oliver, 1991; Janney & Folta, 2006); even more so if the family firm continues to carry the family name. We hypothesize:

Hypothesis 6: Family sellers moderate the role of reputation for affective deal commitment. Specifically, the strength of the positive relationship between reputation and deal commitment is stronger.

All hypotheses postulate a positive moderation of family sellers on factors that contribute to higher affective deal commitment in buyout deals. Thus, we hypothesize:

Hypothesis 7: Family sellers show higher levels of affective deal commitment compared to non-family sellers.

Figure 20 illustrates our research model and corresponding hypotheses.

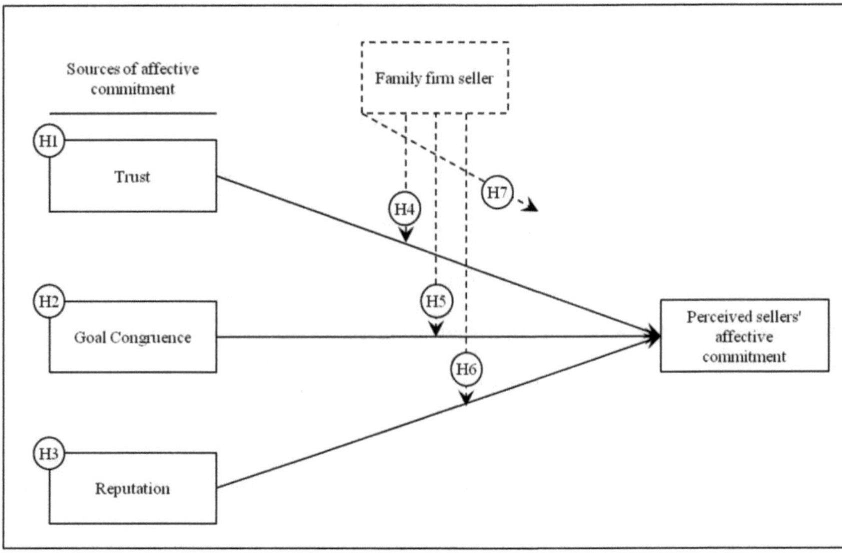

Figure 6-20: Research model for perceived sellers' affective commitment
Source: Author

6.4 Research design

6.4.1 Sample

Membership directories of European PE industry associations and internet search helped us to identify 856 PE firms located across Europe. However, 348 PE firms were dropped because the investment focus was on early stage businesses, no deal track record was observable, and/or the firms already discontinued operations. 508 PE firms remained in the sample group and members of their management were sent a personalized survey. We received responses from 188 PE firms between September 2011 and March 2012, which represented a response rate of 37%. Fourteen questionnaires could not be used due to incompleteness and were removed from the sample. One respondent per firm reported on a single buyout that the PE firm had invested in. Thus, we used a key informant approach (Kumar et al., 1993).

Respondents were supposed to fulfil three requirements for answering the survey. Firstly, they should report on a single deal their PE firm had invested. Secondly, respondents had to be actively involved in the deal-making and the negotiation process with the selling side. Thirdly, the deal should not date back more than three years. We guaranteed all participants confidentiality and anonymity in handling their questionnaires. Most respondents identified themselves as partners or managing directors (43%), investment directors (44%) or investment associates (13%). The majority of completed questionnaires came from Germany (27%), Italy (14%), France (10%), UK (9%), and Spain (6%).

We checked the sample for multicollinearity and a potential non-response bias. Regarding multicollinearity, only moderate levels of correlation were observed among the variables and indicators such as variance inflation factors (VIF) (all < 1.543), tolerance (all > 0.648), and condition index (all < 2.508) all suggested no issues of multicollinearity (Field, 2009; Hair, 1987). Furthermore, the split into early and late respondents and testing with ANOVA revealed no statistically significant differences, which indicated the absence of a non-response bias (Kanuk & Berenson, 1975; Armstrong & Overton, 1977).

6.4.2 Model and measures

We made use of five-point Likert scales with the endpoints "strongly disagree" (1) and "strongly agree" (5) to measure items for our constructs (except for PE reputation which was measured differently). All construct items and alphas (all a > .70) are included in the appendix of this paper. The outcome of a confirmatory factor analysis was positive and showed a good fit with χ^2 (48, n=174) = 63.89) (p < .01), a comparative fit index (CFI) of .971, an incremental index of fit (IFI) of .972, a Tucker–Lewis Index (TLI) of .961, and a root mean square error of approximation (RMSEA) of .044 (Hu & Bentler, 1999).

Dependent variable. We developed three items to measure perceived *affective deal commitment* in buyout transactions based on Allen & Meyer (1990). The items were all adapted to the context of management buyouts. The alpha of the composite is .70.

Independent variables. Three items were used to measure *trust*—adapted to the context of buyouts from Morgan and Hunt (1994) and Zaheer, McEvily, & Perrone, (1998). The alpha of the composite is .77. Four items were adapted from De Clercq & Sapienza (2006) and Sapienza (1992) to measure *goal congruence*. The items covered coal congruence related to degree of control, degree of leverage, and future involvement of the seller. We had to drop one item that was related to the future strategy of the business, in order to reach a sufficient α. The alpha of the composite is .70. The *PE firm reputation* was measured using three items from Dimov, Shepherd, Sutcliffe (2007). These items are (1) Total amount of invested capital by the PE firm, (2) Total number of companies in its portfolio, and (3) Age of PE firm. The alpha of the composite was .79.

Control variables. Various control variables were used to improve reliability of our statistical analysis. Firstly, five dummy codes allowed to control for the industry in which the buyout transaction took place, such as consumer, IT, healthcare, manufacturing and other industries. This was required because the proportion of family ownership in different industries varies (Lee, 2006). "Manufacturing" was left out as the reference category. Secondly, the year of the buyout transaction was controlled for because buyout markets are cyclical, which might affect affective commitment (Scholes et al., 2009). "2011" is the omitted reference category. Thirdly, we controlled for the deal size because larger deals could involve more intermediaries, which might provide less opportunities for affective commitment.

Moderating variable. There is considerable debate on how to define family firms, but ownership and participation of family members in the business are used most frequently (Ling & Kellermanns, 2010; Sharma, 2004; Anderson & Reeb, 2003). In this study, family firm sellers were classified as firms with an ownership level of at least 50% and participation of family members in management or governance roles (Eddleston & Kellermanns, 2007). To ensure robustness of our findings, we tested for different ownership levels ranging from 20% to 100% family ownership. We found moderating effects shown at a 50% ownership level to be stable and representative across different ownership levels.

6.5 Data analysis and results

A summary of means, standard deviations and correlations is provided in ***Table 8.*** The table reveals some significant positive correlations of the two independent variables of trust and goal congruence with the dependent variable being perceived sellers' affective commitment. Thus, these correlations provide some preliminary evidence that trust and goal congruence are positively associated with perceived sellers' affective commitment.

Variable	*Mean*	*SD*	*1*	*2*	*3*	*4*	*5*	*6*	*7*	*8*	*9*	*10*	*11*	*12*	*13*	*14*	*15*
1. Consumer	.29	.45	1														
2. Industry	.36	.48	-.478**	1													
3. IT	.11	.32	-.229**	-.271**	1												
4. Life Sciences	.10	.31	-.216**	-.256**	-.122	1											
5. Other	.13	.34	-.248**	-.294**	-.141	-.133	1										
6. 2011	.49	.50	-.087	.029	.080	-.030	.026	1									
7. 2010	.29	.46	.065	-.065	-.034	.030	.010	-.629**	1								
8. 2009	.09	.28	-.059	.067	-.046	.030	.001	-.300**	-.198**	1							
9. 2008	.13	.34	.090	-.012	-.034	-.021	-.052	-.381**	-.251**	-.120	1						
10. Transact. Value[1]	4.46	1.53	.202**	-.227**	-.017	-.012	.079	.030	-.012	-.012	-.018	1					
11. Trust	4.30	.56	-.169*	.058	.033	.019	.095	.078	.022	.066	-.200**	-.066	1				
12. Goal Congruence	3.80	.72	.004	-.067	-.048	.091	.053	.148	-.073	-.095	-.041	-.101	.269**	1			
13. Reputation	4.06	.91	.070	-.275**	.166*	-.005	.145	.120	.017	-.146	-.079	.532**	.019	-.048	1		
14. Family Seller	.48	.50	-.080	.062	.012	.049	-.037	-.024	-.016	-.010	.064	-.332**	-.004	.229**	-.267**	1	
15. Affective Commitm.	3.18	.84	-.304**	.101	.028	.085	.159*	-.006	-.013	-.001	.027	-.147	.427**	.286**	-.178*	.282**	1

**. Correlation is significant at the 0.01 level (2-tailed). ; *. Correlation is significant at the 0.05 level (2-tailed).

[1] Logarithmized

Table 6-8: Correlation matrix, means, and standard deviations

Source: Author

We tested our hypotheses with hierarchical regression analysis. Avoidance of multicollinearity issues during moderation analysis was achieved by centering interaction variables (Aiken & West, 1991). Results are displayed in ***Table 9***.

	Model 1	*Model 2*	*Model 3*	*Model 4*
Step 1: Control				
Consumer	-.270**	-.202**	-.192*	-.200**
IT	-.011	.029	.019	-.001
Healthcare	.035	.036	.033	.049
Other	.106	.107	.108	.102
2010	.007	.031	.029	.004
2009	-.015	-.024	-.021	-.037
2008	.055	.124†	.114†	.099
Transaction Value[1]	-.076	-.030	-.001	.000
Step 2: Independent				
Trust		.365***	.374***	.361***
Goal Congruence		.177*	.132†	.145*
PE Reputation		-.162*	-.125	-.123
Step 3: Moderators				
Family Seller			.200**	.194**
Step 4: Interaction Terms				
Family x Trust				.146*
Family x Goal Congruence				.074
Family x Reputation				-.087
Change in R^2	.111*	.213***	.034**	.038*
R^2	.111	.324	.358	.396
Adjusted R^2	.068	.278	.310	.339
F	2.566	7.044***	7.470***	6.908***

Notes: Beta weights are reported for the final stage in each model; n = 174; *** $p < 0.001$; ** $p < 0.01$; * $p < 0.05$; † $p < 0.1$

[a] Regression coefficients are reported as betas.
[1] Logarithmized.

Table 6-9: Results of regression analysis
Source: Author

All of our control variables were inserted in model 1. Only the variable "consumer" turned out to be significant ($p < 0.01$). For a test of hypotheses 1, 2, and 3 we inserted all independent variables in model 2. R^2 changed significantly in model 2 ($\Delta R^2 = 0.21$, $p < 0.001$) and trust ($\beta = 0.37$, $p < 0.001$) as well as goal congruence ($\beta = 0.18$, $p < 0.05$) showed a significant effect on sellers' affective commitment. PE reputation was observed to have a significant effect on sellers' affective commitment ($\beta = -0.16$, $p < 0.05$). Thus, we can confirm hypothesis 1 and 2, but we cannot confirm hypothesis 3, because although PE reputation shows significance, the effect on affective commitment is negative and thus contrary to our hypothesis.

A further test was conducted for verification of the moderation effects hypothesized. A family firm seller moderator variable was included for model 3. Model 3 indicated that family sellers show indeed higher levels of affective commitment ($\beta = 0.19$, $p < 0.01$) and a significant change in R^2 is observed ($\Delta R^2 = 0.03$, $p < 0.01$). Thus, hypothesis 7 is confirmed.

Model 4 shows the interaction effects of family firm seller. For model 3, a significant change in R^2 is given ($\Delta R^2 = 0.04$, $p < 0.05$). For model 4, trust and family firm influence interaction is significant ($\beta = 0.15$, $p < 0.05$). The other interaction terms of family influence with goal congruence and PE reputation are insignificant. The overall R^2 change of model 4 showed significance ($\Delta R^2 = 0.04$, $p < 0.05$). Thus, we can confirm hypothesis 4, but reject hypothesis 5 and 6. The significant interaction effect is graphically displayed in ***Figure 21*** to ensure ease of interpretation.

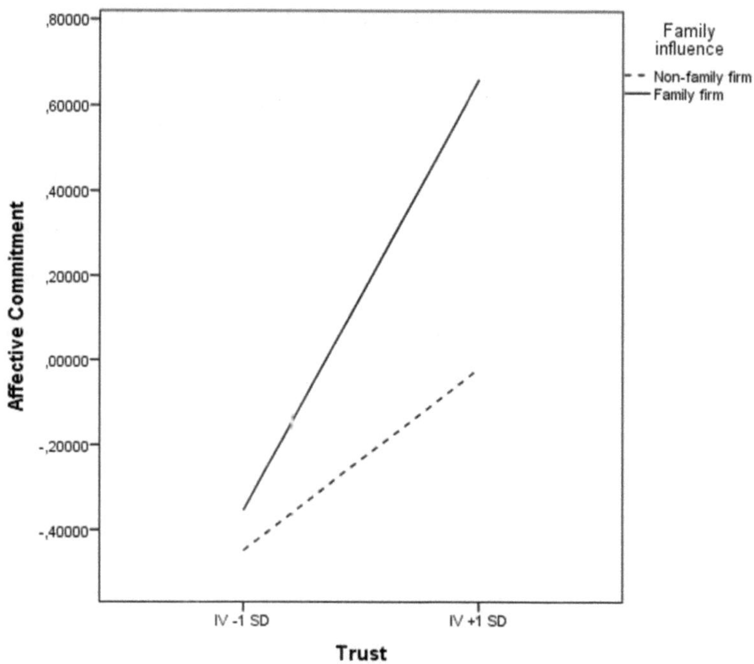

Figure 6-21: Interaction between trust and family seller
Source: Author

Figure 21 pictures the interaction effect of trust and family influence. Family firm sellers moderate the effect of trust on sellers' perceived affective commitment. Thus, family sellers induce to a stronger effect of trust on affective deal commitment.

6.6 Discussion and conclusion

Prior research in the context of buyouts has largely neglected the relational or affective dimension of buyouts, especially where the selling side is concerned. In particular, the role and antecedents of sellers' affective deal commitment in buyouts have not been studied before. Furthermore, it is not clear whether sources of affective deal commitment are dependent on a particular type of seller. The role and antecedents of sellers' affective commitment in buyout deals and the moderating family influence, to the best of our knowledge, have not been studied before. This paper has helped begin to close this research gap. We have highlighted two factors such as trust and goal congruence which induce sellers' affective deal commitment in buyouts. We found no evidence that PE firms' reputation has a positive effect as antecedent of sellers' affective commitment. Moreover, we have demonstrated whether and how family sellers moderate the role of trust for affective commitment; while we cannot confirm a significant family sellers' moderating effect on goal congruence, and PE firms' reputation for affective deal commitment.

Our research generally indicates that buyout deals also give rise to non-financial considerations for the selling side. Affective commitment, in contrast to calculative commitment, is about emotional attachment, closeness, and positive feelings under which the maximization of financial gains can be compromised (Allen & Meyer, 1990; Meyer, Allen, & Gellatly, 1990). We found evidence that affective commitment in buyout deals plays a role. Thus, we further confirm and extend case study based research in this context that portrays the change of ownership as *courtship* rather than *takeover*—emphasizing the need for mutual agreement of buying and selling side and the importance of relational factors that go beyond financial considerations (Graebner & Eisenhardt, 2004). Indeed, we have explicitly asked whether sellers would be willing to incur financial losses as part of our affective commitment scale.

Furthermore, we highlight the role of trust and goal congruence as antecedents of affective commitment in buyout deals. Trust has long been considered as an essential determinant for the performance of exchange relationships, facilitating knowledge exchange and safeguarding against opportunism in situations involving uncertainty (Blau, 1964; Zaheer et al., 1998; Gulati & Nickerson, 2008). Our research shows that the importance of trust for inter-organizational relationships is equally true in the context of buyout deals. In a similar vein, we have highlighted the importance of the buying and selling sides sharing similar goals and how this affects sellers' commitment. Goal congruence as a factor in buyouts, according to our research, goes beyond pure economic motivations, but considers the future of and involvement in the business once a deal is closed. We could not confirm a positive role of PE reputation for affective commitment. This suggests that reputable PE firms find other means to secure deals. Indeed, reputation in our analysis has a negative effect on affective commitment.

Our research also indicates that family sellers are different from non-family sellers. Our hypothesis has been that family sellers have moderating effects on affective commitment and that affective commitment is higher for family firms. We could confirm that the level of affective commitment is indeed higher for family sellers. This finding is consistent with previous literature on SEW that stresses the importance of affective needs for the family firms (Berrone et al., 2012). We further confirmed trust to be moderated by family sellers in its effects on affective commitment. On the contrary, goal congruence and PE firm reputation are unconfirmed as being moderated by family firms. Consequently, our research provides important insights for the family business literature. Firstly, our research shows that family firms demonstrate higher levels of affective commitment and that family influence moderates the role of trust for affective commitment due to the existence of SEW. Thus, we have provided further evidence for the existence of SEW that distinguishes family from non-family firms.

Secondly, our research might complement the concept of emotional value—one of the cornerstones of SEW in family firm research. Prior research has shown that family sellers have a higher emotional attachment to their business due to SEW and will aim to translate SEW into a higher selling price (Zellweger et al., 2011; Zellweger & Astrachan, 2008). Indeed, prior research shows that family firm CEOs would sell the firm to family members for 30% less than they would to non-family members (Zellweger et al., 2011). SEW literature has used "prospect theory" and the "endowment effect" to explain why family sellers want to be financially compensated above a market price for the loss of SEW when selling their business (Zellweger et al., 2011; Thaler, 1980; Kahneman & Tversky, 1979, Tversky & Kahneman, 1986, Tversky & Kahneman, 1991). However, it is unlikely that any non-family buyer will price-in SEW to such an extent in the marketplace. In our research, PE firms represent non-family acquirers, and family sellers nevertheless exhibit affective commitment. Thus, our research indicates that emotional value might not necessarily translate into a higher price, but rather could the role of *trust* in the PE acquirer affectively compensate for the loss of SEW.

Thirdly, we find no evidence for the decline of trust over the lifecycle of the family firm. Prior research has argued that trust in family firms might diminish over time and family firms need to identify ways to secure trust in order to maintain one source of their competitive advantage (Sundaramurthy, 2008). The sale of the business usually marks a late or the end stage of a family firm's lifecycle. As demonstrated, family influence strengthens the role of trust in buyout deals. Thus, we provide evidence for the importance of trust throughout a family firm's lifecycle.

Taken together these findings could also have practical implications for PE firms. Sellers will give affective commitment to buying PE firms that match their goals and in whom they can trust. Thus, sellers seem to value the relationship side of deal-making. PE firms that excel in these dimensions are likely to succeed when buyout markets further consolidate and bidding competition becomes even fiercer. Efforts of PE firms to develop networks in particular industries might be beneficial to strengthen sellers' trust and could help to develop a better understanding of sellers to target their needs (Hochberg, Ljungqvist, & Lu, 2007). The oft-mentioned "winners' curse", which assumes that winning bidders succeed, but will overpay for deals (Capron & Pistre, 2002) might not hold entirely given our research findings. To the contrary, sellers could mitigate overpayment for relationship fit. Furthermore, PE firms might be advised to target certain groups of owners, such as family firms, differently to succeed in deal-making.

6.7 Limitations and guidance for future research

Some limiting factors require consideration when discussing the findings above. Firstly, survey respondents represented only the buying side of buyout deals, i.e. the PE firm. The selling sides' affective commitment was not surveyed directly due to confidentiality restrictions and risks of social desirability response bias (Randall & Fernandes, 1991). However, PE firms routinely accomplish buyout deals and respondents to our survey were high-profile PE managers; both factors should provide our analysis with a credible source of information.

Secondly, we have not analyzed calculative commitment. Calculative commitment stems from an analysis of anticipated termination, switching, and sunk costs as well as attractive alternatives available, independent of the non-economic relationship value itself (Meyer & Allen, 1991; Bendapudi & Berry, 1997). It would be interesting to investigate the relationship of affective commitment and calculative commitment, i.e. the relative strength of the two in sellers' decision-making in buyout deals. Furthermore, future research might investigate how antecedents of affective commitment such as trust, goal congruence, and PE reputation affect the calculative form of commitment.

Third, we have not discussed the potential antecedents of trust. Given the pronounced role of trust in our research and the moderating effect of family sellers, further research into the specific antecedents of trust, i.e. how trust can be generated in buyouts, is needed. There is some preliminary evidence that the "respect" which is given to sellers and the seniority of PE mangers might have an effect on trust generation in buyout deals (Tappeiner et al., 2012). However, more detailed and comprehensive analysis is needed.

Finally, in line with other researchers, our paper further emphasizes the need for future research in the context of buyouts and the relationship between PE and family firms respectively (Howorth et al., 2004; Granata & Chirico, 2010; Dawson, 2011). Given the fact that family firms face considerable challenges to secure family succession (Sharma et al., 2003), selling the family firm in buyouts could be a promising way to secure survival and certainly deserves future research attention (Wennberg et al., 2011; Wright et al., 2001).

7 Conclusion

The last chapter of this thesis is structured as follows. Firstly, the main findings of the chapters 3–6 are summarized. Secondly, the theoretical and practical implications of this thesis are presented. Lastly, limitations are acknowledged and opportunities for future research are outlined.

7.1 Thesis summary

In ***chapter 1***, the basic terms of this research project were explained and defined. Furthermore, a literature review outlined literature gaps based on which research questions were raised. ***Chapter 2*** dealt with the theories and methodologies used to address the research questions in the subsequent chapters.

For ***chapter 3***, the research question was posed: *"How can the role of the family be understood for value creation in family firm buyouts?"* In order to answer this question, a conceptual family firm valuation model, based on the theory of real options, was developed. Through the theoretical reasoning with the model, one can conclude that the involvement and influence of a family provides the PE buyer with distinct real options. As a result, the PE buyer receives real options for external (economic) value creation due to the family's departure (non-family options, NfO). Alternatively, the family's exit after the sale implies a loss of family-dependent real options, which could reduce economic value for the new owner (family options at risk, FOaR). Thus, the opportunities in the post-buyout period available to the new owner determine the value of the business at the time of buying. Consequently, two opposing effects as well as mitigation measures need to be considered when accounting for the value implications of the family. Different valuation cases are outlined—depending on how strongly family vs. non-family options (and mitigation measures) play out, the family buyout can be valued equally or differently to non-family firms (discount or premium).

In ***chapter 4***, the research question 2 *"What factors give bargaining power in buyout negotiations?"* received consideration. This question was answered by identifying three factors which provide PE firms with negotiation power in buyouts—bidder competition, expertise advantage, and sellers' time pressure. Fiercer bidder competition for a buyout target leads to lower bargaining power of PE firms and expertise advantage as well as sellers' time pressure lead to higher bargaining power. Moreover, the PE firms' type of specialization affects power in buyout negotiations positively if PE firms specialize in "size". The benefit of size specialization is attributed to higher investment flexibility, advantages of horizontal networks, the importance of "size" knowledge, quicker execution of investment activities such as due diligence, and greater confidence in valuation projections.

In ***chapter 5***, research question 3 was addressed: *"What factors give bargaining power in buyout negotiations when different family firm characteristics are concerned?"*. Chapter 5 complements chapter 4 on the role of the family and confirms the sources of bargaining power outlined in chapter 4 for family firm buyouts. Factors contributing to the heterogeneity of family firms were found to have moderating effects on competition and expertise sources of bargaining power. Moderating effects are attributed to different degrees or compositions of SEW associated with differences in family influence—a rising "number of family members" in the business triggers higher importance of SEW whereas higher "generational ownership distribution" reduces the importance of SEW. For competition, rising "generational ownership distribution" strengthens the negative relationship between bidder competition and the PE's perceived bargaining power because lower SEW drives exploitation of bidder competition. On the contrary, more active "family members in the business" emphasize non-financial goals associated with the sale which allow preferred PE bidders to advantageously sustain situations of higher bidder competition. For expertise, the number of family members in the business positively moderates the effect of expertise advantage on PE firms' bargaining power; a stronger emphasis of SEW strengthens the families' need for relational aspects and cooperation in interactions with the PE firm.

In ***chapter 6***, research question 4 is targeted: *"What is the role of relationship factors in buyout transactions and how are family firms different from non-family firms?"* In Chapter 6, buyouts are characterized as "courtship" in order to underline the importance of the selling side and non-financial/relationship factors in buyout deals. Trust and goal congruence are confirmed as positive antecedents of affective deal commitment, whereas PE reputation has negative effects. It is shown that family-firm sellers moderate sources of affective deal commitment for the role of trust and overall show higher levels of affective commitment. Thus, trust might play a particularly important role for family firm sellers in management buyouts.

An overview of the key research insights of chapters 3–6 is given in ***Table 10***.

	Chapter 3 (Essay 1)	Chapter 4 (Essay 2)	Chapter 5 (Essay 3)	Chapter 6 (Essay 4)
Research question	• *How can the role of the family be understood for value creation in family firm buyouts?*	• *What factors give bargaining power in buyout negotiations?*	• *What factors give bargaining power in buyout negotiations when different family firm characteristics are concerned?*	• *What is the role of relationship factors in buyout transactions and how are family firms different from non-family firms?*
Main findings	• Conceptualization of a family-firm-specific valuation model • Family can be conceived as providing the buying PE firm with value-enhancing real options (non-family options), but also value-decreasing real options (family options) • Continuous involvement/ association of the family with the buyout business might mitigate risks of losing family options • Valuation discounts can be explained by the weight of family vs. non-family options	• Bidder competition, time pressure, and expertise are identified as sources of bargaining power • Bidder competition decreases PE firms' bargaining power whereas expertise and time pressure have increasing effects • Specialization strategies of PE firms related to size could moderate sources of bargaining power whereas industry specialization has limited effect • Size specialization is effective due to investment flexibility, networks, knowledge, quicker investment execution, and higher valuation confidence	• Bidder competition, time pressure, and expertise are confirmed as sources of bargaining power in family firm buyouts • Transgenerational ownership distribution and the number of family members in the business could moderate sources of bargaining power such as competition and expertise • SEW is hypothesized to be higher with rising family members in the business and lower with higher generational ownership dispersion	• Affective deal commitment of sellers is positively influenced by trust and goal congruence, but not by the reputation of the PE firm • Family sellers positively moderate the importance of trust for affective deal commitment • Family sellers show higher affective commitment • Relational/non-financial factors play a role in management buyouts and trust is key for family firm sellers

Table 7-10: Key findings of the chapters 3–6 (essays)
Source: Author

7.2 Theoretical implications

In general, theoretical implications of this thesis concern two fields of research: family firms and PE. For some theoretical implications only one or the other field of research is touched upon. An overview and summary is given in ***Table 11***.

Theoretical implication	Chapter 3	Chapter 4	Chapter 5	Chapter 6	*Family business research*	*PE research*
External succession route	✓	✓	✓	✓	✓	
Competitive advantage of PE firms	✓	✓	✓	✓		✓
Valuation of family firms	✓				✓	✓
Negotiation of buyouts		✓	✓		✓	✓
Behavioral factors of buyout deals				✓	✓	✓
New applications for existing theories	✓	✓	✓	✓	✓	✓
SEW theory	✓		✓	✓	✓	
Distinctiveness of family firms	✓		✓	✓	✓	
Heterogeneity of family firms			✓		✓	

Table 7-11: Theoretical implications: overview per chapter and field of research
Source: Author

Most importantly, this thesis has implications for the previously neglected external succession route of family firms and thus for the field of family business research. Additionally, the thesis contributes to the field of PE research because it provides insights on the process of management buyouts and on how PE firms could create competitive advantage along the process steps. More specifically, this thesis has theoretical implications related to the valuation and negotiation stage in buyouts, as well as for the relationship between PE buyers and (family) firm sellers. Furthermore, it stimulates the discussion on the theories of ROA, bargaining power, and commitment-trust by extending the scope of previous research and by offering new areas of applicability. In particular, SEW, as a promising theory of family business research, is further re-emphasized in its importance. Moreover, this thesis underlines the distinctiveness of family firms (as a group of firm sellers) and simultaneously the heterogeneity among the group of family firms.

In the following section, theoretical implications are discussed in a more detailed manner referring to the thesis' chapters. The paper that forms ***chapter 3*** contributes to the literature on puzzling findings related to the valuation of family firms (Scholes et al., 2009; Granata & Chirico, 2010; Dawson, 2011; Zellweger & Astrachan, 2008; Zellweger et al., 2011). The paper reconciles lower valuation of family targets given findings in prior research related to lower valuations in the market (Granata & Chirico, 2010; Granata, 2010), but higher perceived valuations by family sellers (Zellweger et al., 2011; Zellweger & Astrachan, 2008). Previous literature which attributed a family-firm valuation-discount to negative perceptions of PE firms on family firm targets was partially contradicted (Granata & Chirico, 2010). More precisely, a new explanation for the family-firm discount was given by attributing the discount to the loss of valuable "family options".

Furthermore, ***chapter 3*** is among the first research attempts to apply the theory of ROA to family firms. By doing so, the traditional boundaries of ROA are extended and simultaneously traditional family firm research is enriched by a new form of theoretical reasoning. Additionally, the importance of SEW theory is emphasized—SEW is viewed as primary cause for the creation of family-induced real options.

Chapters 4 and *5* contribute to theory on the negotiation stage of (family firm) buyouts. Prior research neglected the negotiation phase of buyouts, although buyout negotiations are considered a very important and a highly complex process (Reed et al., 2007; Cumming & Johan, 2009; Tyebjee & Bruno, 1984; Birley, 1984). Moreover, negotiation power theory has no universally applicable framework, but is dependent on the individual negotiation situation (Astley & Sachdeva, 1984; Leap & Grigsby, 1986). **Chapters 4** and **5** show theoretically how buyout negotiations are conceived as interactions between a buying and a selling coalition in which each side derives power from specific sources and whose distribution of power might be unequal. Thus, this thesis extends bargaining power theory to the new situational context of management buyouts.

In ***chapter 4***, research findings add to previous literature on the effects of PE firm specialization. Prior research does not investigate PE specialization on the negotiation stage of buyouts and is merely focused on industry specialization (Cressy et al., 2007). Consequently, this chapter reaffirms existing research on how PE firms are able to realize competitive advantage among peers, but also in relation to the selling side in deal negotiations.

Further evidence given in ***chapter 5*** confirms the importance of SEW and heterogeneous nature of family firms. Chapter 5 points out that higher SEW can be detrimental to the bargaining power of family firms and can imply negative consequences for financial performance. Thus, this chapter further illuminates the "dark side" of SEW, similar to other researchers who, for example, observed excessive risk-taking by family firms triggered by families' desire for SEW (Gómez-Mejía et al., 2007). Additionally, existing theory on the heterogeneity of family firms is re-emphasized. "Family members in the business" and "transgenerational ownership" are highlighted as primary factors contributing to differences among the population of family firms in negotiations of buyouts (due to SEW).

In ***chapter 6***, theoretical contributions are related to behavioral aspects of buyout deals, i.e. the importance of relationship factors between deal parties in a buyout. Previous research has indicated in general, and for family firms in particular, that decision-making of buyout vendors is not purely financially motivated, but is also motivated by non-financial aspects (Graebner & Eisenhardt, 2004; Niedermeyer et al., 2010; Berrone et al., 2012). The quantitative empirical confirmation of non-financial aspects, such as factors of trust, goal congruence, and affective commitment proves the validity and importance of non-financial aspects, especially in the buyout of family businesses. Thus, chapter 6 confirms and extends previous anecdotal evidence and non-quantitative case-study research. Furthermore, commitment-trust theory, which to date was primarily applied in marketing research (Morgan & Hunt, 1994), is extended to the context of management buyouts.

Chapter 6 also adds to previous literature related to the distinctiveness of family firms and SEW when the role of trust is concerned. The importance of trust for family sellers is confirmed in chapter 6 and is explained by the families' desire for SEW. Furthermore, there is no evidence for the decline of trust over the lifecycle of the family firm as previous research argues (Sundaramurthy, 2008). On the contrary, family influence strengthens the role of trust in buyout deals, although the sale of the business usually defines the end of a business lifecycle. Overall, family firms show higher affective commitment compared to non-family firms. Additionally, this thesis may has theoretical implications for the concept of emotional value; emotional value is known to be one of the cornerstones of SEW in family firm research. Prior research argued that family sellers show higher emotional attachment to their business due to SEW and will aim to translate SEW into a higher selling price to compensate for loss of SEW or sell at a significant discount to family members (Zellweger et al., 2011; Zellweger & Astrachan, 2008). In chapter 6, PE firms represent non-family acquirers and family sellers nonetheless exhibit affective commitment at the expense of financial objectives. Thus, this research indicates that emotional value might not necessarily translate into a higher price, but instead could the role of trust in the PE acquirer affectively compensate for the loss of SEW even if the acquirer is not part of the family.

7.3 Practical implications

This thesis provides practical insights for PE firms and vendors of (family) firms in management buyouts which again are highlighted in the chapters of the thesis. The key insights are summarized in ***Figure 22***.

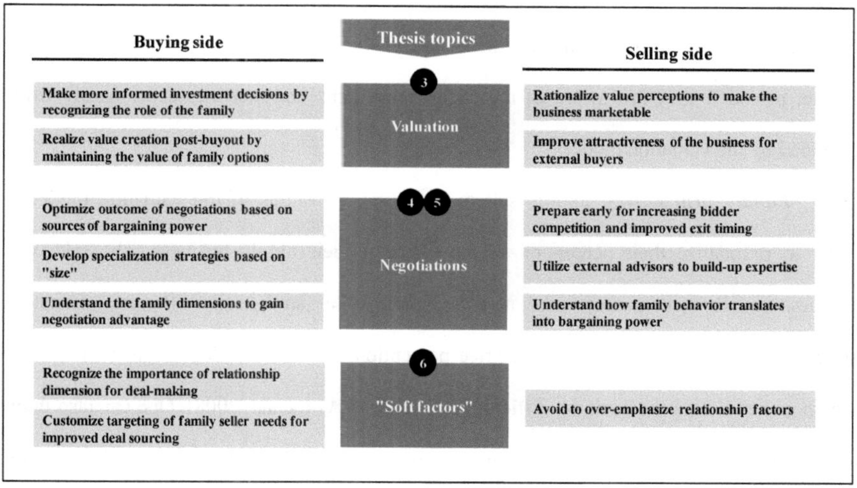

Figure 7-22: Practical implication of this thesis for buyers and sellers
Source: Author

Chapter 3 furthers the practical discussion about investment decisions and value creation of PE buyers while providing family sellers with implications for the "rationalization" of value perceptions as well as acting on its consequences.

PE buyers. PE buyers could improve investment decision-making and dealing with family firms in the post-buyout period. In chapter 3, PE firm buyers are provided with a framework to analyze opportunities and risks related to the value of family firms. PE firms could generate insights into how the family is beneficial for the business (family options), how it can be detrimental to value creation (non-family options), and how mitigation measures could help secure part of the value the family previously created for the business.

Overall, this framework can help PE firms analyze family firm targets appropriately and to more confidently assess their "true" value. Investment decisions made by PE firms might be rendered less biased towards the negative by applying the valuation model of chapter 3—for previous research has suggested a rather negative perception of family firms by PE firms (Granata & Chirico, 2010; Dawson, 2011). Moreover, PE firms could be able to act more considerately when trying to increase the value of the former family business in the post-buyout period if they are aware of the specific strengths and weaknesses in family firms provided by the valuation model.

Family firm sellers. Family sellers could apply insights of the valuation model in order to rationalize their perception of the value of their family business. The sale of a business usually occurs only once in the lifetime of a family seller. Previous literature suggests that due to emotional value, price perceptions of family sellers might be too high, which makes selling the business difficult (Zellweger & Astrachan, 2008). One can also think of situations when family sellers have price perceptions which are too low, i.e. they are not aware of how much the business is worth to an external buyer who recognizes its upside potential. If this is the case, the family seller might sell the business at too low a price. The valuation model of chapter 3 could help family sellers better rationalize their price perceptions based on standards considered legitimate by acquirers. Moreover, family sellers might be able to act upon the assessment in order to improve the attractiveness of their business as an investment target.

Chapter 4 has practical suggestions for how PE buyers and (family) sellers alike could improve their respective negotiation position.

PE buyers. Firstly, PE firms can favorably improve their bargaining position by keeping in mind sources of bargaining power such as competition, expertise, and time pressure and by trying to maximize them accordingly when selecting investment targets.

Secondly, PE firms might consider the role of size specialization as a means of creating a competitive advantage over PE peers and sellers in buyouts respectively (for the negotiation stage). In addition to widely observable industry specializations, size specialization might trigger superior knowledge and greater networks as well as flexible investment decision-making. Thirdly, PE firms are advised to think about even more advanced investment strategies in which different specializations are combined to achieve competitive advantages at different stages of the investment process. Also, superior specialization strategies of PE firms could be achieved by cooperation with other PE firms so that mutually enhancing specializations could be created.

(Family) firm sellers. The selling side of the buyout deal is advised to limit situations which lead to lower bargaining power. Long-term preparation of the sale can help (family) sellers to search for appropriate buyers and to generate a number of alternative potential acquirers (i.e. increase bidder competition). Early preparation might also help to prepare the business for the sale by selectively improving weaknesses ("window-dressing") and by providing more opportunities to exit the business when markets provide favorable conditions for selling the business. External advice regarding the sale might enable family sellers to utilize external expertise for the sale process. By doing so, sellers could make up for a potential expertise disadvantage when dealing with PE firms.

Chapter 5 has practical implications for the effects of family influence on negotiations and how both PE buyers and family sellers might favorably handle them.

PE buyers. In addition to insights on sources of bargaining power which generally hold true for the family firms in the study, PE firms can gain insights on how different factors of family influence could affect the negotiation behavior of the family seller to PE firms' advantage or disadvantage. The moderating effects of a family seller might indicate to PE firms how much complexity is involved when dealing with family sellers. Also, PE firms are advised to take into account the family side of the deal as it can have implications for negotiations. PE firms might be able to incorporate these insights and develop strategies and expertise on how to deal with family sellers in order to maximize bargaining outcomes.

Family firm sellers. Family firm sellers are also advised to take into account the practical implications from chapter 4. In addition, family firm sellers gain practical insights on how their specific family configuration is beneficial or can harm their negotiation position. These insights can help family firm sellers to recognize how family-triggered behavior is translated into bargaining power. By using these insights, family sellers could improve their negotiation position.

Chapter 6 engages in the practical discussion about the role of non-financial aspects in (family firm) buyout deals.

PE buyers. Sellers will give affective commitment to buying PE firms who match their objectives and in whom they can trust. Thus, sellers seem to value the relationship side of deal-making. PE firms that excel in these dimensions are likely to succeed in deal-making with family firm targets when buyout markets further consolidate and bidding competition becomes fiercer. Thus, PE firms might be advised to build up knowledge on how to deal with family sellers appropriately by specifically targeting their needs since they are different from non-family firms. Additionally, PE firms might be advised to focus more on the relationship side of deal-making by building up trust which is likely tied to the duration of the relationship with the seller, respect for the family firms' achievements, and a strong interest in the sustainable development of portfolio firms.

Family firm sellers. The findings in chapter 6 also offer further practical insights for family sellers. Family sellers might recognize their "vulnerability" when it comes to relationship dimensions such as affective commitment and trust in deal-making. By excessively stressing the relationship side of deals, whether it is consciously or unconsciously, family sellers might neglect other important factors such as PE firms' expertise in the industry or PE firms' track record. Moreover, family firms might put their bargaining power position at a disadvantage. Thus, family sellers are advised to be aware of how their way of doing business might entail risks for the sale process of the business.

7.4 Limitations & avenues for future research

This thesis certainly has a number of limitations which need to be acknowledged. Additionally, opportunities for future research are mentioned in this section. Limitations and future research opportunities are again outlined according to chapter.

In ***chapter 3***, four limitations must be considered. Firstly, the proposed valuation model needs modifications/simplifications to be ready to use in practice, as the calculation of real option models is usually challenging, especially if multiple options are considered simultaneously (Philippe, 2005). Thus, any practical application of our model would imply a focus on real options that significantly influence value creation while neglecting others. Alternatively, the combination of DCF models and real option models might prove to be fruitful. Secondly, the valuation framework needs some degree of adjustment to different buyer types (e.g. family firm buyers) which might have different capabilities and objectives for the acquisition. Thirdly, the valuation model needs empirical examination. It might be of particular interest to empirically investigate how family firm valuation is affected by NfO and FOaR, and how strong these effects are relative to each other. Fourthly, additional factors (e.g. bargaining disadvantage) to those covered in the valuation model could contribute to a potential valuation discount of family firms.

Future research might improve the proposed model while accounting for the aforementioned limitations. Specifically, future research might design real option valuation models for easier implementation while offering acceptable accuracy. Avenues of future research are also offered by adjustment of the valuation model to different type of buyers such as family firms. Most importantly, future research might be concerned with empirical investigation of how factors of family influence could affect the composition of the model.

For the empirical studies in ***chapter 4, 5*** and ***6***, two main limitations need to be acknowledged. Firstly, only the buying side was investigated. However, as PE firms regularly engage in transactions, the PE side of the buyout deal provides a reliable source of information. Additionally, the sample of this thesis primarily contains responses of managing and investment directors who have profound deal experience, which consequently increases response validity. Secondly, the sample used is limited to Europe and may be biased towards the "big" European countries of Germany, the UK, and France. It is not entirely clear whether these findings also have validity for the U.S., Asia or emerging economies.

Future research is encouraged to conduct studies which rely on multiple respondents, i.e. buying and selling side simultaneously, to increase the reliability of quantitative research in this research context. Additionally, future research might verify the empirical results of this thesis for other geographic regions and point out potential differences.

For the empirical studies in ***chapter 4*** and ***5***, two limitations should be acknowledged. Firstly, the papers on bargaining power exclude bargaining tactics (Leap & Grigsby, 1986; Dreu & van Kleef, 2004; Kim & Fragale, 2005), which for example explain dilution of previously stronger bargaining power. Secondly, conflicts in negotiations might negatively affect the team play of selling coalitions. In particular, family firms often suffer from conflicts which could give rise to weaker negotiation power. Thirdly, there might be other sources of bargaining power as yet not identified by this thesis.

Future research related to ***chapters 4*** and ***5*** should be concerned with negotiation tactics in the context of buyouts and other potential sources of bargaining power not yet identified. New research might also investigate whether conflicts of family firms could negatively affect bargaining outcomes. Additionally, it might be fruitful to analyze whether and under what circumstances buyout negotiations are characterized by cooperative rather than competitive negotiation behavior, because cooperative bargaining behavior is known for increasing mutually beneficial bargaining outcomes (Lewicki et al., 2010).

In ***chapter 4***, size specialization of PE firms proves to be successful for bargaining power. However, it has to be mentioned that size specialization in other than negotiation phases of the buyout process might be less beneficial. Future research should investigate the effects of specialization in stages of the investment process other than the negotiation stage and also test how cooperation/co-investing of other PE firms could create superior PE strategies.

For ***chapter 6***, a number of limitations should be acknowledged. Firstly, the role of calculative commitment was not analyzed. The relative strength of the two forms of commitment (affective vs. calculative) could provide more evidence on the role of non-financial factors in buyout deals. Future research might rely on conjoint-analysis, which is particularly valuable when trade-offs in decision-making have to be investigated. Secondly, future research might analyze how antecedents of affective commitment such as trust, goal congruence, and PE reputation affect the calculative form of commitment. Thirdly, given the pronounced role of trust, further research could shed light on the specific antecedents of trust. Lastly, the empirical study relied on a rather simple definition of a family firm, which was essential, however, in establishing a general distinction between family and non-family firms. Future research is encouraged to more specifically examine the variances among family firms in the aforementioned factors.

Beyond limitations and future research opportunities, this thesis broadly encourages and re-emphasizes the need for future research in the context of family firm buyouts. Given the fact that family firms face considerable challenges involving family succession (Sharma et al., 2003), selling the family firm could be a promising way to secure their survival (Wright et al., 2001) and could also lead to positive macroeconomic effects for economies if the sale process works effectively. Additionally, ***chapter 2*** has outlined current research gaps when it comes to *"market"* characteristics, *"information asymmetries"*, *"PE perceptions and decision-making"*, *"family firm perceptions and decision-making"*, and *"value creation"* which all certainly deserve research attention in the future.[32] Future research might be also concerned with the role of advisors and intermediaries in buyouts and paths for buyout deal initiation. Overall, much remains to be explored about family firm buyouts and hopefully this thesis has inspired future research.

[32] See also chapter 1.3.

8 Appendix

Chapter 4: Scale items and reliabilities

Construct	Items	α
Dependent variable		
Perceived Bargaining Power	My PE firm had a more powerful initial negotiation position than the seller.	0.78
	My PE firm had the potential to be the stronger party during negotiations.	
	My PE firm had all prerequisites to negotiate a favorable deal.	
	My PE firm realized a very lucrative deal price compared to other deals.	
	My PE firm was the stronger party during negotiations.	
Independent variables		
Competition	Please rate the degree of other potential buyers interested in the buyout target.	0.79
	Please rate the degree of buyers who extended an offer for the buyout target.	
Expertise	My PE firm was able to challenge the seller's valuation.	0.70
	My PE firm knew more than the seller about the management of the sale process.	
	My PE firm knew more than the seller about synergies applicable to the seller's business.	
Time Pressure	The seller was under pressure to reach an agreement quickly.	0.87
	The seller had limited time available to reach an agreement.	
	The seller would have faced negative consequences if no agreement had been reached.	
Moderator		
Industry specialization	My PE firm has a particular deal focus on the buyout target's industry affiliation.	N/A

Size specialization	My PE firm has a particular deal focus on the buyout target's firm size.	N/A

Chapter 5: Scale items and reliabilities

Construct	Items	α
Dependent variable		
Perceived Bargaining Power	My PE firm had a more powerful initial negotiation position than the seller.	0.80
	My PE firm had the potential to be the stronger party during negotiations.	
	My PE firm had all prerequisites to negotiate a favorable deal.	
	My PE firm realized a very lucrative deal price compared to other deals.	
	My PE firm was the stronger party during negotiations.	
Independent variables		
Competition	Please rate the degree of other potential buyers interested in the buyout target.	0.82
	Please rate the degree of buyers who extended an offer for the buyout target.	
Expertise	My PE firm was able to challenge the seller's valuation.	0.70
	My PE firm knew more than the seller about the management of the sale process.	
	My PE firm knew more than the seller about synergies applicable to the seller's business.	
Time Pressure	The seller was under pressure to reach an agreement quickly.	0.83
	The seller had limited time available to reach an agreement.	
	The seller would have faced negative consequences if no agreement had been reached.	

Moderator		
Family Members	The number of family members in the business ("family members") comprises the number of family members that actively participate in the family business.	N/A
Family Generation	Generational ownership dispersion ("family generation") refers to who controls the ownership of the family firm and answers include "1st generation" (founding), "2nd generation" or "3rd generation".	N/A

Chapter 6: Scale items and reliabilities

Construct	Items	α
Dependent variable		
Affective commitment	The seller preferred dealing with my PE firm over others because our business philosophies were matching.	0.70
	The seller preferred dealing with my PE firm over others because we shared a strong personal relationship.	
	The seller preferred dealing with my PE firm over others because of a strong partnership even at the expense of financial advantages for my PE firm.	
Independent variables		
Trust	The seller believed that promises made by my PE firm were reliable.	0.77
	The seller perceived my PE firm as an honest and trustworthy partner.	
	The seller trusted my PE firm to serve his/her specific needs well.	
Goal congruence	The seller and my PE firm shared the same opinion about the seller's involvement in the buyout target after deal closure.	0.70
	The seller and my PE firm shared the same opinion about the acceptable degree of leverage.	
	The seller and my PE firm shared the same opinion about the degree of control.	

PE firm's reputation	Total amount of invested capital by the PE firm. Total number of companies in its portfolio. Age of PE firm.	0.79
Moderator		
Family firm	Firms with an ownership level of at least 50% and participation of family members in management or governance roles.	N/A

9 References

Acharya, V. V., Kehoe, C., & Reyner, M. (2009). Private Equity vs. PLC Boards in the U.K.: A Comparison of Practices and Effectiveness. Journal of Applied Corporate Finance, 21(1), 45–56.

Achleitner, A.-K., & Fingerle, C. (2003). Unternehmenswertsteigerung durch Management Buyout, from http://www.cefs.de/files/EF-WP-01-03.pdf.

Achleitner, A.-K., Herman, K., Lerner, J., & Lutz, E. V. (2010). Family Business and Private Equity: Conflict or Collaboration? The Case of Messer Griesheim. Journal of Private Equity, 13(3), 7–20.

Achrol, R. S. (1991). Evolution of the Marketing Organization: New Forms for Turbulent Environments. Journal of Marketing, 55(4), 77–93.

Ackert, L. F., & Deaves, R. (2010). Behavioral finance: Psychology, decision-making, and markets. Mason, OH: South-Western Cengage Learning.

Adler, N. J. (1997). International dimensions of organizational behavior. Cincinnati, OH: South-Western College Publishing.

Adler, P. S., & Kwon, S.-W. (2002). Social capital: prospects for a new concept. Academy of Management Review, 27(1), 17–40.

Admati, A. R., & Pfleiderer, P. (1994). Robust Financial Contracting and the Role of Venture Capitalists. Journal of Finance, 49(2), 371–402.

Adner, R., & Levinthal, D. A. (2004). What is not a real option: considering boundaries for the application of real options to business strategy. Academy of Management Review, 29(1), 74–85.

Ahlers, O., Hack, A., & Kellermanns, F. W. (2012). “Stepping into the buyers’ shoes”: looking at the value of family firms through the eyes of private equity investors. Unpublished Working Paper.

Ahlers, O., Hack, A., Kellermanns, F. W., & Wright, M. (2013). Opening the black box: power in buyout negotiations and the moderating role of private equity specialization. Unpublished Working Paper.

Ahlers, O., Hack, A., & Kellermanns, F. W. (2013). Bargaining Power in Family Firm Buyouts: Does Family Influence Make a Difference?. Unpublished Working Paper.

Ahlers, O., Hack, A., & Kellermanns, F. W. (2013). Sellers’ affective deal commitment – Buyout transactions as courtship. Unpublished Working Paper.

Aiken, L. S., & West, S. G. (1991). Multiple regression: Testing and interpreting interactions. Newbury Park, CA: Sage

Akerlof, G. A. (1970). The Market for "Lemons": Quality Uncertainty and the Market Mechanism. The Quarterly Journal of Economics, 84(3), 488–500.

Aldrich, H. E. (1977). Visionaries and villains: the politics of designing interorganizational relations. Organization Administration, 8(1), 23–40.

Allen, F. (1984). Reputation and Product Quality. The RAND Journal of Economics, 15(3), 311–327.

Allen, N. J., & Meyer, J. P. (1990). The measurement and antecedents of affective, continuance and normative commitment to the organization. Journal of Occupational Psychology, 63(1), 1–18.

Allen, N. J., & Meyer, J. P. (1996). Affective, Continuance, and Normative Commitment to the Organization: An Examination of Construct Validity. Journal of Vocational Behavior, 49(3), 252–276.

Allen, N. J., & Meyer, J. P. (1990). The Measurement and Antecedents of Affective, Continuance and Normative Commitment to the Organisation. Journal of Occupational Psychology, 63(1), 1–18.

Amess, K. (2002). Management Buyouts and Firm Level Productivity: Evidence from a Panel of UK Manufacturing Firms. Scottish Journal of Political Economy, 49(3), 304–317.

Amess, K. (2003). The effect of Management Buyouts on Firm-Level Technical Inefficiency: Evidence from a panel of UK Machinery and Equipment Manufacturers. Journal of Industrial Economics, 51(1), 35–44.

Amram, M., & Kulatilaka, N. (1999). Real options: Managing strategic investment in an uncertain world. Boston, Mass: Harvard Business School Press.

Anand, J., & Singh, H. (1997). Asset redeployment, acquisitions and corporate strategy in declining industries. Strategic Management Journal, 18(1), 99–118.

Andaleeb, S. S. (1996). An experimental investigation of satisfaction and commitment in marketing channels: The role of trust and dependence. Journal of Retailing, 72(1), 77–93.

Anderson, E., & Weitz, B. (1992). The Use of Pledges to Build and Sustain Commitment in Distribution Channels. Journal of Marketing Research, 29(1), 18–34.

Anderson, E., & Weitz, B. (1989). Determinants of continuity in conventional industrial channel dyads. Marketing Science, 8(4), 310–323

Anderson, J. C., & Narus, J. A. (1990). A Model of Distributor Firm and Manufacturer Firm Working Partnerships. Journal of Marketing, 54(1), 42–58.

Anderson, N., & Schalk, R. (1998). The psychological contract in retrospect and prospect. Journal of Organizational Behavior, 7(Special Issue), 637–647.

Anderson, R. C., & Reeb, D. M. (2003). Founding-Family Ownership and Firm Performance: Evidence from the S&P 500. Journal of Finance, 58(3), 1301–1328.

Apfelbaum, E. (1974). On Conflicts and Bargaining. In Leonard Berkowitz (Ed.), Advances in Experimental Social Psychology (pp. 103–156). Academic Press.

Argyris, N., & Liebeskind, J. P. (1999). Contractual commitments, bargaining power, and governance inseparability: incorporating history into transaction cost theory. Academy of Management Review, 24(1), 49–63.

Armstrong, J. S., & Overton, T. S. (1977). Estimating Nonresponse Bias in Mail Surveys. Journal of Marketing Research, 14(3), 396–402.

Arora, P. K., & Chakraborty, S. (2012). An Analysis of Factors Affecting Private Equity Investments Decision: Evidence from Singapore. International Journal of Business Research, 12(2), 104–113.

Arregle, J.-L., Hitt, M. A., Sirmon, D. G., & Very, P. (2007). The Development of Organizational Social Capital: Attributes of Family Firms. Journal of Management Studies, 44(1), 73–95.

Arthurs, J. D., & Busenitz, L. W. (2003). The Boundaries and Limitations of Agency Theory and Stewardship Theory in the Venture Capitalist/Entrepreneur Relationship. Entrepreneurship: Theory and Practice, 28(2), 145–162.

Astley, W. G., & Sachdeva, P. S. (1984). Structural Sources of Intraorganizational Power: A Theoretical Synthesis. The Academy of Management Review, 9(1), 104–113.

Astrachan, J. H. (2010). Strategy in family business: Toward a multidimensional research agenda. Journal of Family Business Strategy, 1(1), 6–14.

Astrachan, J. H., & Jaskiewicz, P. (2008). Emotional Returns and Emotional Costs in Privately Held Family Businesses: Advancing Traditional Business Valuation. Family Business Review, 21(2), 139–149.

Astrachan, J. H., & Shanker, M. C. (2003). Family Businesses' Contribution to the U.S. Economy: A Closer Look, 16(3), 211–219.

Astrachan, J. H., Klein, S. B., & Smyrnios, K. X. (2002). The F-PEC Scale of Family Influence: A Proposal for Solving the Family Business Definition Problem. Family Business Review, 15(1), 45–58.

Axelson, U. L., Strömberg, P. E., & Weisbach, M. S. (2009). Why Are Buyouts Levered? The Financial Structure of Private Equity Funds. Journal of Finance, 64(4), 1549–1582.

Bacharach, S. B., & Lawler, E. J. (1976). The Perception of Power. Social Forces, 55(1), 123–134.

Bacharach, S. B., & Lawler, E. J. (1980). Power and politics in organizations: The social phsychology of conflict, coalitions, and bargaining (1st edition). San Francisco: Jossey-Bass.

Bacharach, S. B., & Lawler, E. J. (1981). Power and Tactics in Bargaining. Industrial and Labor Relations Review, 34(2), 219–233.

Bacharach, S. B., & Lawler, E. J. (1984). Bargaining: power, tactics, and outcomes. San Francisco, CA: Jossey-Bass.

Balboa, M., & Martí, J. (2007). Factors that determine the reputation of private equity managers in developing markets. Journal of Business Venturing, 22(4), 453–480.

Bansal, H. S., Irving, P. G., & Taylor S. F. (2004). A Three-Component Model of Customer Commitment to Service Providers. Journal of the Academy of Marketing Science, 32(3), 234–250.

Barber, F., & Goold, M. (2007). The Strategic Secret of Private Equity. Harvard Business Review, 85(9), 53–61.

Barkema, H. G., & Schijven, M. (2008a). How Do Firms Learn to Make Acquisitions? A Review of Past Research and an Agenda for the Future. Journal of Management, 34(3), 594–634.

Barkema, H. G., & Schijven, M. (2008b). Toward unlocking the full potential of acquisitions: the role of organizational restructuring. Academy of Management Journal, 51(4), 696–722.

Barney, J. (1991). Firm Resources and Sustained Competitive Advantage. Journal of Management, 17(1), 99–120.

Barney, J. B. (1986). Strategic factor markets: expectations, luck, and business strategy. Management Science, 32(10), 1231-1241.

Baron, R. M., & Kenny, D. A. (1986). The moderator–mediator variable distinction in social psychological research: Conceptual, strategic, and statistical considerations. Journal of Personality and Social Psychology, 51(6), 1173–1182.

Barron, D. R., Boehler, M. G., & Cook, M. F. (2010). Selling your business for more: Maximizing returns for you, your family, and the business. New York, NY: Palgrave Macmillan.

Barzelay, M. (2007). Learning from Second-Hand Experience: Methodology for Extrapolation-Oriented Case Research. Governance, 20(3), 521–543.

Basdeo, D. K., Smith, K. G., Grimm, C. M., Rindova, V. P., & Derfus, P. J. (2006). The impact of market actions on firm reputation. Strategic Management Journal, 27(12), 1205–1219.

Batjargal, B., & Liu, M. (2004). Entrepreneurs' Access to Private Equity in China: The Role of Social Capital. Organization Science, 15(2), 159–172.

Baum, J. A. C., & Oliver, C. (1991). Institutional Linkages and Organizational Mortality. Administrative Science Quarterly, 36(2), 187–218.

Beamish, P. W. (1984). Joint venture performance in developing countries. London, Ontario, Canada: Doctoral dissertation, University of Western Ontario.

Beamish, P. W., & Banks, J. C. (1987). Equity Joint Ventures and the Theory of the Multinational Enterprise. Journal of International Business Studies, 18(2), 1–16.

Bean, L. (2008). Mezzanine Financing: Is It for You? Journal of Corporate Accounting & Finance, 19(2), 33–35.

Becker, H. S. (1960). Notes on the Concept of Commitment. American Journal of Sociology, 66(1), 32–40.

Bendapudi, N., & Berry, L. L. (1997). Customers' motivations for maintaining relationships with service providers. Journal of Retailing, 73(1), 15–37.

Benjamin, B. A., & Podolny, J. M. (1999). Status, Quality, and Social Order in the California Wine Industry. Administrative Science Quarterly, 44(3), 563–589.

Bergman, M. E. (2006). The relationship between affective and normative commitment: review and research agenda. Journal of Organizational Behavior, 27(5), 645–663.

Berrone, P., Cruz, C., & Gómez-Mejía, L. R. (2012). Socioemotional Wealth in Family Firms: Theoretical Dimensions, Assessment Approaches, and Agenda for Future Research. Family Business Review, 25(3), 258–279.

Berrone, P., Cruz, C., Gómez-Mejìa, L. R., & Larraza-Kintana, M. (2010). Socioemotional Wealth and Corporate Responses to Institutional Pressures: Do Family-Controlled Firms Pollute Less? Administrative Science Quarterly, 55(1), 82–113.

Bertrand, M., & Schoar, A. (2006). The Role of Family in Family Firms. Journal of Economic Perspectives, 20(2), 73–96.

Bird, B., Welsch, H., Astrachan, J. H., & Pistrui, D. (2002). Family Business Research: The Evolution of an Academic Field. Family Business Review, 15(4), 337–350.

Birley, S. (1984). Success and failure in management buyouts. Long Range Planning, 17(3), 32–40.

Black, B. S., & Gilson, R. J. (1998). Venture capital and the structure of capital markets: banks versus stock markets. Journal of Financial Economics, 47(3), 243–277.

Black, F., & Scholes, M. (1973). The Pricing of Options and Corporate Liabilities. Journal of Political Economy, 81(3), 637–654.

Blanco-Mazagatos, V., Quevedo-Puente, E. de, & Castrillo, L. A. (2007). The Trade-Off Between Financial Resources and Agency Costs in the Family Business: An Exploratory Study. Family Business Review, 20(3), 199–213.

Blau, P. M. (1964). Exchange and power in social life. New York: Wiley.

Bleackley, M., & Hay, M. (1994). Management buy-outs and the economic cycle: The pattern and determinants of activity. In W. Bygrave, M. Hay, & J. Peeters (Eds.), Realizing investment value (pp. 110–131). London: Pitman.

Blyler, M., & Coff, R. W. (2003). Dynamic capabilities, social capital, and rent appropriation: ties that split pies. Strategic Management Journal, 24(7), 677–686.

Bottazzi, L., Da Rin, M., & Hellmann, T. (2008). Who are the active investors?: Evidence from venture capital. Journal of Financial Economics, 89(3), 488–512.

Boucly, Q., Sraer, D., & Thesmar, D. (2011). Growth LBOs. Journal of Financial Economics, 102(2), 432–453.

Bowman, C., & Ambrosini, V. (2007). Identifying Valuable Resources. European Management Journal, 25(4), 320–329.

Bowman, E. H., & Hurry, D. (1993). Strategy through the option lens: an integrated view of resource investements and the incremental-choice process. Academy of Management Review, 18(4), 760–782.

Braun, M., Zacharias, L., & Latham, S. (2011). Family firms versus leveraged buyouts: a conceptual comparison of distinctive governance structures. Journal of Family Business Management, 1(2), 89–106.

Bresman, H., Birkinshaw, J., & Nobel, R. (1999). Knowledge transfer in international acquisitions. Journal of International Business Studies, 30(3), 439–462.

Brockner, J. (1992). The escalation of commitment to a failing course of action: toward theoretical progress. Academy of Management Review, 17(1), 39–61.

Brophy, D. J., & Guthner, M. W. (1988). Publicly traded venture capital funds: implications for institutional "fund of funds" investors. Journal of Business Venturing, 3(3), 187–206.

Brown, D. T., Fee, C. E., & Thomas, S. E. (2009). Financial leverage and bargaining power with suppliers: Evidence from leveraged buyouts. Journal of Corporate Finance, 15(2), 196–211.

Burkhardt, C. (2008). Private Equity als Nachfolgeinstrument für Schweizer KMU. Bern: Dissertation, Haupt-Verlag.

Busenitz, L. W., & Barney, J. B. (1997). Differences between entrepreneurs and managers in large organizations: Biases and heuristics in strategic decision-making. Journal of Business Venturing, 12(1), 9–30.

Busenitz, L. W., Fiet, J. O., & Moesel, D. D. (2004). Reconsidering the venture capitalists' "value added" proposition: An interorganizational learning perspective. Journal of Business Venturing, 19(6), 787–807.

Busenitz, L. W., Moesel, D. D., Fiet, J. O., & Barney, J. B. (1997). The Framing of Perceptions of Fairness in the Relationship Between Venture Capitalists and New Venture Teams. Entrepreneurship: Theory & Practice, 21(3), 5–21.

Bygrave, W. D. (1987). Syndicated investments by venture capital firms: A networking perspective. Journal of Business Venturing, 2(2), 139–154.

Bygrave, W. D. (1988). The structure of the investment networks of venture capital firms. Journal of Business Venturing, 3(2), 137–157.

Cable, D. M., & Shane, S. (1997). A prisoner's dilemma approach to entrepreneur-venture capitalist relationships. Academy of Management Review, 22(1), 142–176.

Cabrera-Suárez, K., Saá-Pérez, P. de, & García-Almeida, D. (2001). The Succession Process from a Resource- and Knowledge-Based View of the Family Firm. Family Business Review, 14(1), 37–46.

Calogirou, C. F. K., Houdard-Duval, E., & Perrin-Boulonne, H. (2010). Business Dynamics: Start-ups, Business Transfers and Bankruptcy. PLANET S.A., CCIP, DTI and GFA, Published by the European Commission, DG Enterprise and Industry.

Capron, L., & Pistre, N. (2002). When do acquirers earn abnormal returns?. Strategic Management Journal, 23(9), 781–794.

Capron, L., & Shen, J.-C. (2007). Acquisitions of private vs. public firms: Private information, target selection, and acquirer returns. Strategic Management Journal, 28(9), 891–911.

Carlock, R. S., & Ward, J. L. (2001). Strategic planning for the family business: Parallel planning to unify the family and business. Houndmills, Basingstoke, Hampshrie, New York: Palgrave.

Carney, M. (2005). Corporate Governance and Competitive Advantage in Family-Controlled Firms. Entrepreneurship: Theory & Practice, 29(3), 249–265.

Casillas, J., & Acedo, F. (2007). Evolution of the Intellectual Structure of Family Business Literature: A Bibliometric Study of FBR. Family Business Review, 20(2), 141–162.

Chrisman, J. J., Chua, J. H., & Litz, R. (2003). A unified systems perspective of family firm performance: an extension and integration: Theories of Family Business. Journal of Business Venturing, 18(4), 467–472.

Chrisman, J. J., Chua, J. H., & Litz, R. A. (2004). Comparing the Agency Costs of Family and Non-Family Firms: Conceptual Issues and Exploratory Evidence. Entrepreneurship: Theory and Practice, 28(4), 335–354.

Chrisman, J. J., Chua, J. H., & Sharma, P. (2005). Trends and Directions in the Development of a Strategic Management Theory of the Family Firm. Entrepreneurship: Theory and Practice, 29(5), 555–575.

Chrisman, J. J., Chua, J. H., & Zahra, S. A. (2003). Creating Wealth in Family Firms through Managing Resources: Comments and Extensions. Entrepreneurship: Theory and Practice, 27(4), 359–365.

Chrisman, J. J., Chua, J. H., Kellermanns, F. W., & Chang, E. P. C. (2007). Are family managers agents or stewards? An exploratory study in privately held family firms: Family Influences on Firms. Journal of Business Research, 60(10), 1030–1038.

Chrisman, J. J., Chua, J. H., Steier, L. P., Wright, M., & McKee, D. N. (2012). An agency theoretic analysis of value creation through management buy-outs of family firms. Journal of Family Business Strategy, 3(4), 197–206.

Chrisman, J., Chua, J., Pearson, A. W., & Barnett, T. (2012). Family involvement, family influence and family-centered non-economic goals in small firms. Entrepreneurship: Theory and Practice, 36(2), 267–293.

Chua, J. H., Chrisman, J. J., & Sharma, P. (1999). Defining the Family Business by Behavior. Entrepreneurship: Theory & Practice, 23(4), 19–39.

Chua, J. H., Chrisman, J. J., Steier, L. P., & Rau, S. B. (2012). Sources of Heterogeneity in Family Firms: An Introduction. Entrepreneurship: Theory and Practice, 36(6), 1103–1113.

Cialdini, R. B. (1984). Influence: the psychology of persuasion. New York: Quill.

Clercq, D. de, & Dimov, D. (2008). Internal Knowledge Development and External Knowledge Access in Venture Capital Investment Performance. Journal of Management Studies, 45(3), 585–612.

Clercq, D. de, & Sapienza, H. J. (2006). Effects of relational capital and commitment on venture capitalists' perception of portfolio company performance. Journal of Business Venturing, 21(3), 326–347.

Coff, R. W. (1999). When competitive advantage doesn't lead to performance: the resource-based view and stakeholder bargaining power. Organizational Science, 10(2), 119–133.

Cohen, H. (1980). You can negotiate anything. How to get what you want. NJ: Lyle Stuart, Secaucus.

Coleman, J. S. (1988). Social capital in the creation of human capital. The American Journal of Sociology, 94, 95–120.

Copeland, T. E., & Keenan, P. T. (1998). How much is flexibility worth?. McKinsey Quarterly, (2), 38–49.

Copeland, T., & Antikarov, V. (2001). Real options: A practitioner's guide. New York, NY: Texere.

Corbetta, G., & Salvato, C. (2004). Self-Serving or Self-Actualizing? Models of Man and Agency Costs in Different Types of Family Firms: A Commentary on "Comparing the Agency Costs of Family and Non-family Firms: Conceptual Issues and Exploratory Evidence". Entrepreneurship: Theory and Practice, 28(4), 355–362.

Cressy, R., Munari, F., & Malipiero, A. (2007). Playing to their strengths? Evidence that specialization in the private equity industry confers competitive advantage: Private Equity, Leveraged Buyouts and Corporate Governance. Journal of Corporate Finance, 13(4), 647–669.

Crilly, W. M. (1998). Due diligence handbook. New York: American Management Association.

Cronkhite, G., & Liska, J. (1976). A critique of factor analytic approaches to the study of credibility. Communication Monographs, (32), 91–107.

Cruz, C., Justo, R., & Castro, J. O. de (2012). Does family employment enhance MSEs performance?: Integrating socioemotional wealth and family embeddedness perspectives. Journal of Business Venturing, 27, 62–76.

Cullen, J. B., Johnson, J. L., & Sakano, T. (1995). Japanese and Local Partner Commitment to IJVs: Psychological Consequences of Outcomes and Investments in the IJV Relationship. Journal of International Business Studies, 26(1), 91–115.

Cumming, D., & Johan, S. A. (2009). Venture capital and private equity contracting: An international perspective. Malden, MA: Academic Press.

Cumming, D., & Walz, U. (2009). Private equity returns and disclosure around the world. Journal of International Business Studies, 41(4), 727–754.

Cumming, D., Siegel, D. S., & Wright, M. (2007). Private equity, leveraged buyouts and governance. Journal of Corporate Finance, 13(4), 439–460.

Currall, S. C., & Judge, T. A. (1995). Measuring Trust between Organizational Boundary Role Persons. Organizational Behavior and Human Decision Processes, 64(2), 151–170.

Cyert, R. M., & March, J. G. (1963) A behavioral theory of the firm (2nd). Malden, MA: Blackwell Publisher Inc.

Daily, C. M., & Dollinger, M. J. (1992). An Empirical Examination of Ownership Structure in Family and Professionally Managed Firms. Family Business Review, 5(2), 117–136.

Damodaran, A. (2002). Investment valuation: Tools and techniques for determining the value of any asset (2. ed.). Wiley finance. New York: Wiley.

Danes, S. M., Haberman, H. R., & McTavish, D. (2005). Gendered Discourse about Family Business. Family Relations, 54(1), 116–130.

Danes, S. M., Stafford, K., Haynes, G., & Amarapurkar, S. S. (2009). Family Capital of Family Firms. Family Business Review, 22(3), 199–215.

Davis, J. H., Allen, M. R., & Hayes, H. D. (2010). Is Blood Thicker Than Water? A Study of Stewardship Perceptions in Family Business. Entrepreneurship: Theory and Practice, 34(6), 1093–1116.

Davis, J. H., Schoorman, F. D., & Donaldson, L. (1997). Toward a stewardship theory of management. Academy of Management Review, 22(1), 20–47.

Davis, P. S., & Harveston, P. D. (1998). The Influence of Family on the Family Business Succession Process: a Multi-Generational Perspective. Entrepreneurship: Theory & Practice, 22(3), 31.

Dawson, A. (2011). Private equity investment decisions in family firms: The role of human resources and agency costs. Journal of Business Venturing, 26(2), 189–199.

Debicki, B. J., Matherne III, C. F., Kellermanns, F. W., & Chrisman, J. J. (2009). Family Business Research in the New Millennium: An Overview of the Who, the Where, the What, and the Why. Family Business Review, 22(2), 151–166.

Dehlen, T., Zellweger, T. M., Kammerlander, N., & Halter, F. (2012). The role of information asymmetry in the choice of entrepreneurial exit routes. Journal of Business Venturing, Forthcoming.

Demiroglu, C., & James, C. M. (2010). The role of private equity group reputation in LBO financing. Journal of Financial Economics, 96(2), 306–330.

Denis, D. J., Denis, D. K., & Sarin, A. (1997). Agency Problems, Equity Ownership, and Corporate Diversification. Journal of Finance, 52(1), 135–160.

DeNoble, A., Ehrlich, S., & Singh, G. (2007). Toward the Development of a Family Business Self-Efficacy Scale: A Resource-Based Perspective. Family Business Review, 20(2), 127–140.

DeTienne, D. R. (2010). Entrepreneurial exit as a critical component of the entrepreneurial process: Theoretical development. Journal of Business Venturing, 25(2), 203–215.

DeTienne, D. R., & Cardon, M. (2012). Impact of founder experience on exit intentions. Small Business Economics, 38(4), 351–374.

DiMaggio, P. J., & Powell, W. W. (1983). The Iron Cage Revisited: Institutional Isomorphism and Collective Rationality in Organizational Fields. American Sociological Review, 48(2), 147–160.

Dimov, D., Shepherd, D. A., & Sutcliffe, K. M. (2007). Requisite expertise, firm reputation, and status in venture capital investment allocation decisions. Journal of Business Venturing, 22(4), 481–502.

Dixit, A. K., & Pindyck, R. S. (1994). Investment under uncertainty. Princeton, N.J: Princeton University Press.

Doney, P. M., & Cannon, J. P. (1997). An Examination of the Nature of Trust in Buyer-Seller Relationships. Journal of Marketing, 61(2), 35–51.

Dreu, C. K. W. de (1995). Coercive Power and Concession Making in Bilateral Negotiation. The Journal of Conflict Resolution, 39(4), 646–670.

Dreu, C. K. W. de, Giebels, E., & van de Vliet, E. (1998). Social motives and trust in integrative negotiation: The disruptive effects of punitive capability. Journal of Applied Psychology, 83(3), 408–422.

Dreu, C. K. W., & van Kleef, G. A. (2004). The influence of power on the information search, impression formation, and demands in negotiation. Journal of Experimental Social Psychology, 40(3), 303–319.

Dreux, D. R. (1990). Financing Family Business: Alternatives to Selling Out or Going Public. Family Business Review, 3(3), 225–243.

Druckman, D. (1994). Determinants of Compromising Behavior in Negotiation: A Meta-Analysis. The Journal of Conflict Resolution, 38(3), 507–556.

Dunn, B. (1995). Success Themes in Scottish Family Enterprises: Philosophies and Practices Through the Generations. Family Business Review, 8(1), 17–28.

Dwyer, F. R., Schurr, P. H., & Oh, S. (1987). Developing Buyer-Seller Relationships. Journal of Marketing, 51(2), 11–27.

Dyck, B., Mauws, M., Starke, F. A., & Mischke, G. A. (2002). Passing the baton: The importance of sequence, timing, technique and communication in executive succession. Journal of Business Venturing, 17(2), 143–162.

Dyer, W. G. (2003). The Family: The Missing Variable in Organizational Research. Entrepreneurship: Theory & Practice, 27(4), 401–416.

Dyer, W. G., & Whetten, D. A. (2006). Family Firms and Social Responsibility: Preliminary Evidence from the S&P 500. Entrepreneurship: Theory and Practice, 30(6), 785–802.

Eastlick, M. A., Lotz, S. L., & Warrington, P. (2006). Understanding online B-to-C relationships: An integrated model of privacy concerns, trust, and commitment. Journal of Business Research, 59(8), 877–886.

Eddleston, K. A., & Kellermanns, F. W. (2007). Destructive and productive family relationships: A stewardship theory perspective. Journal of Business Venturing, 22(4), 545–565.

Eddleston, K. A., Kellermanns, F. W., & Sarathy, R. (2008). Resource Configuration in Family Firms: Linking Resources, Strategic Planning and Technological Opportunities to Performance. Journal of Management Studies, 45(1), 26–50.

Eddleston, K. A., Kellermanns, F. W., & Zellweger, T. M. (2012). Exploring the Entrepreneurial Behavior of Family Firms: Does the Stewardship Perspective Explain Differences? Entrepreneurship: Theory & Practice, 36(2), 347–367.

Eddleston, K. A., Otondo, R. F., & Kellermanns, F. W. (2008). Conflict, Participative Decision-Making, and Generational Ownership Dispersion: A Multilevel Analysis. Journal of Small Business Management, 46(3), 456–484.

Ehrhardt, O., & Nowak, E. (2003). The effect of IPOs on German family-owned firms: governance changes, ownership structure, and performance. Journal of Small Business Management, 41, 25–32.

Eisenhardt, K. M. (1989). Agency Theory: An Assessment and Review. The Academy of Management Review, 14(1), 57–74.

Eisenhardt, K. M., & Graebner, M. E. (2007). Theory building from cases: opportunities and challenges. Academy of Management Journal, 50(1), 25–32.

Emerson, R. M. (1962). Power-Dependence Relations. American Sociological Review, 27(1), 31–41.

Engelskirchen, C. (2007). The role of family influence in M&A transactions (1st ed.). Lohmer-Cologne: Eul-Verlag.

Etemad, H., & Wright, R. W. (2003). Internationalization of SMEs: Toward a New Paradigm. Small Business Economics, 20(1), 1–4.

EVCA (2011). Member Directory, from European Private Equity and Venture Capital Association: Brussels – Belgium.

Fama, E. F. (1980). Agency Problems and the Theory of the Firm. Journal of Political Economy, 88(2), 288–307.

Fama, E. F. (1991). Efficient Capital Markets: II. Journal of Finance, 46(5), 1575–1617.

Fama, E. F., & Jensen, M. C. (1983). Separation of ownership and control. Journal of Law & Economics, 26(2), 301–326.

Fenn, G. W., Liang, N., & Prowse, S. (1997). The Private Equity Market: An Overview. Financial Markets, Institutions & Instruments, 6(4), 1–106.

Field, A. (2009). Discovering statistics using spss (3rd ed.). Thousand Oaks, CA: SAGE Publications.

Fiet, J. O. (1995). Risk Avoidance Strategies in Venture Capital Markets. Journal of Management Studies, 32(4), 551–574.

Fisher, R. (1981). Getting to yes: Negotiating agreement without giving in. New York: Penguim Books.

Folta, T. B. (1998). Governance and uncertainty: The tradeoff between administrative control and commitment. Strategic Management Journal, 19(11), 1007–1028.

Folta, T. B., & Miller, K. D. (2002). Real options in equity partnerships. Strategic Management Journal, 23(1), 77–88.

Fombrun, C., & Shanley, M. (1990). What's in a name? Reputation building and corporate strategy. Academy of Management Journal, 33(2), 233–258.

French, J. R. P., & Raven, B. H. (1959). The basis of social power. In D. Cartwright (Ed.), Studies in social power. Ann Arbor: University of Michigan Press.

Freudenberger, H. J., Freedheim, D. K., & Kurtz, T. S. (1989). Treatment of individuals in family businesses. Psychotherapy: Theory, Research, Practice, Training, 26(1), 47–53.

Fullerton, G. (2003). When Does Commitment Lead to Loyalty? Journal of Service Research, 5(4), 333–344.

Ganesan, S. (1994). Determinants of Long-Term Orientation in Buyer-Seller Relationships. Journal of Marketing, 58(2), 1–19.

Gedajlovic, E., & Carney, M. (2010). Markets, Hierarchies, and Families: Toward a Transaction Cost Theory of the Family Firm. Entrepreneurship: Theory and Practice, 34(6), 1145–1172.

Gelman, A., & Hill, J. (2007). Data analysis using regression and multilevel/hierarchical models. Cambridge: University Press.

Gerbing, D. W., & Anderson, J. C. (1988). An Updated Paradigm for Scale Development Incorporating Unidimensionality and Its Assessment. Journal of Marketing Research, 25(2), 186–192.

Gersick, K. E. (1997). Generation to generation: Life cycles of the family business. Boston, Mass: Harvard Business School Press.

Geyskens, I., Steenkamp, J.-B. E. M., & Kumar, N. (1998). Generalizations about trust in marketing channel relationships using meta-analysis. International Journal of Research in Marketing, 15(3), 223–248.

Geyskens, I., Steenkamp, J.-B. E. M., Scheer, L. K., & Kumar, N. (1996). The effects of trust and interdependence on relationship commitment: A trans-Atlantic study. International Journal of Research in Marketing, 13(4), 303–317.

Ghemawat, P. (1991). Commitment: The dynamic of strategy. New York: Free Press.

Gifford, S. (1997). Limited attention and the role of the venture capitalist. Journal of Business Venturing, 12(6), 459–482.

Gilligan, J., & Wright, M. (2008). Private equity demystified: An explanatory guide. London.

Gómez-Mejía, L. R., Cruz, C., Berrone, P., & Castro, J. de (2011b). The Bind that Ties: Socioemotional Wealth Preservation in Family Firms. The Academy of Management Annals, 5(1), 653–707.

Gómez-Mejía, L. R., Haynes, K. T., Nuñez-Nickel, M., Jacobson, K. J. L., & Moyano-Fuentes, J. (2007). Socioemotional Wealth and Business Risks in Family-controlled Firms: Evidence from Spanish Olive Oil Mills. Administrative Science Quarterly, 52(1), 106–137.

Gómez-Mejía, L. R., Makri, M., & Larraza-Kintana, M. (2010). Diversification decisions in family-controlled firms. Journal of Management Studies, 47(2), 223–252.

Gómez-Mejía, L. R., Nuñez-Nickel, M., & Gutierrez, I. (2001). The role of family ties in agency contracts. Academy of Management Journal, 44(1), 81–95.

Gómez-Mejía, L. R., Wiseman, R. M., & Dykes, B. J. (2005). Agency Problems in Diverse Contexts: A Global Perspective. Journal of Management Studies, 42(7), 1507–1517.

Gompers, P. A. (1996). Grandstanding in the venture capital industry. Journal of Financial Economics, 42(1), 133–156.

Gompers, P. A., & Lerner, J. (2001) The money of invention: How venture capital creates new wealth. Boston: Harvard Business School Press.

Gompers, P., Kovner, A., Lerner, J., & Scharfstein, D. (2008). Venture capital investment cycles: The impact of public markets. Journal of Financial Economics, 87(1), 1–23.

Goossens, L., Manigart, S., & Meuleman, M. (2008). The Change in Ownership After a Buyout: Impact on Performance. Journal of Private Equity, 12(1), 31–41.

Gottschalg, O., & Wright, M. (2008). Understanding the buyers' role in private equity returns — the influence of skills, strategy and experience. Paper presented at Strategic Management Society Conference, Cologne.

Gouldner, A. W. (1960). The Norm of Reciprocity: A Preliminary Statement. American Sociological Review, 25(2), 161–178.

Gounaris, S. P. (2005). Trust and commitment influences on customer retention: insights from business-to-business services: Business-to-business relationship architecture and networks among Australia, NZ, and Asian firms. Journal of Business Research, 58(2), 126–140.

Graebner, M. E., & Eisenhardt, K. M (2004). The Seller's Side of the Story: Acquisition as Courtship and Governance as Syndicate in Entrepreneurial Firms. Administrative Science Quarterly, 49(3), 366–403.

Granata, D. (2010). Sale: An Alternative Succession Route for Family Firms. Valuation Issues and Acquirers' Perception: PhD thesis, University of Lugano, Switzerland.

Granata, D., & Chirico, F. (2010). Measures of Value in Acquisitions: Family Versus Nonfamily Firms. Family Business Review, 23(4), 341–354.

Granovetter, M. S. (1973). The Strength of Weak Ties. American Journal of Sociology, 78(6), 1360–1380.

Grant, A. M., Dutton, J. E., & Rosso, B. D. (2008). Giving Commitment: Employee Support Programs and The Prosocial Sensemaking Process. Academy of Management Journal, 51(5), 898–918.

Greenhalgh, L., Neslin, S. A., & Gilkey, R. W. (1985). The effects of negotiator preferences, situational power, and negotiator personality on outcomes of business negotiations. Academy of Management Journal, 28(1), 9–33.

Grenadier, S. R. (2002). Option Exercise Games: An Application to the Equilibrium Investment Strategies of Firms. Review of Financial Studies, 15(3), 691–721.

Grundström, C., Öberg, C., & Öhrwall Rönnbäck, A. (2012). Family-owned manufacturing SMEs and innovativeness: A comparison between within-family successions and external takeovers: Culture and values: Understanding the long-term perspectives of family businesses. Journal of Family Business Strategy, 3(3), 162–173.

Gulati, R. (1995). Does familiarity breed trust? The implications of repeated ties for contractual choice in alliances. Academy of Management Journal, 38(1), 85–112.

Gulati, R., & Nickerson, J. A. (2008). Interorganizational Trust, Governance Choice, and Exchange Performance. Organization Science, 19(5), 688–708.

Gundlach, G. T., Achrol, R. S., & Mentzer, J. T. (1995). The Structure of Commitment in Exchange. The Journal of Marketing 59(1), 78–92.

Gupta, A. K., & Sapienza, H. J. (1992). Determinants of Venture Capital Firms' Preferences Regarding the Industry Diversity and Geographic Scope of Their Investments. Journal of Business Venturing, 7(5), 347–362.

Habbershon, T. G., & Williams, M. L. (1999). A Resource-Based Framework for Assessing the Strategic Advantages of Family Firms. Family Business Review, 12(1), 1–25.

Habbershon, T. G., Williams, M. L., & Daniel, J. (1998). Toward a definition of 'familiness'. Working Paper. Snider Entrepreneurial Research Center, Wharton School, University of Pennsylvania.

Habbershon, T. G., Williams, M., & MacMillan, I. C. (2003). A unified systems perspective of family firm performance. Journal of Business Venturing, 18(4), 451–465.

Hack, A. (2009). Sind Familienunternehmen anders? Eine kritische Bestandsaufnahme des aktuellen Forschungsstands. Zeitschrift für Betriebswirtschaftslehre, 79(2/Special Issue), 1–29.

Hagen, B., Zucchella, A., Cerchiello, P., & Giovanni, N. de (2012). International strategy and performance: clustering strategic types of SMEs. International Business Review, 21(3), 369–382.

Hair, J. F. (1987). Multivariate data analysis (3rd ed.). Upper Saddle River, NJ: Macmillan Publishing Company.

Hambrick, D. C., & Mason, P. A. (1984). Upper Echelons: The Organization as a Reflection of Its Top Managers. The Academy of Management Review, 9(2), 193–206.

Handler, W. C. (1994). Succession in Family Business: A Review of the Research, 7(2), 133–157.

Harris, D., Martinez, J. I., & Ward, J. L. (1994). Is Strategy Different for the Family-Owned Business?. Family Business Review, 7(2), 159–174.

Harris, R., Siegel, D. S., & Wright, M. (2005). Assessing the Impact of Management Buyouts on Economic Efficiency: Plant-Level Evidence from the United Kingdom. Review of Economics and Statistics, 87(1), 148–153.

Harvey, M. G., & Lusch, R. F. (1995). Expanding the nature and scope of due diligence. Journal of Business Venturing, 10(1), 5–22.

Haspeslagh, P. C., & Jemison, D. B. (1991). Managing acquisitions: Creating value through corporate renewal. New York, Toronto: Free Press; Collier Macmillan Canada; Maxwell Macmillan International.

Hauser, H.-E., Kay, R., & Boerger, S. (2010). Unternehmensnachfolgen in Deutschland 2010 bis 2014 - Schätzung mit weiterentwickeltem Verfahren. Bonn: Institut für Mittelstandsforschung (Hrsg.): IfM-Materialien Nr. 198.

Haveman, H. A. (1993). Ghosts of Managers Past: Managerial Succession and Organizational Mortality. The Academy of Management Journal, 36(4), 864–881.

Haveman, H. A., & Khaire, M. V. (2004). Survival beyond succession? The contingent impact of founder succession on organizational failure: Evolutionary approaches to entrepreneurship: Honoring Howard Aldrich. Journal of Business Venturing, 19(3), 437–463.

Heel, J., & Kehoe, C. (2005). Why some private equity firms do better than others. McKinsey Quarterly, (1), 24–26.

Heerwegh, D., Vanhove, T., Matthijs, K., & Loosveldt, G. (2005). The effect of personalization on response rates and data quality in web surveys. International Journal of Social Research Methodology, 8(2), 85–99.

Heide, J. B., & John, G. (1992). Do Norms Matter in Marketing Relationships? Journal of Marketing, 56(2), 32–44.

Heil, O., & Robertson, T. S. (1991). Toward a theory of competitive market signaling: a research agenda. Strategic Management Journal, 12(6), 403–418.

Hellmann, T. (2002). A theory of strategic venture investing. Journal of Financial Economics, 64(2), 285–314.

Henderson, V., & Hobson, D. G. (2002). Real options with constant relative risk aversion. Journal of Economic Dynamics & Control, 27(2), 329–355.

Hill, C. W. L. (1990). Cooperation, Opportunism, and the Invisible Hand: Implications for Transaction Cost Theory. Academy of Management Review, 15(3), 500–513.

Hitt, M. A., Biermant L., Shimizu K., & Kochhar R. (2001). Direct and Moderating Effects of Human Capital on Strategy and Performance in Professional Service Firms: A Resource-Based Perspective. Academy of Management Journal, 44(1), 13–28.

Hitt, M. A., Ireland, R. D., Camp, S. M., & Sexton, D. L. (2001). Strategic entrepreneurship: entrepreneurial strategies for wealth creation. Strategic Management Journal, 22(6-7), 479–491.

Hochberg, Y., Ljungqvist, A., & Lu, Y. (2007). Whom You Know Matters: Venture Capital Networks and Investment Performance. Journal of Finance, 62(1), 251–301.

Hoffman, J., Hoelscher, M., & Sorenson, R. (2006). Achieving Sustained Competitive Advantage: A Family Capital Theory. Family Business Review, 19(2), 135–145.

Holmes, J. G., & Rempel, J. K. (1989). Trust in close relationships. In C. Hendrick (Ed.), Close relationships (pp. 187–220). Newbury Park: Sage.

Horton, T. (1986). Managing in a family way. Management Review, 75(2),3.

Howell, S. (2001). Real options: Evaluating corporate investment opportunities in a dynamic world. London [u.a.]: Financial Times Prentice Hall.

Howorth, C. A. (2001). Small Firms' Demand for Finance: A Research Note. International Small Business Journal, 19(4), 78–86.

Howorth, C., Westhead, P., & Wright, M. (2004). Buyouts, information asymmetry and the family management dyad. Journal of Business Venturing, 19(4), 509–534.

Hoy, F., & Verser, T. G. (1994). Emerging, business, emerging field: entrepreneurship and the family firm. Entrepreneurship Theory and Practice, 19(1), 9–23.

Hsu, D. H. (2004). What Do Entrepreneurs Pay for Venture Capital Affiliation? Journal of Finance, 59(4), 1805–1844.

Hsu, D. H. (2006). Venture Capitalists and Cooperative Start-up Commercialization Strategy. Management Science, 52(2), 204–219.

Hu, L., & Bentler, P. M. (1999). Cutoff criteria for fit indexes in covariance structure analysis: Conventional criteria versus new alternatives. Structural Equation Modeling: A Multidisciplinary Journal, 6(1), 1–55.

Hull, J. C. (2009). Options, futures, and other derivatives (7th ed.). Upper Saddle River, NJ: Pearson Prentice Hall.

Hunt, S. D., & Morgan, R. M. (1994). Organizational Commitment: One of Many Commitments or Key Mediating Construct? The Academy of Management Journal, 37(6), 1568–1587.

Hurry, D., Miller, A. T., & Bowman, E. H. (1992). Calls on high-technology: Japanese exploration of venture capital investments in the United States. Strategic Management Journal, 13(2), 85–101.

IFB (2011). The UK Family Business Sector Working to grow the UK economy, from Institute for Family Business: http://www.ifb.org.uk/media/44219/theukfamilybusinesssectorreport nov2011_final.pdf.

IFERA (2003). Family Businesses Dominate. Family Business Review, 16(4), 235–240.

Inkpen, A. C., & Beamish, P. W. (1997). Knowledge, Bargaining Power, and the Instability of International Joint Ventures. The Academy of Management Review, 22(1), 177–202.

Iverson, R. D., & Buttigieg, D. M. (1999). Affective, Normative and Continuance Commitment: Can the 'Right Kind' of Commitment be Managed? Journal of Management Studies, 36(3), 307–333.

Jain, B. A., & Kini, O. (1995). Venture capitalist participation and the post-issue operating performance of IPO firms. Managerial and Decision Economics, 16(6), 593–606.

Jakoby, S. (2000). Erfolgsfaktoren von Management Buyouts in Deutschland: Eine empirische Untersuchung. Lohmar: Eul.

James, H. S. (1999). What Can the Family Contribute to Business?. Examining Contractual Relationships. Family Business Review, 12(1), 61–71.

Janney, J. J., & Folta, T. B. (2006). Moderating effects of investor experience on the signaling value of private equity placements. Journal of Business Venturing, 21(1), 27–44.

Jap, S. D. (1999). Pie-Expansion Efforts: Collaboration Processes in Buyer-Supplier Relationships. Journal of Marketing Research, 36(4), 461–475.

Jap, S. D., & Anderson, E. (2003). Safeguarding Interorganizational Performance and Continuity under Ex Post Opportunism. Management Science, 49(12), 1684–1701.

Jaros, S. J., Jermier, J. M., Koehler, J. W., & Sincich, T. (1993). Effects of continuance, affective, and moral commitment on the withdrawel process: an evaluation of eight structural equation models. Academy of Management Journal, 36(5), 951–995.

Jayaraman, N., Khorana, A., Nelling, E., & Covin, J. (2000). CEO founder status and firm financial performance. Strategic Management Journal, 21(12), 1215–1224.

Jensen, M. C. (1986). Agency Costs of Free Cash Flow, Corporate Finance, and Takeovers. American Economic Review, 76(2), 323–329.

Jensen, M. C. (1989). Eclipse of the Public Corporation. Harvard Business Review, 67(5), 61–74.

Jensen, M. C., & Meckling, W. H. (1976). Theory of the firm: managerial behavior, agency costs and ownership structure. Journal of Financial Economics, 3(4), 305–360.

Jensen, M., & Roy, A. (2008). Staging Exchange Partner Choices: When Do Status and Reputation Matter? Academy of Management Journal, 51(3), 495–516.

Jones, G. R. (1983). Transaction Costs, Property Rights, and Organizational Culture: An Exchange Perspective. Administrative Science Quarterly, 28(3), 454–467.

Kahneman, D., & Tversky, A. (1979). Prospect Theory: An Analysis of Decision under Risk. Econometrica, 47(2), 263–291.

Kahneman, D., Slovic, P., & Tversky, A. (1999). Judgement under uncertainty: Heuristics and biases (Reprint.). Cambridge: Cambridge University Press.

Kang, D. L. (1999). Ownership Structure and the Corporate Dividend Policy: How Large-Block Family Owners Increase Dividend Payouts and Achieve Superior Firm Performance. Working Papers -- Harvard Business School Division of Research, 1.

Kanuk, L., & Berenson, C. (1975). Mail Surveys and Response Rates: A Literature Review. Journal of Marketing Research, 12(4), 440–453.

Kaplan, S. (1989). The effects of management buyouts on operating performance and value. Journal of Financial Economics, 24(2), 217–254.

Kaplan, S. (2007). Private Equity: Past, Present, and Future. Journal of Applied Corporate Finance, 19(3), 8–16.

Kaplan, S. N., & Schoar, A. (2005). Private Equity Performance: Returns, Persistence, and Capital Flows. Journal of Finance, 60(4), 1791–1823.

Kaplan, S. N., & Strömberg, P. (2009). Leveraged Buyouts and Private Equity. Journal of Economic Perspectives, 23(1), 121–146.

Kellermanns, F. W., Eddleston, K. A., & Zellweger, T. M. (2012). Extending the Socioemotional Wealth Perspective: A look at the Dark Side. Entrepreneurship Theory and Practice, 36(2), 347–367.

Kellermanns, F. W., Eddleston, K., Sarathy, R., & Murphy, F. (2012). Innovativeness in family firms: a family influence perspective. Small Business Economics, 38(1), 85–101.

Kelley, H. H., & Thibaut, J. (1978) Interpersonal relations: A theory of interdependence. New York: Academic Press.

Kensinger, J. W., Martin, J. D., & William Petty, J. (2000). Harvesting value from entrepreneurial success. Journal of Applied Corporate Finance, 12(4), 81–93.

Kester, W. C. (1984). Today options for tomorrow's growth. Harvard Business Review, 62(2), 153–160.

Kets de Vries, M. F. R. (1993). The dynamics of family controlled firms: The good and the bad news. Organizational Dynamics, 21(3), 59–71.

Kim, P. H., & Fragale, A. R. (2005). Choosing the Path to Bargaining Power: An Empirical Comparison of BATNAs and Contributions in Negotiation. Journal of Applied Psychology, 90(2), 373–381.

Kim, P. H., Pinkley, R. L., & Fragale, A. R. (2005). Power Dynamics in negotiation. Academy of Management Review, 30(4), 799–822.

Klein, S. B. (2000). Family Businesses in Germany: Significance and Structure. Family Business Review, 13(3), 157–181.

Klein, S. B., Astrachan, J. H., & Smyrnios, K. X. (2005). The F-PEC Scale of Family Influence: Construction, Validation, and Further Implication for Theory. Entrepreneurship: Theory & Practice, 29(3), 321–339.

Kline, R. B. (2005). Principles and practice of structural equation modeling (2nd ed.). New York: Guilford Press.

Klöckner, O. (2009). Buy-outs in Family Businesses: Changes in corporate governance, instruments of managerial control, and financial practices. Wiesbaden: Gabler.

Knill, A. (2009). Should Venture Capitalists Put All Their Eggs in One Basket? Diversification versus Pure-Play Strategies in Venture Capital. Financial Management, 38(3), 441–486.

Koch, C. (1999). Optionsbasierte Unternehmensbewertung: Realoptionen im Rahmen von Akquisitionen. Wiesbaden: Gabler.

Kogut, B., & Kulatilaka, N. (1994). Operating Flexibility, Global Manufacturing, and the Option Value of a Multinational Network. Management Science, 40(1), 123–139.

Kogut, B., & Kulatilaka, N. (2001). Capabilities as Real Options. Organization Science, 12(6), 744–758.

Konovsky, M. A., & Cropanzano, R. (1991). Perceived fairness of employee drug testing as a predictor of employee attitudes and job performance. Journal of Applied Psychology, 76(5), 698–707.

Kouser, R., Durani, A., Hussain, F. Z., & Hassan, M. (2012). Investigation of Banker's Lending Criteria to SMEs and Assessment Thereof. International Research Journal of Finance & Economics, 89, 158–186.

Kreps, D. M., & Wilson, R. (1982). Reputation and imperfect information. Journal of Economic Theory, 27(2), 253–279.

Krishnan, C. N. V., Ivanov, V. I., Masulis, R. W., & Singh, A. K. (2011). Venture Capital Reputation, Post-IPO Performance, and Corporate Governance. Journal of Financial & Quantitative Analysis, 46(5), 1295–1333.

Krychowski, C., & Quelin, B. V. (2010). Real Options and Strategic Investment Decisions: Can They Be of Use to Scholars? Academy of Management Perspectives, 24(2), 65–78.

Kulatilaka, N. (1993). The Value of Flexibility: The Case of a Dual-Fuel Industrial Steam Boiler. Financial Management, 22(3), 271–280.

Kulatilaka, N. (1995). The value of flexibility: a general model of real options. In L. Trigeorgis (Ed.), Real options in capital investment. Models, strategies, and applications. Westport, Conn: Praeger.

Kulatilaka, N., & Perotti, E. C. (1998). Strategic Growth Options. Management Science, 44(8), 1021–1031.

Kumar, N., Scheer, L. K., & Steenkamp, J.-B. E. M. (1995). The Effects of Perceived Interdependence on Dealer Attitudes. Journal of Marketing Research, 32(3), 348–356.

Kumar, N., Stern, L. W., & Anderson, J. C. (1993). Conducting Interorganizational Research Using Key Informants. The Academy of Management Journal, 36(6), 1633–1651.

La Porta, R., Lopez-de-Silanes, F., & Shleifer, A. (1999). Corporate Ownership Around the World. Journal of Finance, 54(2), 471–517.

Landis, R. S., Beal, D. J., & Tesluk, P. E. (2000). A Comparison of Approaches to Forming Composite Measures in Structural Equation Models. Organizational Research Methods, 3(2), 186–207.

Landsberg, I. (1983). Human resources in family firms: the problem of institutional overlap. Organizational Dynamics, 12(1), 17–35.

Lane, C., & Bachmann, R. (1996). The Social Constitution of Trust: Supplier Relations in Britain and Germany. Organization Studies, 17(3), 365–395.

Lansberg, I. (1988). The Succession Conspiracy. Family Business Review, 1(2), 119–143.

Lansberg, I. (1999). Succeeding generations: Realizing the dream of families in business. Boston: Harvard Business School Press.

Larsson, R., Bengtsson, L., Henriksson, K., & Sparks, J. (1998). The Interorganizational Learning Dilemma: Collective Knowledge Development in Strategic Alliances. Organization Science, 9(3), 285–305.

Larzelere, R. E., & Huston, T. L. (1980). The Dyadic Trust Scale: Toward Understanding Interpersonal Trust in Close Relationships. Journal of Marriage and Family, 42(3), 595–604.

Lawler, E. J., & Yoon, J. (1993). Power and the Emergence of Commitment Behavior in Negotiated Exchange. American Sociological Review, 58(4), 465–481.

Le Breton-Miller, I., Miller, D., & Steier, L. P. (2004). Toward an Integrative Model of Effective FOB Succession. Entrepreneurship: Theory and Practice, 28(4), 305–328.

Leap, T. L., & Grigsby, D. W. (1986). A Conceptualization of Collective Bargaining Power. Industrial and Labor Relations Review, 39(2), 202–213.

Lee, J. (2006). Family Firm Performance: Further Evidence. Family Business Review, 19(2), 103–114.

Lee, J.-R., Chen, W.-R., & Kao, C. (1998). Bargaining power and the trade-off between the ownership and control of international joint ventures in China. Journal of International Management, 4(4), 353–385.

Lee, K. S., Lim, G. H., & Lim, W. S (2003). Family business succession: appropriation risk and choice of successor. Academy of Management Review, 28(4), 657–666.

Lee, M.-S., & Rogoff, E. G. (1996). Research Note: Comparison of Small Businesses with Family Participation versus Small Businesses Without Family Participation: An Investigation of Differences in Goals, Attitudes, and Family/Business Conflict. Family Business Review, 9(4), 423–437.

Leeds, R., & Sunderland, J. (2003). Private Equity Investing in Emerging Markets. Journal of Applied Corporate Finance, 15(4), 111–119.

Leiblein, M. J. (2003). The Choice of Organizational Governance Form and Performance: Predictions from Transaction Cost, Resource-based, and Real Options Theories. Journal of Management, 29(6), 937–961.

Leonidou, L. C., Barnes, B. R., & Talias, M. A. (2006). Exporter–importer relationship quality: The inhibiting role of uncertainty, distance, and conflict: Global Marketing of Industrial Products: Contemporary Developments and Future Directions. Industrial Marketing Management, 35(5), 576–588.

Lerner, J. (1994). The Syndication of Venture Capital Investments. Financial Management, 23(3), 16–27.

Lewicki, R. J., Saunders, D. M., & Barry, B. (2010). Essentials of Negotiation (3rd ed.). New York: Mcgraw Hill Book Co.

Li, J., & Labig, C. E. (2001). Negotiating With China: Exploratory Study Of Relationship-Building. Journal of Managerial Issues, 13(3), 345–359.

Lindblom, C. E. (1948). "Bargaining Power" In Price and Wage Determination. The Quarterly Journal of Economics, 62(3), 396–417.

Lindgren, P. (2012). Business Model Innovation Leadership: How Do SME's Strategically Lead Business Model Innovation?. International Journal of Business and Management, 7(14), 53–66.

Ling, Y., & Kellermanns, F. W. (2010). The Effects of Family Firm Specific Sources of TMT Diversity: The Moderating Role of Information Exchange Frequency. Journal of Management Studies, 47(2), 322–344.

Lipman, D. L. (2001). The complete guide to valuing and selling your business. Roseville: CA: Prima Publishing.

Litz, R. A. (1995). The Family Business: Toward Definitional Clarity. Family Business Review, 8(2), 71–81.

Lockett, A., & Wright, M. (1999). The syndication of private equity: evidence from the UK. Venture Capital, 1(4), 303–324.

Lohrke, F. T., Holloway, B. B., & Woolley, T. W. (2009). Conjoint Analysis in Entrepreneurship Research: A Review and Research Agenda. Organizational Research Methods, 13(1), 16–30.

Lohtia, R., Bello, D. C., Yamada, T., & Gilliland, D. I. (2005). The role of commitment in foreign–Japanese relationships: mediating performance for foreign sellers in Japan: Special Section: Retailing Research. Journal of Business Research, 58(8), 1009–1018.

Lossen, U. (2007). Portfolio Strategies of Private Equity Firms: Theory and Evidence (1st ed.): Deutscher Universitätsverlag.

Lund, M. (1985). The Development of Investment and Commitment Scales for Predicting Continuity of Personal Relationships. Journal of Social and Personal Relationships, 2(1), 3–23.

Luo, Y. (2006). Opportunism in Inter-firm Exchanges in Emerging Markets. Management and Organization Review, 2(1), 121–147.

MacMillan, I. C., Kulow, D. M., & Khoylian, R. (1989). Venture capitalists' involvement in their investments: Extent and performance. Journal of Business Venturing, 4(1), 27–47.

Majd, S., & Pindyck, R. S. (1987). Time to build, option value and investment decisions. Journal of Financial Economics, 18(1), 7–27.

Mäkelä, M. M., & Maula, M. V. (2006). Interorganizational Commitment in Syndicated Cross-Border Venture Capital Investments. Entrepreneurship: Theory and Practice, 30(2), 273–298.

Makri, M., Hitt, M. A., & Lane, P. J. (2010). Complementary technologies, knowledge relatedness, and invention outcomes in high technology mergers and acquisitions. Strategic Management Journal, 31(6), 602–628.

Manigart, S., Lockett, A., Meuleman, M., Wright, M., Landström, H., Bruining, H., et al. (2006). Venture Capitalists' Decision to Syndicate. Entrepreneurship: Theory and Practice, 30(2), 131–153.

Manigart, S., Waele, K. de, Wright, M., Robbie, K., Desbrières, P., Sapienza, H. J., Beekman, A. (2002). Determinants of required return in venture capital investments: a five-country study. Journal of Business Venturing, 17(4), 291–312.

Margrabe, W. (1978). The Value of an Option to Exchange One Asset for Another. Journal of Finance, 33(1), 177–186.

Marsh, H. W., Balla, J. R., & McDonald, R. P. (1988). Goodness-of-fit indexes in confirmatory factor analysis: The effect of sample size. Psychological Bulletin, 103(3), 391–410.

Massis, A. de, Chua, J. H., & Chrisman, J. J. (2008). Factors Preventing Intra-Family Succession. Family Business Review, 21(2), 183–199.

Mathieu, J. E., & Zajac, D. M. (1990). A review and meta-analysis of the antecedents, correlates, and consequences of organizational commitment. Psychological Bulletin, 108(2), 171–194.

Mayer, R. C., Davis, J. H., & Schoorman, F. D. (1995). An Integrative Model of Organizational Trust. The Academy of Management Review, 20(3), 709–734.

McConaughy, D. L., & Phillips, G. M. (1999). Founders versus Descendants: The Profitability, Efficiency, Growth Characteristics and Financing in Large, Public, Founding-Family-Controlled Firms. Family Business Review, 12(2), 123–131.

McGrath, R. G. (1996). Options and the enterprise: Toward a strategic theory of entrepreneurial wealth creation. Academy of Management Best Papers Proceedings, 101–105.

McGrath, R. G. (1999). Falling forward: real options reasoning and entrepreneurial failure. Academy of Management Review, 24(1), 13–30.

McGrath, R. G., & Nerkar, A. (2004). Real options reasoning and a new look at the R&D investment strategies of pharmaceutical firms. Strategic Management Journal, 25(1), 1–21.

McGrath, R. G., Ferrier, W. J., & Mendelow, A. L. (2004). Real options as engines of choice and heterogeneity. Academy of Management Review, 29(1), 86–101.

Melin, L., & Nordqvist, M. (2007). The reflexive dynamics of institutionalization: the case of the family business. Strategic Organization, 5(3), 321–333.

Meuleman, M., Amess, K., Wright, M., & Scholes, L. (2009). Agency, Strategic Entrepreneurship, and the Performance of Private Equity-Backed Buyouts. Entrepreneurship Theory and Practice, 33(1), 213–239.

Meyer, J. P., & Allen, N. J. (1991). A three-component conceptualization of organizational commitment. Human Resource Management Review, 1(1), 61–89.

Meyer, J. P., & Herscovitch, L. (2001). Commitment in the workplace: Toward a general model. Human Resource Management Review, 11(3), 299–326.

Meyer, J. P., Allen, N. J., & Gellatly, I. R. (1990). Affective and Continuance Commitment to the Organization: Evaluation of Measures and Analysis of Concurrent and Time-Lagged Relations. Journal of Applied Psychology, 75(6), 710–720.

Meyer, J. P., Becker, T. E., & Vandenberghe, C. (2004). Employee Commitment and Motivation: A Conceptual Analysis and Integrative Model. Journal of Applied Psychology, 89(6), 991–1007.

Meyer, J. W., & Rowan, B. (1977). Institutionalized Organizations: Formal Structure as Myth and Ceremony. American Journal of Sociology, 83(2), 340–363.

Mickelson, R. E., & Worley, C. (2003). Acquiring a Family Firm: A Case Study. Family Business Review, 16(4), 251–268.

Miles, M. B., & Huberman, A. M. (1985). Qualitative data analysis. Thousand Oaks: Sage.

Milgrom, P., & Roberts, J. (1982). Predation, reputation, and entry deterrence. Journal of Economic Theory, 27(2), 280–312

Miller, D., & Le Breton-Miller, I (2005). Managing for the Long Run: Lessons in Competitive Advantage from Great Family Businesses. Harvard Business School Press.

Miller, D., & Le Breton-Miller, I. (2006). Family Governance and Firm Performance: Agency, Stewardship, and Capabilities. Family Business Review, 14(1), 73–87.

Miller, D., Le Breton-Miller, I., & Scholnick, B. (2008). Stewardship vs. Stagnation: An Empirical Comparison of Small Family and Non-Family Businesses. Journal of Management Studies, 45(1), 51–78.

Miller, D., Le Breton-Miller, I., Lester, R. H., & Cannella Jr., A. A. (2007). Are family firms really superior performers? Journal of Corporate Finance, 13(5), 829–858.

Miller, D., Lee, J., Chang, S., & Le Breton-Miller, I. (2009). Filling the institutional void: The social behavior and performance of family vs non-family technology firms in emerging markets. Journal of International Business Studies, 40(5), 802–817.

Miller, D., Steier, L., & Le Breton-Miller, I. (2003). Lost in time: intergenerational succession, change, and failure in family business: Theories of Family Business. Journal of Business Venturing, 18(4), 513–531.

Minor, N. (2003). Deciding to sell your business: The key to wealth and freedom (1st ed.). Denver, CO: Business Entreprise Institute.

Mjoen, H., & Tallman, S. (1997). Control and Performance in International Joint Ventures. Organization Science, 8(3), 257–274.

Modigliani, F., & Miller, M. H. (1958). The cost of capital, corporation finance and the theory of investment. American Economic Review, 48(3), 261–297.

Moorman, C., Zaltman, G., & Deshpande, R. (1992). Relationships between Providers and Users of Market Research: The Dynamics of Trust within and between Organizations. Journal of Marketing Research, 29(3), 314–328.

Morck, R., & Yeung, B. (2003). Agency Problems in Large Family Business Groups. Entrepreneurship: Theory & Practice, 27(4), 367–382.

Morgan, R. M., & Hunt, S. D. (1994). The Commitment-Trust Theory of Relationship Marketing. Journal of Marketing, 58(3), 20–38.

Mosakowski, E. (1993). A resource-based perspective on the dynamic strategy-performance relationship: An empirical examination of the focus and differentiation strategies. Journal of Management, 19(4), 819–839.

Mosakowski, E. (2002). Overcoming resource disadvantages in entrepreneurial firms: when less is more. In M. Hitt, S. Ireland, S. Camp, & D. Sexton (Eds.), Strategic entrepreneurship: Creating a new integrated mindset (pp. 106–126). Oxford, U.K.: Blackwell Publishing Ltd.

Mowday, R. T., Porter, L. W., & Steers, R. M. (1982). Employee-organization linkages: The psychology of commitment, absenteeism, and turnover. New York: Academic Press.

Mowday, R. T., Steers, R. M., & Porter, L. W. (1979). The measurement of organizational commitment. Journal of Vocational Behavior, 14(2), 224–247.

Myers, S. C. (1977). Determinants of corporate borrowing. Journal of Financial Economics, 5(2), 147–175.

Myers, S. C. (1984). Capital Structure Puzzle. Journal of Finance, 39(3), 575–592.

Myers, S. C. (1996). Fischer Black's Contributions to Corporate Finance. FM: The Journal of the Financial Management Association, 25(4), 95–103.

Myers, S. C., & Majd, S. (1990). Abandonment value and project life. Advances in Futures and Operations Research, 4, 1–21.

Nahapiet, J., & Ghoshal, S. (1998). Social capital, intellectual capital, and the organizational advantage. Academy of Management Review, 23(2), 242–266.

Nair, A., Narasimhan, R., & Bendoly, E. (2011). Coopetitive Buyer-Supplier Relationship: An Investigation of Bargaining Power, Relational Context, and Investment Strategies. Decision Sciences, 42(1), 93–127.

Newburry, W., & Zeira, Y. (1997). Generic Differences Between Equity International Joint Ventures (EIJVs), International Acquisitions (IAs) and International Greenfield Investments (IGIs): Implications for Parent Companies. Journal of World Business, 32(2), 87–102.

Niedermeyer, C., Jaskiewicz, P., & Klein, S. B. (2010). 'Can't get no satisfaction?' Evaluating the sale of the family business from the family's perspective and deriving implications for new venture activities. Entrepreneurship & Regional Development, 22(3/4), 293–320.

Nikoskelainen, E., & Wright, M. (2007). The impact of corporate governance mechanisms on value increase in leveraged buyouts: Private Equity, Leveraged Buyouts and Corporate Governance. Journal of Corporate Finance, 13(4), 511–537.

Nonaka, I., & Takeuchi, H. (1995). The knowledge-creating company: How Japanese companies create the dynamics of information. New York: Oxford University Press.

Nooteboom, B. (1996). Trust, Opportunism and Governance: A Process and Control Model. Organization Studies, 17(6), 985–1010.

Nooteboom, B., Berger, H., & Noorderhaven, N. G. (1997). Effects of trust and governance on relational risk. Academy of Management Journal, 40(2), 308–338.

Nordqvist, M. (2005). Familiness in Top Management Teams: Commentary on Ensley and Pearson's "An Exploratory Comparison of the Behavioral Dynamics of Top Management Teams in Family and Nonfamily New Ventures: Cohesion, Conflict, Potency, and Consensus". Entrepreneurship: Theory and Practice, 29(3), 285–292.

Norton, E. (1995). Venture Capital as an Alternative Means to Allocate Capital: An Agency-Theoretic View. Entrepreneurship: Theory & Practice, 20(2), 19–29.

Norton, E., & Tenenbaum, B. H. (1993). Specialization versus diversification as a venture capital investment strategy. Journal of Business Venturing, 8(5), 431–442.

Olekalns, M., & Smith, P. L. (2009). Mutually Dependent: Power, Trust, Affect and the Use of Deception in Negotiation. Journal of Business Ethics, 85(3), 347–365.

Olson, P. D., Zuiker, V. S., Danes, S. M., Stafford, K., Heck, R. K. Z., & Duncan, K. A. (2003). The impact of the family and the business on family business sustainability. Journal of Business Venturing, 18(5), 639–666.

Oriani, R., & Sobrero, M. (2008). Uncertainty and the market valuation of R&D within a real options logic. Strategic Management Journal, 29(4), 343–361.

Overbeck, J. R., Neale, M. A., & Govan, C. L. (2010). I feel, therefore you act: Intrapersonal and interpersonal effects of emotion on negotiation as a function of social power. Organizational Behavior and Human Decision Processes, 112(2), 126–139.

Pablo, A. L., Sitkin, S. B., & Jemison, D. B. (1996). Acquisition Decision-Making Processes: The Central Role of Risk. Journal of Management, 22(5), 723–746.

Parkhe, A. (1993). Strategic alliance structuring: a game theoretic and transaction cost examination of interfirm cooperation. Academy of Management Journal, 36(4), 794–829.

Patchen, M. (1974). The locus and basis of influence on organizational decisions. Organizational Behavior and Human Performance, 11(2), 195–221.

Pearson, A. W., Carr, J. C., & Shaw, J. C. (2008). Toward a Theory of Familiness: A Social Capital Perspective. Entrepreneurship: Theory & Practice, 32(6), 949–969.

Pellegrin, J. G. (1999). Toward a model for making and executing the decision to sell: An exploratory study of the sale of family owned companies. Business School Lausanne, Switzerland: Doctoral dissertation.

Penrose, E. T. (1959). The theory of the growth of the firm. New York: Wiley.

Peteraf, M. A. (1993). The cornerstones of competitive advantage: a resource-based view. Strategic Management Journal, 14(3), 179–191.

Petty, W., Bygrave, W. D., & Shulman, J. M. (1994). Harvesting the entrepreneurial venture: a time for creating value. Journal of Applied Corporate Finance, 7(1), 48–58.

Pfeffer, J. (1981). Power in organizations. Marshfield, Mass: Pitman Pub.

Pfeffer, J., & Nowak, P. P. (1976). Joint ventures and interorganizational interdependence. Administrative Science Quarterly, 21(3), 398–418.

Pfeffer, J., & Salancik, G. R. (1978). The external control of organizations. New York: Harper & Row.

Philippe, D., & Durand, R. (2011). The impact of norm-conforming behaviors on firm reputation. Strategic Management Journal, 32(9), 969–993.

Philippe, H. (2005). Corporate Governance: A New Limit to Real Options Valuation? Journal of Management & Governance, 9(2), 129–149.

Pindyck, R. S. (1988). Irreversible Investment, Capacity Choice, and the Value of the Firm. The American Economic Review, 78(5), 969–985.

Pirson, M., & Malhotra, D. (2011). Foundations of Organizational Trust: What Matters to Different Stakeholders? Organization Science, 22(4), 1087–1104.

Podolny, J. M. (2005). Status signals. Princeton, NJ: Princeton University Press.

Podsakoff, P. M. (1986). Self-Reports in Organizational Research: Problems and Prospects. Journal of Management, 12(4), 531–544.

Podsakoff, P. M., MacKenzie, S. B., Lee, J.-Y., & Podsakoff, N. P. (2003). Common method biases in behavioral research: A critical review of the literature and recommended remedies. Journal of Applied Psychology, 88(5), 879–903.

Poech, A., Achleitner, A.-K., & Burger-Calderon (2005). Private Equity in Familienunternehmen: eine empirische Untersuchung zu psychologischen Aspekten der Transaktionsentscheidung. Finanz Betrieb, 7(5), 289–295.

Poppo, L., Zhou, K. Z., & Ryu, S. (2008). Alternative Origins to Interorganizational Trust: An Interdependence Perspective on the Shadow of the Past and the Shadow of the Future. Organization Science, 19(1), 39–55.

Porter, M. E. (1985). Competitive advantage. New York: The Free Pess.

Portes, A. (1998). Social capital: its origins and applications in modern sociology. Annual Review of Sociology, 24(1), 1–24.

Poutziouris, P. Z. (2001). The Views of Family Companies on Venture Capital: Empirical Evidence from the UK Small to Medium-Size Enterprising Economy. Family Business Review, 14(3), 277–291.

Pruitt, D. (1981). Negotiation Behavior. New York: Academic Press.

Pruitt, D. &. Drews, J. (1969). The effect of time pressure, time elapsed, and the opponent's concession rate on behavior in negotiation. Journal of Experimental Social Psychology, 5, 43–60.

Puranam, P., Powell, B. C., & Singh, H. (2006). Due diligence failure as a signal detection problem. Strategic Organization, 4(4), 319–348.

PWC (2012). Family firm: A resilient model for the 21st century, from PwC Family Business Survey: http://www.pwc.com/en_GX/gx/pwc-family-business-survey/assets/pwc-family-business-survey-2012.pdf.

Ragozzino, R., & Reuer, J. J. (2010). The opportunities and challenges of entrepreneurial acquisitions. European Management Review, 7(2), 80–90.

Randall, D. M., & Fernandes, M. F. (1991). The social desirability response bias in ethics research. Journal of Business Ethics, 10(11), 805–817.

Raub, W., & Weesie, J. (1990). Reputation and Efficiency in Social Interactions: An Example of Network Effects. American Journal of Sociology, 96(3), 626–654.

Raven, B. H. (1993). The Bases of Power: Origins and Recent Developments. Journal of Social Issues, 49(4), 227–251.

Reed, S. F., Lajoux, A. R., & Nesvold, H. P. (2007). The art of M & A: A merger, acquisition, buyout guide (4th ed.). New York: McGraw Hill.

Reichers, A. E. (1986). Conflict and organizational commitments. Journal of Applied Psychology, 71(3), 508–514.

Reuber, A. R. (2010). Strengthening Your Literature Review. Family Business Review, 23(2), 105–108.

Reuer, J. J., & Tong, T. W. (2005). Real Options in International Joint Ventures. Journal of Management, 31(3), 403–423.

Rhee, M., & Valdez, M. E. (2009). Contextual factors surrounding reputation damage with potential implications for reputation repair. Academy of Management Review, 34(1), 146–168.

Rindova, V. P., Pollock, T. G., & Hayward, M. L. A. (2006). Celebrity firms: the social construction of market popularity. Academy of Management Review, 31(1), 50–71.

Ring, P. S. (1996). Fragile and Resilient Trust and Their Roles in Economic Exchange. Business & Society, 35(2), 148–175.

Robichek, A. A., & van Horne, J. C. (1967). Abandonment Value and Capital Budgeting. Journal of Finance, 22(4), 577–589.

Romano, C. A., & Tanewski, G. A. (2001). Capital Structure Decision Making: A Model For Family Business. Journal of Business Venturing, 16(3), 285–310.

Rosenblatt, P. C. (1985). Family corporations; Management; Psychological aspects. San Francisco, United States: Jossey-Bass Publishers.

Ross, S. A. (1973). The Economic Theory of Agency: The Principal's Problem. The American Economic Review, 63(2), 134–139.

Rotter, J. B. (1967). A new scale for the measurement of interpersonal trust. Journal of Personality, 35(4), 651–665.

Rubin, J. Z., & Brown, B. R. (1975). The Social Psychology of Bargaining and Negotiation. New York: Academic Press.

Ruhnka, J. C., & Young, J. E. (1991). Some hypotheses about risk in venture capital investing. Journal of Business Venturing, 6(2), 115–133.

Ruyter, K. de, Moorman, L., & Lemmink, J. (2001). Antecedents of Commitment and Trust in Customer–Supplier Relationships in High Technology Markets. Industrial Marketing Management, 30(3), 271–286.

Sahlman, W. A. (1990). The structure and governance of venture-capital organizations. Journal of Financial Economics, 27(2), 473–521.

Salvato, C., Chirico, F., & Sharma, P (2010). A farewell to the business: Championing exit and continuity in entrepreneurial family firms. Entrepreneurship & Regional Development, 22(3), 321–348.

Saoriniborra, M. (2008). Time pressure in acquisition negotiations: Its determinants and effects on parties' negotiation behaviour choice. International Business Review, 17(3), 285–309.

Sapienza, H. J. (1992). When do venture capitalists add value?. Journal of Business Venturing, 7(1), 9–27.

Sapienza, H. J., & Gupta, A. K. (1994). Impact of agency risks and task uncertainty on venture capitalist-CEO intercation. Academy of Management Journal, 37(6), 1618–1632.

Sapienza, H. J., & Korsgaard, M. A. (1996). Procedural justice in entrepreneur-investor relations. Academy of Management Journal, 39(3), 544–574.

Scheer, L. K., & Stern, L. W. (1992). The Effect of Influence Type and Performance Outcomes on Attitude Toward the Influencer. Journal of Marketing Research, 29(1), 128–142.

Schmelter, R., Mauer, R., Boersch, C., & Brettel, M. (2010). Boosting corporate entrepreneurship through HRM practices: Evidence from German SMEs. Human Resource Management, 49(4), 715–741.

Schmohl, J. (2009). Entrepreneurial exit management - key success factors of the private equity buyout option. Dissertation University of St. Gallen,

Scholes, L., Westhead, P., & Burrows, A. (2008). Family firm succession: The management buy-out and buy-in routes. Journal of Small Business and Enterprise Development, 15(1), 8–30.

Scholes, L., Wright, M., Westhead, P., & Bruining, H. (2010). Strategic changes in family firms post management buyout: Ownership and governance issues. International Small Business Journal, 28(5), 505–521.

Scholes, L., Wright, M., Westhead, P., Bruining, H., & Kloeckner, O. (2009). Family-Firm Buyouts, Private Equity, and Strategic Change. The Journal of Private Equity, 12(2), 7–18.

Scholes, L., Wright, M., Westhead, P., Burrows, A., & Bruining H. (2007). Information Sharing, Price Negotiation and Management Buy-outs of Private Family-owned Firms. Small Business Economics, 29(3), 329–349.

Schulze, W. S., Lubatkin, M. H., & Dino, R. N. (2003a). Exploring the agency consequences of ownership dispersion among the directors of family firms. Academy of Management Journal, 46(2), 179–194.

Schulze, W. S., Lubatkin, M. H., & Dino, R. N. (2003b). Toward a theory of agency and altruism in family firms. Journal of Business Venturing, 18(4), 473–490.

Schulze, W. S., Lubatkin, M. H., Dino, R. N., & Buchholtz, A. K. (2001). Agency Relationships in Family Firms: Theory and Evidence. Organization Science, 12(2), 99–116.

Schurr, P. H., & Ozanne, J. L. (1985). Influences on Exchange Processes: Buyers' Preconceptions of a Seller's Trustworthiness and Bargaining Toughness. Journal of Consumer Research, 11(4), 939–953.

Seppa, T. (2002). Essays on the valuation and syndication of venture capital investments. Helsinki University of Technology: Unpublished Doctoral Dissertation.

Shapiro, C. (1983). Premiums for High Quality Products as Returns to Reputations. The Quarterly Journal of Economics, 98(4), 659–681.

Sharma, P. (2004). An Overview of the Field of Family Business Studies: Current Status and Directions for the Future. Family Business Review, 17(1), 1–36.

Sharma, P., & Irving, P. G. (2005). Four Bases of Family Business Successor Commitment: Antecedents and Consequences. Entrepreneurship: Theory and Practice, 29(1), 13–33.

Sharma, P., & Manikutty, S. (2005). Strategic Divestments in Family Firms: Role of Family Structure and Community Culture. Entrepreneurship: Theory and Practice, 29(3), 293–311.

Sharma, P., Chrisman, J. J., & Chua, J. H. (1997). Strategic management of the family business: past research and future challenges. Family Business Review, 10(1), 1–35.

Sharma, P., Chrisman, J. J., & Chua, J. H. (2003). Predictors of satisfaction with the succession process in family firms: The Evolving Family / Entrepreneurship Business Relationship. Journal of Business Venturing, 18(5), 667–687.

Sharma, P., Chrisman, J. J., Pablo, A. L., & Chua, J. H. (2001). Determinants of Initial Satisfaction with the Succession Process in Family Firms: A Conceptual Model. Entrepreneurship: Theory & Practice, 25(3), 1–19.

Sheehan, K. B. (2001). E-mail Survey Response Rates: A Review. Journal of Computer-Mediated Communication, 6(2), no page numbers available.

Shen, J.-C., & Reuer, J. J. (2005). Adverse Selection in Acquisitions of Small Manufacturing Firms: A Comparison of Private and Public Targets. Small Business Economics, 24(4), 393–407.

Shepherd, D. A. (2009). Grief recovery from the loss of a family business: A multi- and meso-level theory. Journal of Business Venturing, 24(1), 81–97.

Shepherd, D. A., & Zacharakis, A. (2001). The venture capitalist-entrepreneur relationship: Control, trust and confidence in co-operative behaviour. Venture Capital, 3(2), 129–149.

Shepherd, D. A., Zacharakis, A., & Baron, R. A. (2003). VCs' decision processes: Evidence suggesting more experience may not always be better. Journal of Business Venturing, 18(3), 381–401.

Shyam Kumar, M. V. (2005). The value from acquiring and divesting a joint venture: a real options approach. Strategic Management Journal, 26(4), 321–331.

Silva, J. (2006). Venture Capital Investments in Family Firms. In J. E. Butler, A. Lockett, & D. Ucbasaran (Eds.), Venture capital and the changing world of entrepreneurship (pp. 239–247). Greenwich, Conn: Information Age Pub.

Sirmon, D. G., & Hitt, M. A. (2003). Managing Resources: Linking Unique Resources, Management, and Wealth Creation in Family Firms. Entrepreneurship: Theory & Practice, 27(4), 339–358.

Sitkin, S. B., & Pablo, A. L. (1992). Reconceptualizing the determinats of risk behaviour. Academy of Management Review, 17(1), 9–38.

Skinner, W. (1974). The Focused Factory. Harvard Business Review, 52(3), 113–121.

Smith, A. J. (1990). Corporate ownership structure and performance: The case of management buyouts. Journal of Financial Economics, 27(1), 143–164.

Smith, D. L., Pruitt, D. G., & Carnevale, P. J. (1982). Matching and mismatching: The effect of own limit, other's toughness, and time pressure on concession rate in negotiation. Journal of Personality and Social Psychology, 42(5), 876–883.

Smith, K. W., & Triantis, A. J. (1995). The value of options in strategic acquisitions. In L. Trigeorgis (Ed.), Real options in capital investment. Models, strategies, and applications (pp. 135–149). Westport, Conn: Praeger.

Smyrnios, K., Tanewski, G., & Romano, C. (1998). Development of a Measure of the Characteristics of Family Business. Family Business Review, 11(1), 49–60.

Somers, M. J. (2010). Patterns of attachment to organizations: Commitment profiles and work outcomes. Journal of Occupational and Organizational Psychology, 83(2), 443–453.

Sonfield, M. C., & Lussier, R. N. (2004). First-, Second-, and Third-Generation Family Firms: A Comparison. Family Business Review, 17(3), 189–202.

Sorenson, O., & Stuart, T. E. (2001). Syndication Networks and the Spatial Distribution of Venture Capital Investments. American Journal of Sociology, 106(6), 1546–1588.

Sraer, D., & Thesmar, D. (2007). Performance and behavior of family firms: evidence from the French stock market. Journal of the European Economic Association, 5(4), 709–751.

Stahelski, A. J., Frost, D. E., & Patch, M. E. (1989). Use of Socially Dependent Bases of Power: French and Raven's Theory Applied to Workgroup Leadership. Journal of Applied Social Psychology, 19(4), 283–297.

Stavrou, E., Kassinis, G., & Filotheou, A. (2007). Downsizing and Stakeholder Orientation Among the Fortune 500: Does Family Ownership Matter? Journal of Business Ethics, 72(2), 149–162.

Staw, B. M. (1981). The Escalation of Commitment To a Course of Action. Academy of Management Review, 6(4), 577–587.

Steen, A., & Welch, L. S. (2006). Dancing With Giants: Acquisition and Survival of the Family Firm. Family Business Review, 19(4), 289–300.

Stewart, A. (2003). Help One Another, Use One Another: Toward an Anthropology of Family Business. Entrepreneurship: Theory and Practice, 27(4), 383–396.

Stuart, T. E., Hoang, H., & Hybels, R. C. (1999). Interorganizational Endorsements and the Performance of Entrepreneurial Ventures. Administrative Science Quarterly, 44(2), 315–349.

Stuhlmacher, A. F., & Champagne, M. V. (2000). The Impact of Time Pressure and Information on Negotiation Process and Decisions. Group Decision and Negotiation, 9(6), 471–491.

Stuhlmacher, A. F., Gillespie, T. L., & Champagne, M. V. (1998). The impact of time pressure in negotiation: a meta-analysis. International Journal of Conflict Management, 9(2), 97–116.

Sundaramurthy, C. (2008). Sustaining Trust Within Family Businesses. Family Business Review, 21(1), 89–102.

Tagiuri, R., & Davis, J. (1996). Bivalent Attributes of the Family Firm. Family Business Review, 9(2), 199–208.

Tagiuri, R., & Davis, J. A. (1992). On the Goals of Successful Family Companies. Family Business Review, 5(1), 43–62.

Tappeiner, F., Howorth, C., Achleitner, A.-K., & Schraml, S. (2012). Demand for private equity minority investments: A study of large family firms. Journal of Family Business Strategy, 3(1), 38–51.

Telser, L. G. (1980). A Theory of Self-Enforcing Agreements. The Journal of Business, 53(1), 27–44.

Thaler, R. H. (1980). Toward a positive theory of consumer choice. Journal of Economic Behavior & Organization, 1(1), 39–60.

Thaler, R. H. (1993). Advances in behavioral finance. New York: Russell Sage Foundation.

Thomas, J. (2002). Freeing the Shackles of Family Business Ownership. Family Business Review, 15(4), 321–336.

Thompson, B. (2004). Exploratory and confirmatory factor analysis: Understanding concepts and applications. Washington, DC, US: American Psychological Association.

Tokarczyk, J., Hansen, E., Green, M., & Down, J. (2007). A Resource-Based View and Market Orientation Theory Examination of the Role of “Familiness” in Family Business Success. Family Business Review, 20(1), 17–31.

Tong, T. W., Reuer, J. J., & Peng, M. W. (2008). International joint ventures and the value of growth options. Academy of Management Journal, 51(5), 1014–1029.

Tranfield, D., Denyer, D., & Smart, P. (2003). Towards a Methodology for Developing Evidence-Informed Management Knowledge by Means of Systematic Review. British Journal of Management, 14(3), 207–222.

Trigeorgis, L. (1993a). Real Options and Interactions with Financial Flexibility. Financial Management, 22(3), 202–224.

Trigeorgis, L. (1993b). The Nature of Option Interactions and the Valuation of Investments with Multiple Real Options. Journal of Financial & Quantitative Analysis, 28(1), 1–20.

Trigeorgis, L. (1995). Real options: an overview. In L. Trigeorgis (Ed.), Real options in capital investment. Models, strategies, and applications (pp. 1–28). Westport, Conn: Praeger.

Trigeorgis, L. (1996). Real options: Managerial flexibility and strategy in resource allocation. Cambridge, Mass: MIT Press.

Tsang, E. W. K. (2002). Learning from overseas venturing experience: The case of Chinese family businesses. Journal of Business Venturing, 17(1), 21–40.

Tversky, A., & Kahneman, D. (1986). Rational Choice and the Framing of Decisions. The Journal of Business, 59(4), 251–78.

Tversky, A., & Kahneman, D. (1991). Loss Aversion in Riskless Choice: A Reference-Dependent Model. The Quarterly Journal of Economics, 106(4), 1039–1061.

Tyebjee, T. T., & Bruno, A. V. (1984). A Model of Venture Capitalist Investment Activity. Management Science, 30(9), 1051–1066.

Upton, N., & Petty, W. (2000). Venture capital investment and US family business. Venture Capital, 2(1), 27–39.

Vancouver, J. B., & Schmitt, N. W. (1991). An exploratory examination of person-organization fit: organizational goal congruence. Personnel Psychology, 44(2), 333–352.

Vancouver, J. B., Milisap, R. E., & Peters, P. A. (1994). Multilevel Analysis of Organizational Goal Congruence. Journal of Applied Psychology, 79(5), 666–679.

Varaiya, N. P. (1987). Determinants of Premiums in Acquisition Transactions. Managerial and Decision Economics, 8(3), 175–184.

Villalonga, B., & Amit, R. (2006). How do family ownership, control and management affect firm value? Journal of Financial Economics, 80(2), 385–417.

Vroom, V. H. (1960). Some Personality Determinants of the Effects of Participation. Englewood Cliffs, New Jersey: Prentice Hall.

Walton, R. E., & McKersie, R. B. (1965). A behavioral theory of labor negotiations: An analysis of a social interaction system. New York: McGraw-Hill.

Wang, D. (2006). Founding Family Ownership and Earnings Quality. Journal of Accounting Research, 44(3), 619–656.

Wang, H., & Lim, S. S. (2008). Real options and real value: the role of employee incentives to make specific knowledge investments. Strategic Management Journal, 29(7), 701–721.

Ward, J. L. (1987). Keeping the family business healthy: How to plan for continuing growth, profitability and family leadership. San Francisco, Calif.: Jossey-Bass.

Ward, J. L. (1988). The Special Role of Strategic Planning for Family Businesses. Family Business Review, 1(2), 105–117.

Ward, J. L. (1997). Growing the Family Business: Special Challenges and Best Practices. Family Business Review, 10(4), 323–337.

Washington, M., & Zajac, E. J. (2005). Status evolution and competition: theory and evidence. Academy of Management Journal, 48(2), 282–296.

Weigelt, K., & Camerer, C. (1988). Reputation and corporate strategy: a review of recent theory and applications. Strategic Management Journal, 9(5), 443–454.

Weisberg, S. (2005). Applied linear regression (3rd ed.). Hoboken, N.J: Wiley-Interscience.

Wennberg, K., Wiklund, J., DeTienne, D. R., & Cardon, M. S. (2010). Reconceptualizing entrepreneurial exit: Divergent exit routes and their drivers. Journal of Business Venturing, 25(4), 361–375.

Wennberg, K., Wiklund, J., Hellerstedt, K., & Nordqvist, M. (2011). Implications of intra-family and external ownership transfer of family firms: short-term and long-term performance differences. Strategic Entrepreneurship Journal, 5(4), 352–372.

Wernerfelt, B. (1984). A Resource-based View of the Firm. Strategic Management Journal, 5(2), 171–180.

Westhead, P., & Howorth, C. (2007). 'Types' of private family firms: an exploratory conceptual and empirical analysis. Entrepreneurship & Regional Development, 19(5), 405–431.

Westhead, P., Cowling, M., & Howorth, C. (2001). The Development of Family Companies: Management and Ownership Imperatives. Family Business Review, 14(4), 369–385.

Wilson, D. T. (1995). An Integrated Model of Buyer-Seller Relationships. Journal of the Academy of Marketing Science, 23(4), 335–345.

Wilson, N., Wright, M., Siegel, D. S., & Scholes, L. (2012). Private equity portfolio company performance during the global recession: Special Section: Financial and Real Effects of Alternative Investments. Journal of Corporate Finance, 18(1), 193–205.

Wilson, T. E., & Grimlund, R. A. (1990). An Examination of the Importance of an Auditor's Reputation. Auditing, 9(2), 43–59.

Wolfe, R. J., & McGinn, K. L. (2005). Perceived relative power and its influence on negotiations. Group Decision and Negotiaition, 14, 3–20.

Wood, G., & Wright, M. (2009). Private equity: A review and synthesis. International Journal of Management Reviews, 11(4), 361–380.

Wright Robbie, M. K. (1998). Venture Capital and Private Equity: A Review and Synthesis. Journal of Business Finance & Accounting, 25(5-6), 521–570.

Wright, M., & Robbie, K. (1996). Venture Capitalists, Unquoted Equity Investment Appraisal and the Role of Accounting Information. Accounting & Business Research, 26(2), 153–168.

Wright, M., Amess, K., Weir, C., & Girma, S. (2009). Private Equity and Corporate Governance: Retrospect and Prospect. Corporate Governance: An International Review, 17(3), 353–375.

Wright, M., Hoskisson, R. E., & Busenitz, L. W. (2001). Firm rebirth: Buyouts as facilitators of strategic growth and entrepreneurship. Academy of Management Executive, 15(1), 111–125.

Wright, M., Hoskisson, R. E., Busenitz, L. W., & Dial, J. (2000). Entrepreneurial growth through privatization: the upside of management buyouts. Academy of Management Review, 25(3), 591–601.

Wright, M., Lockett, A., & Pruthi, S. (2002). Small Business Economics, 19(1), 13–29.

Wright, M., Renneboog, L., Simons, T., & Scholes, L. (2006). Leveraged Buyouts in the U.K. and Continental Europe: Retrospect and Prospect. Journal of Applied Corporate Finance, 18(3), 38–55.

Wright, M., Thompson, S., & Robbie, K. (1992). Venture capital and management-led, leveraged buy-outs: A European perspective. Journal of Business Venturing, 7(1), 47–71.

Wright, M., Ferris, S. P., Sarin, A., & Awasthi, V. (1996). Impact of Corporate Insider, Blockholder, and Institutional Equity Ownership on Firm Risk Taking. The Academy of Management Journal, 39(2), 441–463.

Wulf, T., Stubner, S., Gietl, R., & Landau, C. (2010). Private Equity and Family Business - Can Private Equity Investors Add to the Success of Formerly Owned Family Firms? HHL Working paper series.

Yan, A., & Gray, B. (1994). Bargaining Power, Management Control, and Performance in United States-China Joint Ventures: A Comparative Case Study. The Academy of Management Journal, 37(6), 1478–1517.

Yan, A., & Gray, B. (2001a). Antecedents and Effects of Parent Control in international Joint Ventures. Journal of Management Studies, 38(3), 393–416.

Yan, A., & Gray, B. (2001b). Negotiating control and achieving performance in international joint ventures: A conceptual model. Journal of International Management, 7(4), 295–315.

Zacharakis, A. L., & Meyer, G. D. (2000). The potential of actuarial decision models: Can they improve the venture capital investment decision? Journal of Business Venturing, 15(4), 323–346.

Zaheer, A., & Venkatraman, N. (1995). Relational governance as an interorganizational strategy: an empirical test of the role of trust in economic exchange. Strategic Management Journal, 16(5), 373–392.

Zaheer, A., McEvily, B., & Perrone, V. (1998). Does Trust Matter? Exploring the Effects of Interorganizational and Interpersonal Trust on Performance. Organization Science, 9(2), 141–159.

Zahra, S. A. (2003). International expansion of U.S. manufacturing family businesses: the effect of ownership and involvement: Theories of Family Business. Journal of Business Venturing, 18(4), 495–512.

Zahra, S. A., Hayton, J. C., & Salvato, C. (2004). Entrepreneurship in Family vs. Non-Family Firms: A Resource-Based Analysis of the Effect of Organizational Culture. Entrepreneurship: Theory and Practice, 28(4), 363–381.

Zaltman, G., & Moorman, C. (1988). The importance of personal trust in the use of research. Journal of Advertising Research, 28(5), 16–24.

Zeira, Y., & Newburry, W. (1999). Equity International Joint Ventures (EIJVs) and International Acquisitions (IAs): Generic Differences in the Pre- and Post-Incorporation Stages. Management International Review, 39(4), 323–352.

Zellweger, T. M. (2007). Time Horizon, Costs of Equity Capital, and Generic Investment Strategies of Firms. Family Business Review, 20(1), 1–15.

Zellweger, T. M. (2006). Risk, return and value in the family firm. Bamberg: Difo-Druck.

Zellweger, T. M., Eddleston, K. A., & Kellermanns, F. W. (2010). Exploring the concept of familiness: Introducing family firm identity. Journal of Family Business Strategy, 1(1), 54–63.

Zellweger, T. M., Kellermanns, F. W., Chrisman, J. J., & Chua, J. H. (2011). Family Control and Family Firm Valuation by Family CEOs: The Importance of Intentions for Transgenerational Control. Organization Science, 23 (3), 851–868.

Zellweger, T. M., & Astrachan, J. (2008). On the Emotional Value of Owning a Firm. Family Business Review, 21(4), 347–363.

MIX
Papier aus verantwortungsvollen Quellen
Paper from responsible sources
FSC® C105338

If you have any concerns about our products,
you can contact us on
ProductSafety@springernature.com

In case Publisher is established outside the EU,
the EU authorized representative is:
Springer Nature Customer Service Center GmbH
Europaplatz 3, 69115 Heidelberg, Germany

Printed by Libri Plureos GmbH
in Hamburg, Germany